counseling american minorities

counseling american minorities

a cross cultural perspective

Second Edition

donald r. atkinson
university of california
santa barbara

george morten
university of wisconsin
milwaukee

derald wing sue
california state university
hayward

wcb Wm. C. Brown Company Publishers
Dubuque, Iowa

Contents

Preface

This second edition of *Counseling American Minorities: A Cross-Cultural Perspective,* like the first, is designed to help counselors and mental health practitioners maximize their effectiveness when working with a culturally diverse population. A major thesis of this book is that counselors can establish the necessary and sufficient conditions of a counseling relationship with clients who are culturally different. While similarity in race, ethnicity, and culture may be highly correlated with counseling success, we believe that other attributes (ability to share a similar world view, appropriate use of counseling strategies, awareness of own values, etc.) may be equally important factors in cross-cultural counseling.

The purposes of this edition remain the same as those of the first. First, as a collection of readings, it is intended to sensitize counselors (minority as well as nonminority) to the life experiences of culturally distinct populations. Minority observers have strongly criticized the counseling profession for its lack of attention to the unique needs and experiences of minority individuals. We hope this text can serve as a first step in sensitizing counselors to these needs and experiences. While direct exposure to the environment of the clientele population is perhaps best, reading relevant materials written by and about minority individuals is at least a starting point.

A second major purpose of the book is to examine the traditional counseling role, which has been heavily criticized by minority authors, and to suggest new directions for the counseling profession when dealing with minorities. By combining the present empirical, theoretical, and conceptual work on counseling minorities, it is our purpose to offer direction for future counseling practice, counselor education, and counseling research.

The actual text of this second edition has changed considerably. Chapter 1, which seeks to clarify concepts and terms related to minority group/cross-cultural counseling, has been expanded to include discussion of the following concepts: oppression, melting pot, cultural assimilation, and cultural pluralism. Chapter 2, which provides a broad overview of the unfulfilled promise of counseling for minorities, has been updated with new references in relevant sections. The chapter in which the Minority Identity Development Model is described has been moved from chapter 15 in the first edition to chapter 3 in the current edition with the hope and expectation that it will enhance reader appreciation of intra- and inter-group differences and similarities in the chapters that follow. Chapter 16, which discusses implications for counseling practice, counselor education, and counseling research, has been updated and expanded considerably.

Perhaps the most significant changes to this edition, however, have been made in parts 2 through 5, which are devoted to minority group readings. The readings in part 2, The American Indian Client, remain intact from the first edition. New readings appear in parts 3 through 5 (The Asian American Client, The Black Client, and The Latino Client, respectively) along with added exercises at the end of parts 2 through 5. Parts 2 through 5 each begin with a reading that provides a historical-social perspective of the ethnic group followed by two readings that examine the dynamics of counseling when members of the group are involved as clients.

In several of the readings male pronouns are employed in the generic sense, a violation of our own standard of avoiding language that perpetuates stereotypes. We apologize for this declension. Our guiding principle in the selection of readings has been to include those articles with relevance for counseling that combine scientific rigor and scholarly presentation with a valid portrayal of the ethnic group involved (for this latter reason we have attempted to include readings by members of the group itself whenever possible). The readings that include the generic use of male pronouns meet these requirements but appeared in print before publication policies which prohibit the use of sexist language were widely adopted. Copyright laws restrict alteration of the text of these articles as they originally appeared.

Another significant change in the second edition is the inclusion of the Position Paper on Cross-Cultural Counseling Competencies. This document, which describes eleven cross-cultural competencies that counselors should have in the areas of beliefs/attitudes, knowledges, and skills, is the product of the American Psychological Association's Education and Training Committee. The Position Paper is reprinted in its entirety in appendix A.

It is the editors' opinion that many of the concepts presented in parts 1 and 6 of this book are applicable to other minority groups, including nonracial/ethnic minorities; it is only due to limitations of time, space, and our own sense of priorities that these groups are not included in this volume. Women and homosexuals, for example, are two other numerically large categories of persons who experience considerable physical, social, and economic oppression; the reader will find reference to these groups throughout parts 1 and 6.

Less widely acknowledged is the minority status of groups like the handicapped, the aged, religious denominations, and others. A great deal has been written about the handicapped; indeed, an entire field of counseling has evolved which is devoted to fulfilling the psychological needs of this group. Little has been written, however, concerning the thesis that handicapped people are a minority *because they are oppressed;* rather, the accepted view is that they are a minority because they are an identifiable group and represent a numerical minority. The elderly represent a minority class whom we will all join sooner or later, barring premature death; in the past counseling has tended to ignore this group. Mandatory retirement, spiraling inflation, social ostracization, and numerous other forces all serve to oppress the aged, rendering them in many ways the most powerless of all minorities. It is evident that the oppression of the aged in the United States has not received the attention it merits. Prison populations have their own unique vocabulary and well defined culture; they too constitute a minority group. Drug users, also, have an identifiable culture of which many counselors, even drug counselors, are quite ignorant. Religious groups like the Jews, Mormons, Amish, Hutterites and others are minorities about whom the average counselor knows little except what he or she learned from the pages of a high school history book. Certainly the economically disadvantaged (referred to by some writers as the "underclass"), a group encompassing other minority categories, constitute a minority group of their own.

The reader, we are sure, can think of other minorities that deserve attention in the counseling literature. We readily admit that the inclusion or exclusion of certain groups is almost indefensible. Our decisions reflect our own priorities and judgments. Nonetheless, we hope the reader will find many of the concepts presented in this book useful when working with any minority client. We also hope additional writing on minority groups not included in this book will be forthcoming.

This book of readings originated because each of us saw the need for a book in the counseling field that would treat a broad range of minority groups in a single volume. The books available on counseling minorities are, for the most part, limited in perspective to the problems of a single category. A few of these texts have demonstrated or at least implied that other minority groups experience similar concerns in an oppressive society. Although this approach has proven somewhat valuable, it runs the risk of glossing over minority differences. This book is designed to foster direct comparison and contrast of various racial/ethnic minority group experiences and concerns that may be similar or dissimilar.

We believe that the current text, as a book of readings, can be used in conjunction with a variety of courses in the broad field of mental health: counseling techniques, theories of counseling, the social worker and urban problems, community psychology, changing roles of the counselor, mental health outreach, and individual and group analysis. Its primary use, however, is likely to be in undergraduate and graduate courses designed specifically to facilitate understanding the minority experience as it relates to such objectives as counseling minority youth, cross-cultural counseling, multicultural counseling. To this end, it can serve as the principal text for such courses.

Parts 2 through 6 conclude with a number of hypothetical cases which require the reader to assume he or she is interacting with a minority client. Each case is followed by several questions designed to induce the reader to examine his/her own biases and stereotypes, and to explore potential obstacles to minority group/cross-cultural counseling. The most effective use of these cases and questions will probably occur when they serve to stimulate group discussion, preferably in settings where a number of racial/ethnic groups are represented.

It would be pleasing if we could report that in the four years since the first edition of *Counseling American Minorities: A Cross-Cultural Perspective* appeared in print oppression of minorities had become a thing of the past. Unfortunately, this is hardly the case. Legislative and judicial achievements of the 1960s and early 1970s are currently under attack at the local, state, and federal levels. Minority persons continue to experience discrimination in employment, housing, and education. Physical harassment and abuse of minorities is on the rise. The need for counselor knowledge of, and sensitivity to, the minority client experience is greater now than it has been at any time in the past decade. We hope this text enhances counselor knowledge and sensitivity in this important area.

D. R. A.
G. M.
D. W. S.

Part 1
Why a Cross-Cultural Perspective?

1 Introduction
Defining Terms

The 1960s and 1970s witnessed a sudden increase in the number of articles that related to minority group counseling appearing in the professional counseling literature. A number of these studies identified such diverse groups as the aged, Asian Americans, Blacks, Chicanos, drug users, gays, the handicapped, Native Americans, prison inmates, students, and women as minority groups; this led to some question about what the term *minority* means. To add to the confusion, a number of terms are often used interchangeably with *minority* and/or with each other when their applicability is questionable. Writers, researchers, and practitioners have frequently failed to clearly distinguish between such important concepts as race, ethnic group, culture, and minority. The rhetoric and emotionalism surrounding the field of counseling minorities have distorted communications sufficiently without added confusion arising from undefined terms. Since counseling effectiveness relies so heavily on accurate and appropriate communication, especially in working with a culturally diverse client, it seems imperative that counselors clarify the meaning of these words. The following discussion is offered to define and elucidate certain basic terms and concepts related to minority group/cross-cultural counseling.

Race, Ethnicity, and Culture

Two terms that are often used interchangeably in the counseling literature are race and ethnicity. According to the *Oxford Dictionary of Words,* the term "race" first appeared in the English language less than three hundred years ago. Yet in that brief time race has come to be one of the most misused and misunderstood terms in the American vernacular (Rose, 1964).

The term race, as it is most frequently used today, borrows much of its meaning from a biological conception. As such, race refers to a system by which both plants and animals are classified into subcategories according to specific physical and structural characteristics. As it pertains to the human group, Krogman (1945) defines race as ". . . a subgroup of peoples possessing a definite combination of physical characters, of genetic origin, the combination of which to varying degrees distinguishes the subgroup from other subgroups of mankind" (p. 49). Physical differences involving skin pigmentation, head form, facial features, stature, and the color distribution and texture of body hair, are among the most commonly recognized factors distinguishing races of people. But, as Anderson (1971) points out, this system is far from ideal, in that not all racial group members fit these criteria precisely. While we commonly recognize three basic racial types—Caucasoid, Mongoloid, and Negroid—a great deal of overlapping occurs among these groups. In fact, when we look beneath the superficial characteristics, we find there are more similarities between groups than differences (owing to the fact that all humanoids originate from a single specie), and more differences within racial groups than between them. The apparent flexibility of this definition poses little difficulty for biologists, whose major intent is to create a schema for showing genetic relationships. Unfortunately, this same level of functional clarity is not shared by the social sciences.

Most of the confusion surrounding the term race occurs when it is used in social context. As Mack (1968) so adequately points out, race in the biological sense has no biological consequences, but what people *believe* about race has very profound social consequences. Through subtle yet effective socializing influences, group members are taught and come to accept as "social fact" a myriad of myths and stereotypes regarding skin color, stature, facial features and so forth. Thus, as Mack (1968) contends, "most of men's discussions about race are discussions about their beliefs, not about biological fact" (p. 103).

Ethnicity, on the other hand, refers to a group classification in which the members share a unique social and cultural heritage passed on from one generation to the next (Rose, 1964). Ethnicity is often erroneously assumed to have a biological or genetic foundation. For instance, Jews, as well as numerous other groups, are frequently identified as a racially distinct group. But, as Thompson and Hughes (1958) point out:

> . . . (Jews) . . . are not a biological race because the people known as Jews are not enough like each other and are too much like other people to be distinguished from them. But as people act with reference to Jews and to some extent connect the attitudes they have about them with real and imagined biological characteristics, they become a socially supposed race (p. 67).

If one accepts the view that ethnicity is the result of shared social and cultural heritage, it is apparent that Jews are an ethnic group. Hence, ethnic differences often involve differences in customs, language, religion and other cultural factors; racial differences may or may not be germane to ethnic differences.

Finally, there is common confusion over the relationship of the term "culture" with race and ethnicity. Moore (1974) hits at the heart of the confusion:

> Sometimes we tend to confuse race and ethnic groups with culture. Great races do have different cultures. Ethnic groups within races differ in cultural

content. But, people of the same racial origin and of the same ethnic groups differ in their cultural matrices. All browns, or blacks, or whites, or yellows, or reds are not alike in the cultures in which they live and have their being. The understanding of the culture of another, or of groups other than our own, demands a knowledge of varied elements within a culture or the variety of culture components within a larger cultural matrix (p. 41).

Numerous definitions of culture have been offered by anthropologists over the years, including Kroeber and Kluckhohn's (1952) attempt to synthesize many of them:

Culture consists of patterns, explicit and implicit, of and for behavior acquired and transmitted by symbols, constituting the distinctive achievement of human groups, including their embodiments in artifacts; the essential core of culture consists of traditional (i.e., historically derived and selected) ideas and especially their attached values; culture systems may, on the other hand, be considered as products of action, on the other as conditioning elements of further action (p. 181).

Needless to say, the myriad of confusing definitions that Kroeber and Kluckhohn set out to eliminate was only augmented by their earnest efforts. The most succinct and useful definition, for our purposes, is that offered by Linton (1945), who sees culture as, ". . . the configuration of learned behavior and results of behavior whose components and elements are shared and transmitted by the members of a particular society" (p. 32). By virtue of this definition of culture and those concepts of race and ethnicity accepted earlier, it is clear that the various ethnic groups within racial and among racial categories have their own unique cultures. It should also be clear that even within ethnic groups, small groups of individuals may develop behavior patterns they share and transmit, which in essence constitute a form of culture.

Before leaving this discussion of culture, it is important to dismiss two terms that have been widely used in the past to describe minority groups: "culturally deprived" and "culturally disadvantaged." The term "culturally deprived" implies the absence of culture, a (perhaps hypothetical) situation that has no relationship to the groups addressed in this book. Notwithstanding the effects of the larger society's culture on minorities through the mass media, minority groups clearly possess and transmit a culture of their own.

The term "culturally disadvantaged" suggests the person to whom it is applied is at a disadvantage because she/he lacks the cultural background formed by the controlling social structure. The use of "disadvantaged" rather than "deprived" is intended to recognize that the individual possesses a cultural heritage, but also suggests it is not the *right* culture. While less noxious than "culturally deprived," "culturally disadvantaged" still implies a cultural deficiency, whereas the real issue is one of ethnocentrism, with the values of the majority culture viewed as more important than those of minority cultures. A person may be economically disadvantaged because he/she has less money than the average person, or educationally disadvantaged due to inferior formal education. We seriously object, however, to any inference that minority peoples have less culture.

Even the currently popular terms "culturally different" and "culturally distinct" can carry negative connotation when they are used to imply that a minority person's culture is at variance (out-of-step) with the dominant (accepted) culture. The inappropriate application of these two terms occurs in counseling when their usage is restricted to minority clients. Taken literally, it is grammatically and conceptually correct to refer to a majority client as "culturally different" or "culturally distinct" from the counselor if the counselor is a minority individual.

Melting Pot, Cultural Assimilation, and Cultural Pluralism Philosophies

Throughout the early stages of its development, the United States projected an image of the cultural melting pot, a nation in which all nationalities, ethnicities, and races melted into one culture. Many Americans took pride in the melting pot image and a play by British playwright Israel Zangwill, entitled *The Melting Pot,* enjoyed widespread popularity in this country when it was first performed in 1908. Inherent in the melting pot concept was the view that a new and unique culture would continually emerge as each new immigrant group impacted upon the existing culture (Krug, 1976).

Not everyone in the United States, however, subscribed to the melting pot theory and philosophy. The Chinese Exclusion Act passed by Congress in 1882 was the first of a number of federal and state laws established to insure that certain immigrant groups would have minimal impact on the emerging American culture. In 1926 Henry Pratt Fairchild, a noted American sociologist of the time, wrote that the melting pot philosophy and unrestricted immigration were "slowly, insidiously, irresistably eating away the very heart of the United States" (Fairchild, 1926, p. 261). According to Fairchild and others, the "heart of the United States," was an (equivocally defined) American culture that was based primarily on the values and mores of early immigrants, principally English, Irish, German, and Scandanavian groups. Instead of melting all cultures into one, opponents of the melting pot philosophy argued that an effort should be made to culturally assimilate ("Americanize") all immigrant groups. To reduce the effects of the melting pot phenomenon and increase the probability of cultural assimilation, immigration quotas were developed for those countries whose culture diverged most from the American culture. Public education, with its universal use of the English language, was viewed as the primary institution for perpetuating the existing American culture (Epps, 1974).

The growing awareness of civil rights that took place in the 1960s and 1970s lead to increased recognition that the melting pot principle had bypassed certain ethnic groups and that the cultural assimilation philosophy was objectionable because it called for relinquishing traditional ethnic values and norms in favor of those of the dominant culture. With the civil rights movement came a growing interest in cultural pluralism. According to the theory of cultural pluralism, individual ethnic groups maintain their own cultural uniqueness while sharing common elements of American culture (Kallen, 1956). Cultural pluralism is often likened to a cultural stew, the various ingredients are mixed together but rather than melting into a single mass, the components remain intact and distinguishable while contributing to a whole that is richer than its parts alone. Cultural pluralism has enjoyed some popularity and acceptance (although hardly widespread) during the 1970s as evidenced by the passage of the Ethnic Heritage Studies Bill by Congress in 1973 and the implementation of bilingual, bicultural education in many metropolitan school districts. Whether support for bilingual, bicultural education will continue in the 1980s, however, remains to be seen.

Minority, Oppression, and the Third World

The term *minority* is frequently used in counseling literature to refer to racial/ethnic minorities or the nonwhite populations. Other authors have defined minority groups as physically or behaviorally identifiable groups that make up less than 50 percent of the United States population. Included in this definition are racial/ethnic minorities, the aged, the poor, "gay" people and others of a non-straight sexual orientation, handicapped persons, drug users, and prison populations.

In common usage, however, numerical size alone does not determine minority status. Over 80 percent of the population of South Africa is nonwhite, yet this group is frequently referred to as a minority by individuals within and outside South Africa (Rose, 1964). Prerequisite to an understanding of this use of the term minority is an understanding of the term, oppression.

Oppression is a state of being a person is forced to accept with respect to self, others, and society in general (Goldenberg, 1978). It is a state of being, in which the oppressed person is deprived of some human right or dignity and is (or feels) powerless to do anything about it. Oppression can manifest itself in many ways. European Jews during World War II and both Black Americans and American Indians throughout much of United States history are examples of groups that have experienced oppression in its most extreme form, genocide. Insidious forms of oppression that continue to plague groups of Americans in the 1980s include political, economic, and social oppression. Examples of oppression currently experienced by minority groups include harrassment of Vietnamese shrimp fishing boats in Louisiana and Texas, an average life expectancy for

American Indians approximately 20 years less than the national norm, and educational and income statistics for Blacks and Hispanics that still trail far behind the national averages.

A definition of minority preferred by the present authors and employed in this book, which incorporates the concept of oppression, has been offered by Wirth (1945) who defines minority as:

> . . . a group of people who, because of physical or cultural characteristics, are singled out from the others in society in which they live for differential and unequal treatment, and who therefore regard themselves as objects of collective discrimination (p. 347).

Since we have already established culture as characterized by shared and transmitted behavior, this definition allows us to accept all those groups included in the racial/ethnic and numerical definitions, plus other groups that are oppressed by society *primarily because of their group membership* as minorities. Most importantly, this definition allows us to include women as minorities, a group of oppressed individuals who constitute a numerical majority in this country.

Another term that is frequently used interchangeably with the word "minority" is "Third World." The term Third World is of French derivation *(tiers monde)*, which enjoys international acceptance to describe the nonindustrialized nations of the world that are neither Western nor Communist (Miller, 1967). Many of these countries are located in Africa, South America, and Asia, primarily nonwhite portions of the world. In the United States, nonwhite individuals are frequently referred to as Third World persons. The term has certain political connotations, however, and to some degree has been used as a symbol of comradeship among all oppressed people. The misuse of the term occurs when it is used in this broader sense to apply to all oppressed people, since oppressed people live in First World (Capitalist societies), Second World (Socialist societies), and Third World nations, and are not necessarily distinguished by skin color.

Minority Group/Cross-Cultural Counseling

Minority group counseling, then, can be defined as any counseling relationship in which the client is a member of a minority group, regardless of the status of the counselor (who may be a member of the same minority group, a different minority group, or the majority group). To date much of the writing on minority group counseling has dealt exclusively with racial minorities and has examined the majority counselor-minority client relationship to the exclusion of other possibilities. This limited view of minority group counseling has fallen into some disfavor, perhaps because it ignores the special conditions of a counseling relationship in which the counselor is also a minority person. Further, there is concern that the term minority group counseling suggests a minority pathology; this is perceived as analogous to "Black pathology," an attempt to explain Black behavior in terms of White norms.

Cross-cultural counseling, by way of contrast, refers to any counseling relationship in which two or more of the participants are culturally different. This definition of cross-cultural counseling includes situations in which both the counselor and client(s) are minority individuals but represent different racial/ethnic groups (Black-Chicano, Asian American-Native American, Puerto Rican-Black and so forth). It also includes the situation in which the counselor is a racial/ethnic minority person and the client is White (Black counselor-White client, Chicano counselor-White client, etc.). Additionally it includes the circumstance in which the counselor and client(s) are racially and ethnically similar but belong to different cultural groups because of other variables such as sex, sexual orientation, socioeconomic factors, and age (White male-White female, Black straight person-Black "gay," poor Asian American-wealthy Asian American).

This book is primarily concerned with counseling situations in which the client is a minority group member and culturally different than the counselor. Although the readings selected for inclusion in this volume relate specifically to racial/ethnic (Third World) minorities, the contributions here included are believed to be applicable to all oppressed people. Since the intention is to include counseling relationships defined as minority group counseling *and* cross-cultural counseling, the editors have elected to identify this focus as *minority-group/cross-cultural counseling.*

References

Anderson, C. H. *Toward a new sociology: A critical view.* Homewood, Ill.: The Dorsey Press, 1971.

Epps, E. G. *Cultural pluralism.* Berkeley, CA.: McCutchan Publishing Co., 1974.

Fairchild, H. P. *The melting pot mistake.* Boston: Little, Brown, & Co., 1926.

Goldenberg, I. I. *Oppression and social intervention.* Chicago: Nelson-Hall, 1978.

Kallen, H. M. *Cultural pluralism and the American idea.* Philadelphia: University of Philadelphia Press, 1956.

Kroeber, A. L., & Kluckhohn, C. *Culture: A critical review of concepts and definitions.* New York: Vintage Books, 1952.

Krogman, W. M. The concept of race. In R. Linton's (Ed.) *The science of man in world crisis.* New York: Columbia University Press, 1945, 38–62.

Krug, M. *The melting of the ethnics.* Bloomington, Indiana: Phi Delta Kappa Educational Foundation, 1976.

Linton, R. *The cultural background of personality.* New York: Appleton-Century Co., 1945.

Mack, R. W. *Race, class, & power,* New York: American Book Co., 1968.

Miller, J. D. B. *The politics of the third world.* London: Oxford University Press, 1967.

Moore, B. M. Cultural differences and counseling perspectives. *Texas Personnel and Guidance Association Journal,* 1974, *3,* 39–44.

Rose, P. I. *They and we: Racial and ethnic relations in the United States.* New York: Random House, 1964.

Thompson, E. T., & Hughes, E. C. Race: *Individual and collective behavior.* Glencoe, Ill.: Free Press, 1958.

Wirth, L. The problem of minority groups. In R. Linton (Ed.) *The science of man in the world crisis.* New York: Columbia University Press, 1945.

2 Minority Group Counseling
An Overview

Until the mid 1960s, the counseling profession demonstrated little interest in or concern for the status of racial, ethnic, or other minority groups. Counseling and Guidance, with its traditional focus on the needs of the "average" student, tended to overlook the special needs of students who, by virtue of their skin color, physical characteristics, socioeconomic status, etc., found themselves disadvantaged in a world designed for White, middle class, physically able, "straight" people. Psychotherapy, with its development and practice limited primarily to middle and upper class individuals, also overlooked the needs of minority populations. By the late 1960s, however, "The winds of the American Revolution II . . . (were) . . . howling to be heard" (Lewis, Lewis & Dworkin, 1971, p. 689). And as Aubrey (1977) points out, the view that counseling and guidance dealt with the normal developmental concerns of individuals to the exclusion of special groups' concerns could no longer be accepted.

> Events in the 1960's, however, would blur this simple dichotomy by suddenly expanding potential guidance and counseling audiences to include minority groups, dissenters to the war in Viet Nam, alienated hippie and youth movements, experimenters and advocates of the drug culture, disenchanted students in high schools and universities, victims of urban and rural poverty and disenfranchised women (p. 293).

The forces that led to this voluminous, and often emotional, outcry in the professional counseling literature go far beyond the condition of social unrest existing in the United States in the late 1960s and early 1970s. The note of dissatisfaction was struck when the guidance movement first began and accepted, intentionally or unintentionally, the practically unfulfilled, idealistic promises of the Declaration of Independence as a guideline (Byrne, 1977). As Shertzer and Stone (1974) suggest, "The pervasive concept of individualism, the lack of rigid class lines, the incentive to exercise one's talents to the best of one's ability may have provided a philosophical base . . ." (p. 22) for the dramatic shift in emphasis the profession took almost 60 years after its inception. Fuel for the fire was added when the Civil Rights movement of the 1950s provided convincing evidence that the educational establishment had failed to make provision for equal educational opportunity to all and that the time had come to correct existing discrepancies. The fire of discontent was fanned into a bright flame as the political activism associated with the Viet Nam war touched almost all phases of American life.

Yet the promise of counseling and guidance for minority individuals remains, as yet, unfulfilled. Nor has counseling to date been able to bring much clarity to issues raised in the minority group literature. Central to all other considerations is the role of the profession itself vis a vis minorities. Should counselors work in the domain of "special" minority needs and experiences or should they continue to aim at serving the "middle American" population? While to some extent the question appears moot, one need only examine the curricula of major counselor training programs to determine that the profession continues to train counselors for working with White, middle class, straight, mainstream clientele. Indeed, this has been a serious bone of contention for many minority professionals.

The Unfulfilled Promise of Counseling for Minorities

Minority group authors, particularly those representing racial/ethnic minority groups, have been vociferous and unequivocal in their denunciations of the counseling profession since the mid 1960s. In a comprehensive review of counseling literature related to racial/ethnic minority groups, Pine (1972) found the following view of counseling to be representative of that held by most minority individuals:

> . . . that it is a waste of time; that counselors are deliberately shunting minority students into dead end non-academic programs regardless of student potential, preferences, or ambitions; that counselors discourage students from applying to college; that counselors are insensitive to the needs of students and the community; that counselors do not give the same amount of energy and time in working with minority as they do with White middle-class students; that counselors do not accept, respect, and understand cultural differences; that counselors are arrogant and contemptuous; and that counselors don't know themselves how to deal with their own hangups (p. 35).

Although Pine's article deals primarily with racial/ethnic minorities, similar views of counseling have been expressed by feminist, "gay," pacifist, and other activist minority groups (Counseling and the Social Revolution, 1971).

To some extent minority group unhappiness with counseling reflects disillusionment with all the organized social sciences because of their poor performance as instruments for correcting social ills (Sanford, 1969). Psychology in particular has been criticized for its role as the "handmaiden of the status quo" (Halleck, 1971, p. 30). Frequently minorities see psychology functioning to maintain and promote the status and power of the Establishment (Sue & Sue, 1972).

To a large degree, minority group dissatisfaction with the counseling profession can be explained as disenchantment with unfulfilled promises. As suggested earlier, counseling has at least covertly accepted such ideal rights as "equal access to opportunity," "pursuit of happiness," "fulfillment of personal destiny," and "freedom" as omnipresent, inherent goals in the counseling process (Adams, 1973; Belkin, 1975; Byrne, 1977). Although these lofty ideals may seem highly commendable and extremely appropriate goals for the counseling profession to promote, in reality they have often been translated in such a way as to justify support for the status quo (Adams, 1973).

While the validity of minority criticisms can and will be argued by professional counselors, there is little doubt that, for whatever reasons, counseling has failed to serve the needs of minorities, and in some cases, has proven counterproductive to their well-being. The fact that various minority groups are underrepresented in conventional counseling programs (Sue, 1973) suggests these groups are counseling as irrelevant to their needs.

There is evidence, for example, that ethnic minorities prefer to discuss emotional and educational/vocational problems with parents, friends, and relatives rather than professional counselors (Webster & Fretz, 1978). The lack of minority counselors in many counseling agencies may be a factor in underutilization and the preference for discussing personal concerns with friends and relatives. Thompson and Cimbolic (1978) found that Black college students were more likely to make use of counseling center services if Black counselors were available than if only White counselors could be seen for appointments. There is also substantial evidence that Asian Americans, Blacks, Chicanos, and Native Americans terminate counseling after an initial counseling session at a much higher rate than do Anglos (Sue, Allen, & Conaway, 1978; Sue & Mc Kinney, 1975; Sue, McKinney, Allen, & Hall, 1974). Clearly, minorities see the counseling process, as currently implemented, as irrelevant to their own life experiences and inappropriate or insufficient for their felt needs.

When minorities do bother to seek treatment there is evidence that they are diagnosed differently and receive "less preferred" forms of treatment than do majority clients. In the area of diagnosis, Lee and Temerlin (1968) found that psychiatric residents were more likely to arrive at a diagnosis of mental illness when the individual's history suggested lower-class origin than when a high socioeconomic class was indicated. Haase (1956) demonstrated that clinical psychologists given identical sets of Rorschach test records made more negative prognostic statements and judgments of greater maladjustment when the records were identified as the products of lower-class individuals than when associated with middle-class persons. Broverman, Broverman, Clarkson, Rosenkrantz, and Vogel (1970) found sex also to be a factor in diagnosis, with less favorable judgments by clinical psychologists with respect to female clients than for male clients. In a related study, Thomas and Stewart (1971) presented counselors with taped interviews of a high school girl in counseling and found the girl's career choice rated more appropriate when identified as traditional than when identified as deviant (traditionally male attitude). Similar results have been cited by Schlossberg and Pietrofesa (1973). Mercado and Atkinson (in press) found that male counselors suggested sex-stereotypic occupations for exploration by a high school girl.

In the area of treatment, Garfield, Weiss, and Pollack (1973) gave two groups of counselors identical printed descriptions (except for social class) of a 9-year-old boy who engaged in maladaptive classroom behavior. The counselors indicated a greater willingness to become ego-involved when the child was identified as having upper-class status than when assigned lower-class status. Habermann and Thiry (1970) found that doctoral degree candidates in Counseling and Guidance more frequently programmed students from low-socioeconomic backgrounds into a noncollege bound track than a college preparation track. Research documentation of the inferior quality of mental health services provided to racial/ethnic minorities are commonplace (Clark, 1965; Cowen, Gardner, & Zox, 1967; Guerney, 1969; Lerner, 1972; Thomas & Sillen, 1972; Torion, 1973; Yamamoto, James, Bloombaum, & Hattem, 1967; Yamamoto, James & Palley, 1968).

Differential diagnoses and treatment of minorities is presumably a function of stereotypes held by counselors. Evidence that counselors do hold stereotypes of minorities is beginning to accumulate. Casas, Wampold, and Atkinson (1981) found that university counselors tend to group student characteristics into constellations reflective of common ethnic stereotypes. In a study employing an illusory correlation paradigm, Wampold, Casas and Atkinson, (1981) found that nonminority counselor trainees are more likely to be influenced by stereotypes when assigning characteristics to ethnic groups than are minority counselor trainees. Finally, even when attempting to be sensitive to the needs of Mexican-American students, university counselors may base their counseling services on stereotypes that are not supported by research (Casas & Atkinson, 1981).

Criticism of the Traditional Counseling Role

Due in part to the unfulfilled promise of counseling for minorities, a great deal of criticism has been directed at the traditional counseling role in which an office-bound counselor engages the client in verbal interaction with the intention of resolving the client's psychological problems. For the most part, this criticism can be summarized as three interrelated concerns: criticism of the intrapsychic counseling model, criticism of how counseling approaches have developed, and criticism related to counseling process variables.

Criticism of Intrapsychic Counseling Model

Perhaps the strongest, most cogent indictment of the traditional counseling role has been criticism of the intrapsychic view of client problems inherent to some degree in all current counseling approaches. The intrapsychic model assumes client problems are the result of personal disorganization rather than institutional or societal dysfunctioning (Bryson & Bardo, 1975). Counselors, these critics argue, should view minority clients as victims of a repressive society and rather than intervene with the victim, counselors should attempt to change the offending portion of the client's environment (Banks, 1972; Williams & Kirkland, 1971).

The issue of whether one focuses on the *person* or *system* is an important one. Counseling in this country has grown out of a philosophy of "rugged individualism" in which people are assumed to be responsible for their own lot in life. Success in society is attributed to outstanding abilities or great effort. Likewise, failures or problems encountered by the person may be attributed to some inner deficiency (lack of effort, poor abilities, etc.). For the minority individual who is the victim of oppression, the person-blame approach tends to deny the existence of external injustices (racism, sexism, age, bias, etc.).

Pedersen (1976) has suggested that the counselor can help the minority client either adopt, or adapt to the dominant culture. Vexliard (1968) has coined the terms autoplastic and alloplastic to define two levels of adaption; the first, ". . . involves accommodating oneself to the givens of a social setting and structure and the latter involves shaping the external reality to suit one's needs" (Draguns, 1976, p. 6). Thus, critics of the traditional counseling role see cultural adoption and the autoplastic model of adaption as repressive but predictable outcomes of the intrapsychic counseling model. The counseling roles they advocate can be viewed as directed toward the alloplastic end of the auto-alloplastic adaption continuum, and will be discussed in some detail in the final chapter of this book.

Criticism of How Counseling Approaches Have Developed

Minority intellectuals have criticized contemporary counseling approaches which they contend have been developed by and for the White, middle class person (Bell, 1971; Gunnings, 1971; Mitchell, 1971). Little or no attention has been directed to the need to develop counseling procedures that are compatible with minority cultural values. Unimodal counseling approaches are perpetuated by graduate programs in counseling that give inadequate treatment to the mental health issues of minorities. Cultural influences affecting personality, identify formation, and behavior manifestations frequently are not a part of training programs. When minority group experiences are discussed, they are generally seen and analyzed from the "White, middle class perspective." As a result, counselors who deal with the mental health problems of minorities often lack understanding and knowledge about cultural differences and their consequent interaction with an oppressive society.

Majority counselors who do not have firsthand experience with the minority client's specific cultural milieu may overlook the fact that the client's behavior patterns have different interpretations in the two cultures represented. Behavior that is diagnosed as pathological in one culture may be viewed as adaptive in another (Wilson & Calhoun, 1974). Grier & Cobbs (1968) in their depiction of Black cultural paranoia as a "healthy" development make reference to the potential for inappropriate diagnoses. Thus, the determination of normality or abnormality tends to be intimately associated with a White, middle class standard.

Furthermore, counseling techniques which are a product of the White middle class culture are frequently applied indiscriminately to the minority population (Bell, 1971). In addition, counselors themselves are often culturally encapsulated (Wrenn, 1962), measuring reality against their own set of monocultural assumptions and values, and demonstrating insensitivity to cultural variations in clients (Pedersen, 1976). New counseling techniques and approaches are needed, it is argued, that take into account the minority experience (Gunnings, 1971).

The issue is perhaps best represented semantically by the emic-etic dichotomy, which was first presented by the linguist, Pike (1954). Draguns (1976) offers the following definition of these two terms:

> Emic refers to the viewing of data in terms indigenous or unique to the culture in question, and etic, to viewing them in light of categories and concepts external to the culture but universal in their applicability (p. 2).

The criticisms relevant to the current discussion, then, focus on what can be called the "pseudoetic" approach to cross-cultural counseling (Triandis, Malpass, & Davidson, 1973); culturally encapsulated counselors assume that their own approach and associated techniques can be culturally generalized and are robust enough to cope with cultural variations. In reality, minority critics argue, we have developed emic approaches to counseling that are designed by and for White, middle-class individuals.

Criticisms Related to Counseling Process Variables—Barriers to Minority Group/Cross-Cultural Counseling

Much of the criticism related to minority group counseling focuses upon the interactions that occur between counselor and client. Counseling is seen as a process of interpersonal interaction and communication which requires accurate sending and receiving of both verbal and nonverbal messages. When the counselor and client come from different cultural backgrounds, barriers to communication are likely to develop, leading to misunderstandings that destroy rapport and render counseling ineffective. Thus, process manifestations of cultural barriers pose a serious problem in minority group/cross-cultural counseling.

Most of the writing on barriers to minority group/cross-cultural counseling has focused on racial/ethnic minorities as clientele with a major portion of these studies examining the White counselor—Black client relationship. It is evident, however, that many of the concepts developed by these authors have relevance to any counseling situation involving an individual from a minority (i.e., oppressed) group. It is equally clear that although presented from a majority counselor-minority client perspective, many of the same barriers may exist between a counselor and client who represent two different minority groups (i.e., two different cultures).

In the present discussion, we make a distinction between cultural barriers that are unique to a minority group/cross-cultural counseling situation (e.g., language differences) and those that are process barriers present in every counseling relationship but are particularly thorny and more likely to occur in a cross-cultural situation (e.g., transference).

Barriers Indigenous to Cultural Differences

In discussing barriers and hazards in the counseling process, Johnson and Vestermark (1970) define barriers as, ". . . real obstacles of varying degrees of seriousness . . ." (p. 5). They go on to describe cultural encapsulation as one of the most serious barriers that can affect the counseling relationship. Padilla, Ruiz, and Alvarez (1975) have identified three major impediments to counseling that a non-Latino counselor may encounter when working with a Latino client. Sue & Sue (1977) have generalized these barriers as relevant to all Third World people. We expand the concept further and attempt to relate the three barriers to all minority group/cross-cultural counseling situations. The three barriers are: (a) language differences; (b) class-bound values; and (c) culture-bound values. These three categories are used to facilitate the present discussion; it should be pointed out, however, that all three categories are recognized as functions of culture broadly defined.

Language Differences—Much of the criticism related to the traditional counseling role has focused on the central importance of verbal interaction and rapport in the counseling relationship. This heavy reliance by counselors on verbal interaction to build rapport presupposes that the participants in a counseling dialogue are capable of understanding each other. Yet many counselors fail to understand the client's language and its nuances sufficiently so as to make rapport building possible (Vontress, 1973). Furthermore, educationally and economically disadvantaged clients may lack the prerequisite verbal skills required to benefit from "talk therapy" (Calia, 1966; Tyler, 1964), especially when confronted by a counselor who relies on complex cognitive and conative concepts to generate client insight.

Sue and Sue (1977) have pointed out that the use of standard English with a lower-class or bilingual client may result in misperceptions of the client's strengths and weaknesses. Certainly the counselor who is unfamiliar with a client's dialect or language system will be unlikely to succeed in establishing rapport (Wilson & Calhoun, 1974). Furthermore, Vontress (1973) suggests that counselors need to be familiar with minority group body language lest they misinterpret the meaning of postures, gestures, and inflections. For example, differences in nonverbal behavior are frequently seen in the comparison of Blacks and Whites. When speaking to another person, Anglos tend to look away from the person (avoid eye contact) more often than do Black individuals. When listening to another person speak, however, Blacks tend to avoid eye contact while Anglos make eye contact. This may account for statements from teachers who feel that Black pupils are inattentive (they make less eye contact when spoken to) or feel that Blacks are more angry (intense stare) when speaking.

Similar observations can be made regarding cross-cultural counseling with other, nonracially-identified minority groups. For instance, prison inmates have developed a language system that tends to change over a period of time. The naive counselor who enters the prison environment for the first time may find that his/her use of standard English may elicit smiles or even guffaws from clients, to say nothing of what this does to the counselor's credibility. Gays, too, have developed a vocabulary that may be entirely foreign to a "straight" counselor. Anyone who doubts this statement need only visit a gay bar in San Francisco or elsewhere and listen to the public dialogue. Any counselor unfamiliar with gay vocabulary is likely to be perceived as too straight by a gay client to be of any help. Gays, like other minority groups, rely heavily upon their own vernacular to convey emotions and, understandably, they prefer a counselor who can grasp these emotions without further translation into standard English.

Unique language patterns can also be associated with poor Appalachian whites, drug users, the handicapped, and to some extent, almost any category that qualifies as a minority group as defined in this book. Often with political activism, minority groups will develop expressive language that is not common to, or has a different connotation than, standard English. Inability to communicate effectively in the client's language may contribute significantly to the poor acceptance which counseling has received from minorities.

Class-bound Values—Differences in values between counselor and client that are basically due to class differences are relevant to minority group/cross-cultural counseling since, almost by definition, many minority group members are also of a lower socioeconomic class. Furthermore, for the purposes of this book, differences in attitudes, behaviors, beliefs, and values among the various socioeconomic groups constitute cultural differences. The interaction of social class and behavior has been well documented by Hollingshead (1949). The importance of social class for school counseling has been discussed by Bernard (1963). Combining the results of several studies, Havighurst and Neugarten (1962) concluded that at least fifty percent of the American population falls into either the upper lower or lower lower socioeconomic classes, suggesting that a large portion of the counselor's potential clientele may be from these socioeconomic classes. The impact of social class differences on counseling in general acquires added significance if one accepts the statement presented earlier in this chapter, that existing counseling techniques are middle and upper class based.

One of the first and most obvious value differences encountered by the middle class counselor and the lower class client involves the willingness to make and keep counseling appointments. As Sue and Sue (1977) point out, ". . . lower-class clients who are concerned with 'survival' or making it through on a day-to-day basis expect advice and suggestions from the counselor . . . (and) . . . appointments made weeks in advance with short weekly 50 minute contacts are not consistent with the need to seek immediate solutions" (p. 424). Vontress (1973) states that Appalachian Whites refuse to be enslaved by the clock and not only do they refuse to adhere to values of promptness, planning, and protocol, but they suspect people who do adhere to these values.

Differences in attitudes toward sexual behavior often enter the counseling relationship between a counselor and client representing different socioeconomic classes. For the most part, open acceptance of sexual promiscuity differs from one socioeconomic level to another, although other factors (e.g., religious beliefs) play heavy roles. Middle class counselors, whether consciously or unconsciously, often attempt to impose middle class sexual mores on lower and upper class clients.

The fact that the clients' socioeconomic status affects the kind of therapeutic treatment clients receive has been well documented. Ryan and Gaier (1968), for instance, found that students from upper socioeconomic backgrounds have more exploratory interviews with counselors than do students representing other social classes. Middle class patients in a veterans administration clinic tend to remain in treatment longer than do lower class patients. And Hollingshead and Redlich (1958) found that the level of therapeutic intensiveness varies directly with socioeconomic background.

Culture-bound Values—Culture, as broadly defined for the purposes of this book, consists of behavior patterns shared and transmitted by a group of individuals. In addition to language and class-bound values already discussed, culture-bound values obviously involve such elements as attitudes, beliefs, customs, and institutions identified as integral parts, of a group's social structure.

Counselors frequently impose their own cultural values upon minority clients in ignorance, reflecting an insensitivity to the clients' values. Referring to clients from racial/ethnic minorities as "culturally deprived" is an example of this imposition. "Straight," male counselors sometimes make sexual remarks about females in front of a male client that may be repugnant to the client if he is gay (to say nothing about how it would affect females who overheard it). Nor is the experience reported by Granberg (1967) in which he found himself incorrectly assuming his homosexual client wanted to become "straight" an unusual example of the counselor's cultural values interfering with the counseling relationship. Drug and prison "counselors" often fulfill roles of instilling the values of the larger society upon their clientele without full awareness of their impact.

For some time the role of the counselor's values in the counseling relationship has been a thorny professional issue. The issue becomes even more poignant when a majority counselor and minority client are involved. In this case, ". . . the values inherent in (the) two different sub-cultures may be realistically as diverse as those of two countries" (Wilson & Calhoun, 1974). While the major concern with this issue, in the broader context, centers on the counselor's influence upon the client, class- and culture-bound value differences can impede further rapport building.

For example, one of the most highly valued aspects of counseling entails self-disclosure, a client's willingness to let the counselor know what he or she thinks or feels. Many professionals argue that self-disclosure is a necessary condition for effective counseling. Jourard (1964) suggests that people are more likely to disclose themselves to others who will react as they do, implying that cultural similarity is an important factor in self-disclosure. Furthermore, self-disclosure may be contrary to basic cultural values for some minorities. Sue and Sue (1972) have pointed out that Chinese American clients, who are taught at an early age to restrain from emotional expression, find the direct and subtle demands by the counselor to self-disclosure very threatening. Similar conflicts have been reported for Chicano (Cross & Maldonado, 1971) and Native American (Trimble, 1976) clients. Poor clients, of whatever racial or ethnic background, frequently resist attempts by the counselor to encourage client self-exploration and prefer to ascribe their problems, often justifiably, to forces beyond their control (Calia, 1966). In addition, many racial minorities have learned to distrust Whites in general and may "shine on" a majority counselor, since this has proven to be adaptive behavior with Whites in the past. Sue and Sue (1977) suggest that self-disclosure is itself a cultural value and counselors who, ". . . value verbal, emotional and behavioral expressiveness as goals in counseling are transmitting their own cultural values" (p. 425).

Related to this last point is the lack of structure frequently provided by the counselor in the counseling relationship. Often, in order to encourage self-disclosure, the counseling situation is intentionally designed to be an ambiguous one, one in which the counselor listens empathically and responds only to encourage the client to continue talking (Sue & Sue, 1972). Minority clients frequently find the lack of structure confusing, frustrating, and even threatening (Haettenschwiller, 1971). Atkinson,

Maruyama, and Matsui (1978) found that Asian Americans prefer a directive counseling style to a nondirective one, suggesting the directive approach is more compatible with their cultural values.

Similar results were found in a replication of the Atkinson et al. (1978) study with American Indian high school students (Dauphinais, Dauphinais, & Rowe, 1981). Black students also were found to prefer a more active counseling role over a passive one (Peoples & Dell, 1975).

Process Manifestations of Cultural Differences

Many of the problems encountered in minority group/cross-cultural counseling which have been identified as cultural barriers might better be conceived of as process manifestations of cultural differences, since they may be present to some extent in any counseling relationship but are aggravated by cultural differences. We will briefly discuss five of them: stereotyping, resistance, transference, countertransference, and client expectations.

Stereotyping—Stereotyping is a major problem for all forms of counseling. It may broadly be defined as rigid preconceptions which are applied to all members of a group or to an individual over a period of time, regardless of individual variations. The key word in this definition is *rigidity,* an inflexibility to change. Thus, a counselor who believes that Blacks are "lazy," "musical," "rhythmic," and "unintelligent"; Asians are "sneaky," "sly," "good with numbers," and "poor with words"; or that Jews are "stingy," "shrewd," and "intellectual" will behave toward representatives of these groups as if they possessed these traits. The detrimental effects of stereotyping have been well documented in professional literature (Rosenthal & Jacobsen, 1968; Smith, 1977; Sue, 1973). First, counselors who have preconceived notions about minority group members may unwittingly act upon these beliefs. If Black students are seen as possessing limited intellectual potential, they may be counseled into terminal vocational trade schools. Likewise, if Asian Americans are perceived as being only good in the physical sciences but poor in verbal-people professions, counselors may direct them toward a predominance of science courses. The second and even more damaging effect is that many minorities may eventually come to believe these stereotypes about themselves. Thus, since the majority of stereotypes about minorities are negative, an inferior sense of self-esteem may develop.

Due to stereotyping or attempts to avoid stereotyping by the counselor, majority counselors frequently have difficulty adjusting to a relationship with a minority client. The most obvious difficulty in this area occurs when the counselor fails to recognize the client as an individual and assigns to the client culturally stereotypic characteristics that are totally invalid for this individual (Smith, 1977). In an effort to treat the client as just another client, on the other hand, the counselor may demonstrate "color or culture blindness" (Wilson & Calhoun, 1974). In this case the counselor may avoid altogether discussing the differences between the two participants, thus implying that the client's attitudes and behaviors will be assessed against majority norms. The content of the counseling dialogue may also be restricted by the preoccupation of the majority counselor with fear that the client will detect conscious or unconscious stereotying on the part of the counselor (Gardner, 1971).

Resistance—Resistance is usually defined as client opposition to the goals of counseling and may manifest itself as self-devaluation, intellectualization, and overt hostility (Vontress, 1976). While it is a potential difficulty in any counseling encounter, the problem becomes particularly acute when the counselor and client are culturally different, since the counselor may misinterpret the resistance as a dynamic of the client's culture.

Transference—Transference occurs when the client responds to the counselor in a manner similar to the way he or she responded to someone else in the past (Greenson, 1964, pp. 151–152), and this may manifest itself as either a liking or disliking of the counselor. Clients may or may not be aware of the transference effect themselves. This phenomena is particularly problematic in the majority counselor-minority client dyad, ". . . because minority group members bring to the relationship intense emotions derived from experiences with and feelings toward the majority group" (Vontress, 1976, p. 49). Minority clients for instance, due to their experiences with an oppressive, majority-controlled society are likely to anticipate authoritarian behavior from the counselor.

Countertransference—Countertransference occurs when the counselor responds to a client as he or she responded to someone in the past (Wilson & Calhoun, 1974, p. 318). Countertransference is particularly difficult for the counselor to recognize and accept since counselors typically view themselves as objective, although empathic, participants in the counseling relationship. It seems highly unlikely, however, that majority counselors in this society are entirely free of the stereotypic attitudes toward minority peoples (Jackson, 1973). An argument can be made that counselors, like everyone else, carry with them conscious and unconscious attitudes, feelings, and beliefs about culturally different people, and that these will manifest themselves as countertransference (Vontress, 1976).

Client Expectation—Closely related to transference, client expectations for success in the counseling relationship can directly affect counseling outcome. When the minority client finds him/herself assigned to a majority counselor, the client's prognostic expectations may be reduced (Wilson & Calhoun, 1974). Prior to the initial counseling session the client may experience feelings of distrust, futility, and anger which generate an expectation that counseling will not succeed. Such an expectation usually dooms the counseling relationship to failure.

Barriers to Minority Counselor-Minority
or Majority Client Counseling

As used in the counseling literture, minority group counseling frequently implies that the counselor is a member of the dominant culture and the client a minority group member, suggesting that this combination is of greatest threat to effective counseling. A few authors have referred to the problems encountered in counseling when the client and counselor are from the same minority group. Virtually none have discussed the difficulties experienced when the counselor is from a different minority group than the client. Lest the impression be given that culturally related barriers only exist for the majority counselor-minority client dyad, we now turn briefly to difficulties experienced by minority counselors and their clients.

Intra-Minority Group Counseling

Several authors have identified problems that the minority counselor may encounter when working with a client from a cultural background similar to that of the counselor. Jackson (1973) points out that the minority client may respond with anger when confronted by a minority counselor. The anger may result from finding a minority person associated with a majority controlled institution. Some clients may experience anger, on the other hand, because they feel a majority counselor would be more competent, thus enhancing the probability of problem resolution. Or the client's anger may reflect jealousy that the counselor has succeeded through personal efforts in breaking out of a repressive environment. In the case of a Third World counselor, the counselor may also be seen as:

> . . . too white in orientation to be interested in helping, as less competent than his colleagues, as too far removed from problems that face the patient, or as intolerant and impatient with the patient's lack of success in dealing with problems (Jackson, 1973, p. 277).

The minority counselor may respond to minority client anger by becoming defensive (Jackson, 1973), thus impeding the counseling process. Minority counselors may also either deny identification with or over-identify with the client (Gardner, 1971). Sattler (1970) has suggested that minority counselors may have less tolerance and understanding of minority clients and view the contact as low status work compared to counseling a majority client.

Calnek (1970) points out the danger that Third World counselors too often adopt stereotypes which Whites have developed, concerning how minority clients think, feel, and act. The counselor may deny that the client is also a minority person, for fear the common identification will result in a loss of professional image for the counselor. Over-identification, on the other hand, may cause the counseling experience to degenerate into a gripe session. Calnek also refers to the danger of the counselor projecting his/her own self image onto the client because they are culturally similar.

While the foregoing comments are, for the most part, directed at the Black counselor-Black client dyad, it is easy to see that the problem could be generalized to include other intra-minority group situations.

Inter-Minority Group Counseling

Counselors representing one minority group who find themselves working with a client representing a different minority group often face the problems associated with both the majority counselor-minority client and the intra-minority group counseling situations. Although the camaraderie of Third World peoples that results from awareness of shared oppression helps to bridge cultural differences on college and university campuses, in the nonacademic world these differences are often as intense or more intense than those between the dominant and minority cultures. One need only observe Chicano students and parents in East Los Angeles or Black students and parents in Bedford-Stuyvesant to gain an appreciation of ethnocentrism and the difficulty which culturally different-minority counselors can perceive in these situations. Furthermore, the counselor representing a different minority than the client may be suspect to the client, for the same reasons counselors of similar minority backgrounds would be suspect.

Potential Benefits in Cross-Cultural Counseling

Almost no attention has been given in the counseling literature to identifying the benefits of cross-cultural counseling. In reference to the minority counselor-majority client dyad, Jackson (1973) suggests that the client may find it easier to, ". . . share information that is looked on as socially unacceptable without censor from the therapist" (p. 275), suggesting self-disclosure, at least of some materials, may be enhanced. Students who are rebelling against the Establishment, for instance, may prefer a minority counselor, feeling that the counselor's experience with oppression qualifies him/her to acquire empathy with the client (Gardner, 1971). Gardner (1971) also suggests majority clients may prefer minority counselors if they are dealing with material that would be embarrassing to share with a majority counselor. Jackson (1973) points out that there is a tendency in this situation to perceive the counselor more as another person than as a superhuman, notwithstanding those cases where the counselor is perceived as a "super-minority." In the latter case, the client may view the minority counselor as more capable than his/her majority counterpart, owing to the obstacles the counselor had to overcome. The net effect in this case may be a positive expectation. The possibility that minority counselors are less likely to let secrets filter back into the client's community is also cited by Gardner (1971) as a positive variable in cross-cultural counseling.

Several authors (Draguns, 1975, 1976; Trimble, 1976), while referring in part to national cultures, have suggested that cross-cultural counseling is a learning experience to be valued in and of itself. The counseling process, with its intentional provision for self-disclosure of attitudes, values and intense emotional feelings, can help the counselor and client gain a perspective on each other's culture, frequently in a way never experienced outside of counseling. Cross-cultural counseling also offers an opportunity to both counselor and client to expand their modes of communication, to learn new ways of interacting. Rather than being viewed as a deficit, client (and counselor) bilingualism should be viewed and treated as a strength.

Again it seems apparent that much of the foregoing can be generalized to apply to nonracially or ethnically identified minorities. It also seems evident that further research and discussion are needed regarding both the barriers and benefits of cross-cultural counseling. Those discussed above, along with several proposed by the current authors, are outlined in table 2.1. In addition to citing positive and negative aspects of cross-cultural situations, the authors have attempted, as shown in table 2.1, to identify their counterparts when counselor and client are culturally similar.

Editors' View

The editors of this book of readings are in agreement with those earlier writers who have suggested that cross-cultural counseling can not only be effective for resolving client difficulties, but can also serve as a forum for a unique learning experience. That barriers to cross-cultural counseling exist is not at issue here. Clearly, cultural differences between counselor and client can result in barriers that are, in some instances, insurmountable. As suggested earlier, however, cross-cultural counseling can involve benefits to both client and counselor that may not be possible in intra-cultural counseling.

Furthermore, it is our contention that the primary barrier to effective counseling and one which underlies many other barriers is the traditional counseling role itself. No one has yet offered conclusive evidence that differences in status variables (e.g., race, ethnicity, sex, sexual orientation) alone create barriers to counseling. The fact that one person in a counseling dyad is born Black and one White, for instance, should not negate the possibility of their working together effectively. From our perspective, it is how we perceive and experience our and our client's Blackness and Whiteness that creates barriers to constructive communication. For the most part, our perceptions and experiences are shaped by a socialization process that begins at birth. We feel that the traditional counseling role (nonequalitarian, intrapsychic model, office, bound, etc.) often helps to perpetuate the very socialization process that creates a barrier between culturally different individuals.

Table 2.1

Culturally Relevant Barriers and Benefits in Inter- and Intra-Cultural Counseling

Inter-Cultural Counseling	
Barriers	*Benefits*
—client resistance	—client's willingness to self-disclose some material
—client transference	
—client cultural restraints on self-disclosure	—client less likely to view counselor as omniscient
—client expectations	—client expectation for success may be enhanced
—counselor countertransference	—potential for considerable cultural learning by both client and counselor
—counselor maladjustment to the relationship	
—counselor misdirected diagnosis	—increased need for counselor and client to focus on their own processing
—counselor patronization of client's culture	
—counselor denial of culturally dissonant component of client problem	—potential for dealing with culturally dissonant component of client problem
—counselor "missionary zeal"	
—language differences	
—value conflicts	

Intra-Cultural Counseling	
Barriers	*Benefits*
—unjustified assumption of shared feelings	—shared experience may enhance rapport
—client transference	—client willingness to self-disclose some materials
—counselor countertransference	
	—common mode of communication may enhance process

Some critics will argue that differences in experiences are paramount, that a counselor who experiences being Black will understand the Black client's perspective better than any White counselor ever can. We agree to a point. There is simply no conclusive evidence, however, that a counselor must experience everything his/her client does. Carried to the extreme, the similarity of experience argument suggests that all counseling is doomed to failure since no two individuals can ever fully share the same life experiences. Furthermore, while cultural differences do result in unique experiences for both the client and the counselor, our experiences as human beings are remarkably similar. This view—that we are more alike than different—is perhaps best expressed by the sociobiologist De vore (1977):

> Anthropologists always talk about crosscultural diversity, but that's icing on the cake. The cake itself is remarkably panhuman. Different cultures turn out only minor variations on the theme of the species—human courtship, our mating systems, child care, fatherhood, the treatment of the sexes, love, jealousy, sharing. Almost everything that's importantly human—including behavior flexibility—is universal, and developed in the context of our shared genetic background. (p. 88)

In chapter 3 we propose an identity development model that assumes a pan human response *across* minority groups to the experience of oppression. A primary purpose of the model, however, is to suggest that attitudes and behaviors vary greatly *within* the various minority groups and are reflective of stages in identity development. One of the great dangers of attempting to study minority groups, despite the best of intentions, is that old stereotypes are replaced by new ones. The Minority Identity Development model is presented prior to the minority group reading to minimize the development of new stereotypes by suggesting that, even within cultural groups, attitudes and behaviors vary greatly.

References

Adams, H. J. The progressive heritage of guidance: A view from the left. *Personnel and Guidance Journal,* 1973, *51,* 531–538.

Atkinson, D. R., Maruyama, M., & Matsui, S. The effects of counselor race and counseling approach on Asian Americans' perceptions of counselor credibility and utility. *Journal of Counseling Psychology,* 1978, *25,* 76–83.

Aubrey, R. F. Historical development of guidance and counseling and implications for the future. *Personnel and Guidance Journal,* 1977, *55,* 288–295.

Banks, W. The Black client and the helping professionals. In R. I. Jones (Ed.) *Black Psychology.* New York: Harper & Row, 1972.

Belkin, G. S. *Practical Counseling in the Schools,* Dubuque, Iowa: William C. Brown, 1975.

Bell, R. L. The culturally deprived psychologist. *Counseling Psychologist,* 1971, *2,* 104–107.

Bernard, H. W. Socioeconomic class and the school counselor. *Theory into practice,* 1963, *2,* 17–23.

Broverman, I., Broverman, D. M., Clarkson, F. E., Rosenkrantz, P. S., & Vogel, S. Sex role stereotype and clinical judgments of mental health. *Journal of Consulting and Clinical Psychology,* 1970, *34,* 1–7.

Bryson, S., & Bardo, H. Race and the counseling process: An overview. *Journal of Non-White Concerns in Personnel and Guidance,* 1975, *4,* 5–15.

Bryne, R. H. *Guidance: A behavioral approach.* Englewood Cliffs, N.J.: Prentice-Hall, 1977.

Calia, V. F. The culturally deprived client: A re-formulation of the counselor's role. *Journal of Counseling Psychology,* 1966, *13,* 100–105.

Calnek, M. Racial factors in the countertransference: The Black therapist and the Black client. *American Journal of Orthopsychiatry,* 1970, *40,* 39–46.

Casas, J. M., & Atkinson, D. R. The Mexican American in higher education: An example of subtle stereotyping. *Personnel and Guidance Journal,* 1981, *59,* 473–476.

Casas, J. M., Wampold, B. E., & Atkinson, D. R. The categorization of ethnic stereotypes by university counselors. *Hispanic Journal of Behavioral Sciences,* 1981, *3,* 75–82.

Clark, K. B. *Dark Ghetto: Dilemmas of Social Power.* New York: Harper and Row, 1965.

Counseling and the Social Revolution. *Personnel and Guidance Journal,* 1971, *49* (9).

Cowen, E. L., Gardner, E. A., & Zox, M. (Eds.) *Emergent approaches to mental health problems.* New York: Appleton-Century-Crofts, 1967.

Cross, W. C., & Maldonado, B. The counselor, the Mexican American, and the stereotype. *Elementary School Guidance and Counseling,* 1971, *6,* 27–31.

Dauphinais, P., Dauphinais, L., & Rowe, W. Effects of race and communication style on Indian perceptions of counselor effectiveness. *Counselor Education and Supervision,* 1981, *21,* 72–30.

De Vore, I. The new science of genetic self-interest. *Psychology Today,* 1977, *10* (9), 42–51, 84–88.

Draguns, J. G. Resocialization into culture: The complexities of taking a worldwide view of psychotherapy. In R. W. Brislin, S. Bochner, & W. J. Lonner (Eds.), *Cross-cultural perspectives in learning.* New York: John Wiley & Sons, Halsted, 1975.

Draguns, J. G. Counseling across cultures: Common themes and distinct approaches. In P. Pedersen, W. J. Lonner, & J. G. Draguns (Eds.), *Counseling across cultures.* Honolulu: The University of Hawaii Press, 1976.

Gardner, L. H. The therapeutic relationship under varying conditions of race. *Psychotherapy: Theory, Research and Practice,* 1971, *8,* (1), 78–87.

Garfield, J. C., Weiss, S. L., & Pollack, E. A. Effects of the child's social class on school counselor's decision making. *Journal of Counseling Psychology,* 1973, *20,* 166–168.

Granberg, L. I. What I've learned in counseling. *Christianity Today,* 1967, *2,* 891–894.

Greenson, R. R. *The technique and practice of psychoanalysis* (Vol. 1). New York: International Universities Press, 1964.

Grier, W. H. & Cobbs, P. M. *Black Rage.* New York: Bantam Books, Inc., 1968.

Guerney, B. G. (Ed.) *Psychotherapeutic agents: New roles for nonprofessionals, parents, and teachers.* New York: Holt, Rinehart & Winston, 1969.

Gunnings, T. S. Preparing the new counselor. *The Counseling Psychologist,* 1971, *2* (4), 100–101.

Haase, W. *Rorschach diagnosis, socio-economic class and examiner bias.* Unpublished doctoral dissertation, New York University, 1956.

Habermann, L., & Thiry, S. *The effect of socio-economic status variables on counselor perception and behavior.* Unpublished master's thesis, University of Wisconsin, 1970.

Haettenschwiller, D. L. Counseling black college students in special programs. *Personnel and Guidance Journal,* 1971, *50,* 29–35.

Halleck, S. L. Therapy is the handmaiden of the status quo. *Psychology Today,* 1971, *4,* 30–34, 98–100.

Havighurst, R. J., & Neugarten, B. L. *Society and Education* (Second edition). Boston: Allyn & Bacon, Inc., 1962.

Hollingshead, A. B. *Elmtown's youth: The impact of social classes on adolescents.* New York: John Wiley and Sons, Inc., 1949.

Hollingshead, A. B. & Redlich, F. C. *Social class and mental health.* New York: John Wiley & Sons, Inc., 1958.

Jackson, A. M. Psychotherapy: Factors associated with the race of the therapist. *Psychotherapy: Theory, Research and Practice,* 1973, *10,* 273–277.

Johnson, D. E., & Vestermark, M. J. *Barriers and hazards in counseling.* Boston: Houghton Mifflin Co., 1970.

Jourard, S. M. *The transparent self.* Princeton, N.J.: D. Van Nostrand Co., 1964.

Lee, S., & Temerlin, M. K. *Social class status and mental illness.* Unpublished doctoral dissertation, University of Oklahoma, 1968.

Lerner, B. *Therapy in the ghetto: Political impotence and personal disintegration.* Baltimore: Johns Hopkins University Press, 1972.

Lewis, M. D., Lewis, J. A., & Dworkin, E. P. Editorial: Counseling and the social revolution. *The Personnel and Guidance Journal,* 1971, *49,* 689.

Mercado, P. & Atkinson, D. R. Effects of counselor sex, student sex, and student attractiveness on counselor's judgments. *Journal of Vocational Behavior,* in press.

Mitchell, H. Counseling black students: A model in response to the need for relevant counselor training programs. *The Counseling Psychologist,* 1971, *2* (4), 117–122.

Padilla, A. M., Ruiz, R. A., & Alvarez, R. Community mental health services for the Spanish-speaking/surnamed population. *American Psychologist,* 1975, *30,* 892–905.

Pedersen, P. B. The field of intercultural counseling. In P. B. Pedersen, W. J. Lonner & J. G. Draguns (Eds.) *Counseling across cultures.* Honolulu: The University of Hawaii Press, 1976.

Peoples, V. Y., & Dell, D. M. Black and white student preferences for counselor roles. *Journal of Counseling Psychology,* 1975, *22,* 529–534.

Pike, K. L. *Language in relation to a unified theory of the structure of human behavior.* Part 1: Preliminary edition. Summer Institute of Linguistics, 1954.

Pine, G. J. Counseling minority groups: A review of the literature. *Counseling and Values,* 1972, *17,* 35–44.

Rosenthal, R., & Jacobson, L. *Pygmalion in the classroom: Teacher expectation and pupils' intellectual development.* New York: Holt, Rinehart & Winston, 1968.

Ryan, D. W., & Gaier, E. L. Student socio-economic status and counselor contact in junior high school. *Personnel and Guidance Journal,* 1968, *46,* 466–472.

Sanford, N. Research with students as action and education. *American Psychologist,* 1969, *24,* 544–546.

Sattler, J. M. Racial "Experimenter Effects" in experimentation, testing, interviewing and psychotherapy. *Psychological Bulletin,* 1970, *73,* 137–160.

Schlossberg, N. K. & Pietrofesa, J. J. Perspectives on counseling bias: Implications for counselor education. *The Counseling Psychologist,* 1973, *4,* 44–54.

Shertzer, B., & Stone, S. C. *Fundamentals of Counseling* (2nd ed.) Boston: Houghton Mifflin, 1974.

Smith, E. J. Counseling Black individuals: Some stereotypes. *Personnel and Guidance Journal,* 1977, *55,* 390–396.

Sue, D. W. Ethnic identity: The impact of two cultures on the psychological development of Asians in America. In S. Sue & Wagner (Eds.) *Asian Americans: Psychological perspectives.* Ben Lomand, California: Science and Behavior Books, Inc., 1973, 140–149.

Sue, D. W., & Sue, S. Counseling Chinese-Americans, *Personnel and Guidance Journal,* 1972, *50,* 637–644.

Sue, D. W. & Sue, D. Barriers to effective cross-cultural counseling. *Journal of Counseling Psychology,* 1977, *24,* 420–429.

Sue, S., Allen, D., & Conaway, L. The responsiveness and equality of mental health care to Chicanos and Native Americans. *American Journal of Community Psychology,* in press.

Sue, S., & McKinney, H. Asian Americans in the community mental health care system. *American Journal of Orthopsychiatry,* 1975, *45,* 111–118.

Sue, S., McKinney, H., Allen, D., & Hall, J. Delivery of community health services to Black and White clients. *Journal of Consulting Psychology,* 1974, *42,* 794–801.

Thomas, A., & Sillen, S. *Racism and psychiatry.* New York: Brunney Mazel, 1972.

Thomas, A. H., & Stewart, N. R. Counselor response to female clients with deviate and conforming career goals. *Journal of Counseling Psychology,* 1971, *18,* 352–357.

Thompson, R. A., & Cimbolic, P. Black students' counselor preference and attitudes toward counseling center use. *Journal of Counseling Psychology,* 1978, *25,* 570–575.

Torion, R. P. Socioeconomic status and traditional treatment approaches reconsidered. *Psychological Bulletin,* 1973, *79,* 263–270.

Triandis, H. C., Malpass, R. S., & Davidson, A. R. Psychology and Culture. *Annual Review of Psychology,* 1973, *24,* 355–378.

Trimble, J. E. Value differences among American Indians: Concern for the concerned counselor. In P. Pedersen, W. J. Lonner, & J. G. Draguns (Eds.), *Counseling across cultures.* Honolulu: The University of Hawaii Press, 1976.

Tyler, L. The methods and processes of appraisal and counseling. In A. S. Thompson and D. E. Super (Eds.) *The professional preparation of counseling psychologists.* New York: Bureau of Publications, Teachers College, Columbia University, 1964.

Vexliard, A. Tempérament et modalités d'adaptation. *Bulletin de Psychologie,* 1968. *21,* 1–15.

Vontress, C. E. Counseling: Racial and ethnic factors. *Focus on Guidance,* 1973, *5,* 1–10.

Vontress, C. E. Racial and ethnic barriers in counseling. In P. Pedersen, W. J. Lonner, & J. G. Draguns (Eds.) *Counseling across cultures.* Honolulu: The University of Hawaii Press, 1976.

Wampold, B. E., Casas, J. M., & Atkinson, D. R. Ethnic bias in counseling: An information processing approach. *Journal of Counseling Psychology,* 1981, *28,* 498–503.

Webster, D. W., & Fretz, B. R. Asian American, Black, and White college students' preferences for help-giving sources. *Journal of Counseling Psychology, Journal of Counseling Psychology,* 1978, *25,* 124–130.

Williams, R. L., & Kirkland, J. The white counselor and the black client. *Counseling Psychologist,* 1971, *2,* 114–117.

Wilson, W. & Calhoun, J. F. Behavior therapy and the minority client. *Psychotherapy: Theory, Research and Practice,* 1974, *11,* 317–325.

Wrenn, C. G. The culturally encapsulated counselor. *Harvard Educational Review,* 1962, *32,* 444–449.

Yamamoto, J., James, Q. C. Bloombaum, M., & Hatten, J. Racial factors in patient selection. *American Journal of Psychiatry,* 1967, *124,* 630–636.

Yamamoto, J., James, Q. C., & Palley, N. Cultural problems in psychiatric therapy. *Archives of General Psychiatry,* 1968, *19,* 45–49.

3 Proposed Minority Identity Development Model

Each minority group has a unique cultural heritage that makes it distinct from other groups. Cultural distinction, however, has often been erroneously interpreted as evidence of cultural conformity and has frequently led to a monolithic view of minority group attitudes and behaviors. Clearly, uniformity of attitudes and behaviors is no more true for minority individuals than it is for members of the dominant culture. With regard to the very issue of cultural distinction, minority attitudes may vary from desire for total assimilation into the dominant culture to total rejection of the dominant culture and immersion in the minority culture (Parks, 1950).

In chapter 8 Derald and Stanley Sue provide evidence of the disparate ways in which Chinese Americans respond to cultural conflict. Some reject their Chinese background entirely and try to assimilate into the dominant society. Others adhere to traditional cultural values and attempt to resist assimilation. Still others stress pride in their racial identity while refraining from the conformity inherent in both the traditional Chinese practices and assimilation into mainstream culture. Ruiz and Padilla suggest in chapter 15 that there is a danger inherent in trying to isolate the "true nature" of the Latino character since each person's attitudes and behaviors are a function of his/her degree of acculturation. Furthermore, these and other readings to follow suggest that not only do intragroup differences exist, but attitudes and behaviors within individuals can fluctuate greatly as their identification with one culture or another changes.

The purpose of this chapter is to explicate a model of minority identity development that acknowledges coincidental identity transformational processes involving minority groups and utilizes these processes to help explain individual differences within minority groups. A number of earlier authors have also attempted to explain individual differences within racial/ ethnic groups. Some of these early attempts took the form of simple typologies in which a particular minority group was divided into smaller subcategories or types based on their degree of ethnic identification. As Hall, Cross, and Freedle (1972) point out, these subgroups generally included both "conservative" and "militant" types, and one or two categories in between. Vontress (1971), for instance, theorized that Afro Americans conformed to three distinct subgroups: (1) Colored, (2) Negro, and (3) Black. Briefly, these subcategories represented decreasing levels of dependence upon White society and culture as the source of self-definition and worth, and an increasing degree of identification with Black society and culture. As another example, Mayovich (1973) typed Japanese Americans according to four separate categories: (1) Conformists, (2) Anomic, (3) Liberal, and (4) Militant. Mayovich (1973) hypothesized that as a result of their acceptance or rejection of traditional values and their involvement or detachment from social issues, all Japanese Americans (at least those of the Sansei generation) fell into one of these four types.

This method of "typing" minority individuals has come under heavy criticism in recent years, however. Banks (1972), for instance, contends that these theorists have mistakenly proposed labels that attribute certain fixed personality traits to people when, in fact, their behavior is a function of a specific situation. Others (Cross, 1970; Hall, Cross, & Freedle, 1972; Jackson, 1975) have suggested that any attempt to define minority "types" must acknowledge movement of individuals across categories. In spite of such criticisms, it is important to recognize the early typologies as pioneering attempts that paved the way for more sophisticated models of identity development.

A second major approach has viewed minority attitudes and behavior as a product of an identity development continuum. This approach differs from earlier typologies in that minority attitudes and behaviors are viewed as flexible and a function of the individual's stage of identity development. Rather than type the individual, stages of development through which any minority person may pass are described. Attitudinal and behavioral attributes are, therefore, not viewed as fixed characteristics, but as related to identity development.

These early attempts to define a process of minority identity development were almost exclusively the work of Black intellectuals who were obviously influenced in their thinking by the impact of social, psychological and cultural events in the 60s. Hall, Cross, and Freedle (1972) describe how these events highlighted the process of Black identity transformation:

> We have seen a change in the nature of black-white relations in America. To be sure, this change has produced many consequences, one of which has been an identity transformation among American blacks. The transformation has been from an older orientation whereby most blacks viewed themselves as inadequate, inferior, incapable of self-determination, and unable to cope with the intricacies of life in a complex society, to one of feeling adequate, self-reliant, assertive and self-determinative (p. 156).

The most highly developed models of Black identity transformation have been offered by Cross (1970, 1971) and Jackson (1975). Each of these men, independent of the other, developed a four-stage identity development process, although each acknowledges the influence of earlier writers

(Crawford & Naditch, 1970; Sherif & Sherif, 1970; Thomas, 1971; Wallace, 1964). Cross (1971) described his model as a "Negro-to-Black Conversion Experience" consisting of preencounter, encounter, immersion, and internalization stages, and an exploratory study by Cross and two colleagues (Hall, Cross, & Freedle, 1972) provides some tentative support for these stages of development. According to the model, Blacks at the preencounter stage are "programmed to view and think of the world as being nonblack, anti-black, or the opposite of Black" (Hall, Cross, & Freedle, 1972, p. 159). At the next stage, the encounter stage, the Black individual becomes aware of what being Black means and begins to validate him/herself as a Black person. During the immersion stage, the Black person rejects all nonblack values and totally immerses him/herself in Black culture. Finally, in the internalization stage, the Black person gains a sense of inner security and begins to focus on ". . . things other than himself and his own ethnic or racial group" (Hall, Cross, & Freedle, 1972, p. 160).

Jackson (1975) identifies a similar four-stage process as the Black Identity Development Model. In stage one—Passive Acceptance—the Black person accepts and conforms to White social, cultural, and institutional standards (p. 21). In stage two—Active Resistance—the Black person rejects all that is White and attempts to remove all White influences upon his/her life (p. 22). In stage three—Redirection—the Black individual no longer admires or despises what is White, but rather considers it irrelevant to Black Culture (p. 23). Finally, in stage four—Internalization—the Black person acknowledges and appreciates the uniqueness of the Black culture, and comes to accept and reject various aspects of American culture based on their own merits.

Although these identity development models pertain specifically to the Black experience, the editors of the present text believe that some of the basic tenets of these theories can be generalized and applied to other minority groups, due to their shared experience of oppression. Several earlier writers (Stonequist, 1937; Berry, 1965) have also observed that minority groups share the same patterns of adjustment to cultural oppression. Parallels are most easily drawn between Blacks and other racial/ethnic groups. During the past two decades, for instance, the social and political activity of Latinos, Asian Americans, and Native Americans has resulted in an identity transformation for persons within these groups, similar to that experienced by Black Americans. A Third World Consciousness has emerged, with the common experience of oppression clearly serving as the unifying force.

Parallels between the Black experience and that of women (Myrdal, 1944; Cox, 1976) and gays (Murphy, 1974) have also been suggested. Women, "gays," the aged, the handicapped, and other oppressed groups have become increasingly conscious of themselves as objects of oppression, and this has resulted in changed attitudes toward themselves, their own minority groups, other minority groups, and members of the dominant culture. Based on views expressed by earlier writers and our own clinical observation that these changes in attitudes and subsequent behavior follow a predictable sequence, we propose a five-stage, Minority Identity Development (MID) model.

The MID model we propose is not presented as a comprehensive theory of personality development, but rather as a schema to help counselors understand minority client attitudes and behaviors within existing personality theories. The model defines five stages of development that oppressed people may experience as they struggle to understand themselves in terms of their own minority culture, the dominant culture, and the oppressive relationship between the two cultures. Although five distinct stages are presented in the model, the MID is more accurately conceptualized as a continuous process in which one stage blends with another and boundaries between stages are not clear.

It is our observation that not all minority individuals experience the entire range of these stages in their lifetimes. Prior to the turbulent 1960s, a decade in which the transition of many individuals through this process was accelerated and, therefore, made more evident, many people were raised and lived out their lives in the first stage. Nor is the developmental process to be interpreted as irreversible. It is our opinion that many minority individuals are raised by parents functioning at level five, but in coming to grips with their own identity, offsprings often move from level five to one of the lower levels. On the other hand, it does not appear that lower levels of development are prerequisite to functioning at higher levels. Some people born and raised in a family functioning at level five appear never to experience a level one sense of identity.

At each level we provide examples of four corresponding attitudes that may assist the counselor to understand behaviors displayed by individuals operating at or near these levels. (It is our contention that minority behavior, like all human behavior, can only be fully understood within the context of the attitudes that motivate it.) Each attitude is believed to be an integral part of any minority person's identity; how he/she views: (a) self, (b) others of the same minority, (c) others of another minority, and (d) majority individuals. It was not our intention to define a hierarchy with more valued attitudes at higher levels of development. Rather, the model is intended to reflect a process that we have observed in our work with minority clients over the past two decades.

Minority Identity Development Model

Stage One—Conformity Stage

Minority individuals in this stage of development are distinguished by their unequivocal preference for dominant cultural values over those of their own culture. Their choice of role models, life styles, value system, etc., all follow the lead of the dominant group. Those physical and/or cultural characteristics that single them out as minority persons are a source of pain, and are either viewed with disdain or are repressed from consciousness. Their views of self, fellow group members, and other minorities in general are clouded by their identification with the dominant culture.

A. *Attitude toward self: Self-depreciating attitude.* Individuals who acknowledge their distinguishing physical and/or cultural characteristics consciously view them as a source of shame. Individuals who repress awareness of their distinguishing physical and/or cultural chracteristics depreciate themselves at a subconscious level.

B. *Attitude toward members of the same minority: Group-depreciating attitude.* Fellow minority group members are viewed according to dominant held beliefs of minority strengths and weaknesses.

C. *Attitude toward members of different minority: Discriminatory attitude.* Other minorities are viewed according to the dominant group's system of minority stratification (i.e., those minority groups that most closely resemble the dominant group in physical and cultural characteristics are viewed more favorably than those less similar).

D. *Attitude toward members of dominant group: Group appreciating attitude.* Members of the dominant group are admired, respected, and often viewed as ideal models. Cultural values of the dominant society are accepted without question.

Stage Two—Dissonance Stage

In the Dissonance stage of identity development, which is typified by cultural confusion and conflict, the minority individual encounters information and/or experiences that are inconsistent with previously accepted values and beliefs, and consequently is led to question and to some degree challenge, attitudes acquired in the Conformity stage.

A. *Attitude toward self: Conflict between self-depreciating and self-appreciating attitudes.* With a growing awareness of minority cultural strengths comes a faltering sense of pride in self. The individual's attitude toward distinguishing physical and/or cultural characteristics is typified by alternating feelings of shame and pride in self.

B. *Attitude toward members of same minority: Conflict between group-depreciating and group-appreciating attitudes.* Dominant-held views of minority strengths and weaknesses begin to be questioned, as new, contradictory information is received. Cultural values of the minority group begin to have appeal.

C. *Attitude toward members of a different minority: Conflict between dominant-held views of minority hierarchy and feelings of shared experience.* The individual begins to question the dominant-held system of minority stratification, and experiences a growing sense of comradeship with other oppressed people. Most of the individual's psychic energy at this level, however, is devoted to resolving conflicting attitudes toward self, the same minority, and the dominant group.

D. *Attitude toward members of dominant group: Conflict between group appreciating and group depreciating attitude.* The individual experiences a growing awareness that not all cultural values of the dominant group are beneficial to him/her. Members of the dominant group are viewed with growing suspicion.

Stage Three—Resistance and Immersion Stage

In this stage of development, the minority individual completely endorses minority-held views and rejects the dominant society and culture. Desire to eliminate oppression of the individual's minority group becomes an important motivation of the individual's behavior.

A. *Attitude toward self: Self-appreciating attitude.* The minority individual at this stage acts as an explorer and discoverer of his/her history and culture, seeking out information and artifacts that enhance his/her sense of identity and worth. Cultural and physical characteristics which once illicited feelings of shame and disgust at this stage become symbols of pride and honor.

B. *Attitude toward members of the same minority: Group-appreciating attitude.* The individual experiences a strong sense of identification with and commitment to his/her minority group, as enhancing information about the group is acquired. Members of the group are admired, respected, and often viewed as ideal models. Cultural values of the minority group are accepted without question.

C. *Attitude toward members of a different minority: Conflict between feelings of empathy for other minority experiences and feelings of culturocentrism.* The individual experiences a growing sense of camarderie with persons from other minority groups, to the degree to which they are viewed as sharing similar forms of oppression. Alliances with other groups tend to be short-lived, however, when their values come in conflict with those of the individual's minority group. The dominant group's system of minority stratification is replaced by a system which values most those minority groups that are culturally similar to the individual's own group.

D. *Attitude toward members of dominant group: Group-depreciating attitude.* The individual totally rejects the dominant society and culture, and experiences a sense of distrust and dislike for all members of the dominant group.

Stage Four—Introspection Stage

In this stage of development, the minority individual experiences feelings of discontent and discomfort with group views rigidly held in the Resistance and Immersion stage, and diverts attention to notions of greater individual autonomy.

A. *Attitude toward self: Concern with basis of self-appreciating attitude.* The individual experiences conflict between notions of responsibility and allegiance to minority group and notions of personal autonomy.
B. *Attitude toward members of same minority: Concern with unequivocal nature of group appreciation.* While attitudes of identification are continued from the preceding Resistance and Immersion stage, concern begins to build up regarding the issue of group-usurped individuality.
C. *Attitude toward members of a different minority: Concern with ethnocentric basis for judging others.* The individual experiences a growing uneasiness with minority stratification that results from culturocentrism and the greater value placed on groups experiencing the same oppression than those experiencing a different oppression.
D. *Attitude toward members of dominant group: Concern with the basis of group depreciation.* The individual experiences conflict between attitude of complete distrust for the dominant society and culture, and attitude of selective trust and distrust according to dominant individuals' demonstrated behaviors and attitudes. The individual also recognizes the utility of many dominant cultural elements, yet is confused as to whether to incorporate such elements into his/her minority culture.

Stage Five—Synergetic Articulation and Awareness Stage
Minority individuals in this stage experience a sense of self-fulfillment with regard to cultural identity. Conflicts and discomforts experienced in the introspection stage have been resolved, allowing greater individual control and flexibility. Cultural values of other minorities as well as those of the dominant group are objectively examined and accepted or rejected on the basis of prior experience gained in earlier stages of identity development. Desire to eliminate *all* forms of oppression becomes an important motivation of the individual's behavior.

A. *Attitude toward self: Self-appreciating attitude.* The individual experiences a strong sense of self-worth, self-confidence, and autonomy as the result of having established his/her identity as an individual, a member of a minority group, and/or a member of the dominant culture.
B. *Attitude toward members of the same minority: Group appreciating attitude.* The individual experiences a strong sense of pride in the group without having to accept group values unequivocally. Strong feelings of empathy with the group experience are coupled with an awareness that each member of the group is an individual.
C. *Attitude towrd members of a different minority: Group appreciating attitude.* The individual experiences a strong sense of respect for the

group's cultural values coupled with an awareness that each member of the group is an individual. The individual also experiences a greater understanding and support for all oppressed people, regardless of their similarity to the individual's minority group.

D. *Attitude toward members of the dominant group: Attitude of selective appreciation.* The individual experiences selective trust and liking for members of the dominant group who seek to eliminate repressive activities of the group. The individual also experiences an openness to the constructive elements of the dominant culture.

Table 3.1
Summary of Minority Identity Development Model

Stages of Minority Development Model	Attitude toward self	Attitude toward others of the same minority	Attitude toward others of different minority	Attitude toward dominant group
Stage 1— Conformity	self-depreciating	group-depreciating	discriminatory	group-appreciating
Stage 2— Dissonance	conflict between self-depreciating and appreciating	conflict between group-depreciating and group-appreciating	conflict between dominant held views of minority hierarchy and feelings of shared experience	conflict between group-appreciating and group-depreciating
Stage 3— Resistance and Immersion	self-appreciating	group-appreciating	conflict between feelings of empathy for other minority experiences and feelings of culturo-centrism	group-depreciating
Stage 4— Introspection	concern with basis of self-appreciation	concern with nature of unequivocal appreciation	concern with ethnocentric basis for judging others	concern with the basis of group depreciation
Stage 5— Synergetic Articulation and Awareness	self-appreciating	group-appreciating	group-appreciating	selective appreciation

Implications of the MID Model for Counseling

As suggested earlier, the MID model is not intended as a comprehensive theory of personality, but rather as a paradigm to help counselors understand minority client attitudes and behaviors. In this respect, the model is intended to sensitize counselors to: (1) the role oppression plays in a minority individual's identity development, (2) the differences that can exist between members of the same minority group with respect to their cultural identity, and (3) the potential which each individual minority person has for changing his/her sense of identity. Beyond helping to understand minority client behavior, the model has implications for the counseling process itself.

The general attitudes and behaviors that describe minority individuals at the Conformity stage (e.g., denial of minority problems, strong dependence and identification with dominant group, etc.) suggest that clients from this stage are unlikely to seek counseling related to their cultural identity. It is more likely that they will perceive problems of cultural identity as problems related to their personal identity. Clients at this stage are more inclined to visit and be influenced by counselors of the dominant group than those of the same minority. Because of the client's strong identification with dominant group members, counselors from the dominant group may find the conformist client's need to please and appease a powerful force in the counseling relationship. Clients at the Conformity stage are likely to present problems that are most amenable to problem solving and goal-oriented counseling approaches.

Minority individuals at the Dissonance stage of development are preoccupied by questions concerning their concept of self, identity, and self-esteem; they are likely to perceive personal problems as related to their cultural identity. Emotional problems develop when these individuals are unable to resolve conflicts which occur between dominant-held views and those of their minority group. Clients in the Dissonance stage are more culturally aware than Conformity clients and are likely to prefer to work with counselors who possess a good knowledge of the client's cultural group. Counseling approaches that involve considerable self-exploration appear to be best suited for clients at this stage of development.

Minority individuals at the Resistance and Immersion stage are inclined to view all psychological problems (whether personal or social in nature) as a product of their oppression. The likelihood that these clients will seek formal counseling regarding their cultural identity is very slim. In those cases when counseling is sought, it will tend to be only between members of the same minority group, and generally in response to a crisis situation. Therapy for Stage Three clients often takes the form of exposure to, and practice of, the ways and artifacts of their culture. An example of this might be a woman who experiences a release of tension and anxiety because of her involvement in a class on women's liberation. Clients at this stage who do seek counseling are likely to prefer group process and/or alloplastic approaches to counseling.

Clients at the Introspection stage are torn between their preponderant identification with their minority group and their need to exercise greater personal freedom. When these individuals are unable to resolve mounting conflict between these two forces, they often seek counseling. While Introspective clients still prefer to see a counselor from their own cultural group, counselors from other cultures may be viewed as credible sources of help if they share world views similar to those of their clientele and appreciate their cultural dilemma. Counselors who use a self-exploration and decision-making approach can be most effective with these clients.

Clients at the fifth stage of identity development have acquired the internal skills and knowledge necessary to exercise a desired level of personal freedom. Their sense of minority identity is well balanced by an appreciation of other cultures. And, while discrimination and oppression remain a painful part of their lives, greater psychological resources are at their disposal in actively engaging the problem. Attitudinal similarity between counselor and client becomes a more important determinant of counseling success than membership-group similarity.

Discussion of the MID model's implications for counseling is admittedly highly speculative at this point, and the model itself requires empirical verification before more definitive inferences are drawn. We hope the model will stimulate much needed research with regard to minority identity development and that it will help the reader distinguish and comprehend intragroup differences that are evident in the readings to follow.

References

Banks, W. The Black client and the helping professionals. In R. I. Jones (Ed.) *Black Psychology*. New York: Harper & Row, 1972.

Berry, B. *Ethnic and race relations*. Boston: Houghton Mifflin, 1965.

Cox, S. *Female psychology: The emerging self*. Chicago: Science Research Associates, 1976.

Crawford, T. J., & Naditch, M. Relative deprivation, powerlessness, and militancy: The psychology of social protest. *Psychiatry*, 1970, *33*, 208–223.

Cross, W. E. The black experience viewed as a process: A crude model for black self-actualization. Paper presented at the Thirty-fourth Annual Meeting of the Association of Social and Behavioral Scientists, April 23–24, 1970, Tallahassee, Florida.

Cross, W. E. The Negro-to-Black conversion experience. *Black World*, 1971, *20*, 13–27.

Hall, W. S.; Cross, W. E.; & Freedle, R. Stages in the development of Black awareness: An exploratory investigation. In Reginald L. Jones' (Ed.) *Black Psychology*, New York: Harper & Row, 1972, 156–165.

Jackson, B. Black identity development. *MEFORM: Journal of Educational Diversity & Innovation,* 1975, *2,* 19–25.

Maykovich, M. K. Political activation of Japanese American youth. *Journal of Social Issues,* 1973, *29,* 167–185.

Murphy, J. *Homosexual Liberation.* New York: Praeger Publishers, 1971.

Myrdal, G. An American dilemma: The Negro problem and modern democracy. New York: Harper and Row, 1944.

Parks, R. E. *Race and culture.* Glencoe, Ill.: The Free Press, 1950.

Sherif, M., & Sherif, C. Black unrest as a social movement toward an emerging self identity. *Journal of Social and Behavioral Sciences,* 1970, *15,* 41–52.

Stonequist, E. V. *The marginal man.* New York: Charles Scubner's Sons, 1937.

Thomas, C. W. *Boys no more.* Beverly Hills, Ca.: Glencoe Press, 1971.

Vontress, C. E. Racial differences: Impediments to rapport. *Journal of Counseling Psychology,* 1971, *18,* 7–13.

Wallace, A. F. C. *Culture and personality.* New York: Random House, 1964.

Part 2
The American Indian Client

Photo by Rohn Engh

We are not free. We do not make choices. Our choices are made for us; we are the poor. For those of us who live on reservations these choices are made by federal administrators, bureaucrats, and their 'yes men,' euphemistically called tribal governments. Those of us who live in non-reservation areas have our lives controlled by local white power elites. We have many rulers. They are called social workers, 'cops,' school teachers, churches, etc., . . . (Warrior, 1967, p. 72).

For nearly 500 years, Native Americans have been fighting a defensive war for their right to freedom, their lands, their organizations, their traditions and beliefs, their way of life, and their very lives. American Indians have experienced massacres by the United States Army, have seen the Bureau of Indian Affairs systematically destroy their leadership and way of life, have known promises broken, have had their land taken from them, and have watched their children die because of inadequate health care, poverty, and suicide. By almost every measure of impoverishment and deprivation, the Native American is the poorest of the poor (Farb, 1968). Their population has decreased from a high of 3,000,000 to about 600,000. While historically Indians were killed in massacres, cultural genocide continues to operate through institutional racism. The following statistics are provided by Josephy (1971) and Richardson (1981):

- The average annual income of Native Americans ($1,500) is 75% below that of the national average, and $1,000 less than that of Blacks;
- Unemployment rate for American Indians is nearly 40% (10 times the average);
- The life expectancy of Indians is 44 years.
- Infant mortality for Native Americans after the first month of life is three times the national average;
- Fifty percent of Indian school children (double the national average) fail to complete high school;
- Suicide rate of Indian teenagers is 100 times that of Whites.
- Until 1975, the Bureau of Indian Affairs was run by non-Indians.

It is ironic that many of the Whites who created these problems refer to them as "Indian problems," and have tried a variety of White-imposed methods to solve them. Deloria, in "Indians Today, the Real and the Unreal," discusses this point at length. In essence, the attempts to solve the problems consisted of imposing White solutions onto the Indian;—turn the Indian into a White and the problem will go away! Such attempts were not only manifestations of cultural oppression; they marked a failure on the part of Whites to understand that the 2500 years of Indian histories and cultures had little in common with European-based cultures.

The fact that the helping professions (counseling, psychotherapy, social work) as practiced in the United States may be instruments of cultural oppression is indirectly discussed by Lewis and Ho in their article "Social Work with Native Americans." They point out how social work and other mental health approaches and strategies arise from the milieu of direct intervention. Native American cultural concepts of noninterference are at odds with such a therapeutic orientation. In addition, certain Native-American values revolving around sharing, time perspectives, patience, and nonverbal communication may also cause problems for the prospective, well-meaning counselor. Youngman and Sadongei in "Counseling the American Indian Child" discuss how misunderstandings can occur when different cultural interpretations of certain behaviors are made. For the young Indian child in a Western school system, the problems are immense.

Counselors must not only recognize the historical Native American experience of oppression and exploitation, but be alert to how their conventional training in mental health practices may be inappropriate to the life styles and values of Native Americans. To impose them blindly is to perpetuate oppression of the most damaging kind.

Farb, P. The American Indian: A Portrait in limbo. *Saturday Review,* October 12, 1967, 26–29.

Josephy, Jr., Alvin M. *Red power,* New York: McGraw-Hill Book Co., 1971.

Richardson, E. Cultural and historical perspectives in counseling American Indians. In Sue, D. W. *Counseling the culturally different:* Theory and practice. New York: John Wiley & Sons, 1981.

Warrior, C. We are not free. In Josephy, Jr., A. (Ed.) *Red power,* New York: McGraw-Hill, 1971.

4 Indians Today, the Real and the Unreal
Deloria, V.

Indians are like the weather. Everyone knows all about the weather, but none
can change it. When storms are predicted, the sun shines. When picnic
weather is announced, the rain begins. Likewise, if you count on the
unpredictability of Indian people, you will never be sorry. ·

One of the finest things about being an Indian is that people are always
interested in you and your "plight." Other groups have difficulties,
predicaments, quandaries, problems, or troubles. Traditionally we Indians
have had a "plight."

Our foremost plight is our transparency. People can tell just by looking
at us what we want, what should be done to help us, how we feel, and what a
"real" Indian is really like. Indian life, as it relates to the real world, is a
continuous attempt not to disappoint people who know us. Unfulfilled
expectations cause grief and we have already had our share.

Because people can see right through us, it becomes impossible to tell
truth from fiction or fact from mythology. Experts paint us as they would like
us to be. Often we paint ourselves as we wish we were or as we might have been.

The more we try to be ourselves the more we are forced to defend what
we have never been. The American public feels most comfortable with the
mythical Indians of stereotype-land who were always THERE. These Indians
are fierce, they wear feathers and grunt. Most of us don't fit this idealized
figure since we grunt only when overeating, which is seldom.

To be an Indian in modern American society is in a very real sense to be
unreal and ahistorical. In this book we will discuss the other side—the
unrealities that face *us* as Indian people. It is this unreal feeling that has been
welling up inside us and threatens to make this decade the most decisive in
history for Indian people. In so many ways, Indian people are re-examining
themselves in an effort to redefine a new social structure for their people.
Tribes are reordering their priorities to account for the obvious discrepancies
between their goals and the goals whites have defined for them.

Indian reactions are sudden and surprising. One day at a conference we
were singing "My Country 'Tis of Thee" and we came across the part that
goes:

> *Land where our fathers died*
> *Land of the Pilgrims' pride . . .*

Some of us broke out laughing when we realized that our fathers undoubtedly died trying to keep those Pilgrims from stealing our land. In fact, many of our fathers died because the Pilgrims killed them as witches. We didn't feel much kinship with those Pilgrims, regardless of who they did in.

We often hear "give it back to the Indians" when a gadget fails to work. It's a terrible thing for a people to realize that society has set aside all non-working gadgets for their exclusive use.

During my three years as Executive Director of the National Congress of American Indians it was a rare day when some white didn't visit my office and proudly proclaim that he or she was of Indian descent.

Cherokee was the most popular tribe of their choice and many people placed the Cherokees anywhere from Maine to Washington State. Mohawk, Sioux, and Chippewa were next in popularity. Occasionally I would be told about some mythical tribe from lower Pennsylvania, Virginia, or Massachusetts which had spawned the white standing before me.

At times I became quite defensive about being a Sioux when these white people had a pedigree that was so much more respectable than mine. But eventually I came to understand their need to identify as partially Indian and did not resent them. I would confirm their wildest stories about their Indian ancestry and would add a few tales of my own hoping that they would be able to accept themselves someday and leave us alone.

Whites claiming Indian blood generally tend to reinforce mythical beliefs about Indians. All but one person I met who claimed Indian blood claimed it on their grandmother's side. I once did a projection backward and discovered that evidently most tribes were entirely female for the first three hundred years of white occupation. No one, it seemed, wanted to claim a male Indian as a forebear.

It doesn't take much insight into racial attitudes to understand the real meaning of the Indian-grandmother complex that plagues certain whites. A male ancestor has too much of the aura of the savage warrior, the unknown primitive, the instinctive animal, to make him a respectable member of the family tree. But a young Indian princess? Ah, there was royalty for the taking. Somehow the white was linked with a noble house of gentility and culture if his grandmother was an Indian princess who ran away with an intrepid pioneer. And royalty has always been an unconscious but all-consuming goal of the European immigrant.

The early colonists, accustomed to life under benevolent despots, projected their understanding of the European political structure onto the Indian tribe in trying to explain its political and social structure. European royal houses were closed to ex-convicts and indentured servants, so the colonists made all Indian maidens princesses, then proceeded to climb a social ladder of their own creation. Within the next generation, if the trend continues, a large portion of the American population will eventually be related to Powhattan.

While a real Indian grandmother is probably the nicest thing that could happen to a child, why is a remote Indian princess grandmother so necessary for many whites? Is it because they are afraid of being classed as foreigners? Do they need some blood tie with the frontier and its dangers in order to experience what it means to be an American? Or is it an attempt to avoid facing the guilt they bear for the treatment of the Indian?

The phenomenon seems to be universal. Only among the Jewish community, which has a long tribal-religious tradition of its own, does the mysterious Indian grandmother, the primeval princess, fail to dominate the family tree. Otherwise, there's not much to be gained by claiming Indian blood or publicly identifying as an Indian. The white believes that there is a great danger the lazy Indian will eventually corrupt God's hard working people. He is still suspicious that the Indian way of life is dreadfully wrong. There is, in fact, something *un-American* about Indians for most whites.

I ran across a classic statement of this attitude one day in a history book which was published shortly after the turn of the century. Often have I wondered how many Senators, Congressmen, and clergymen of the day accepted the attitudes of that book as a basic fact of life in America. In no uncertain terms did the book praise God that the Indian had not yet been able to corrupt North America as he had South America:

> It was perhaps fortunate for the future of America that the Indians of the North rejected civilization. Had they accepted it the whites and Indians might have intermarried to some extent as they did in Mexico. That would have given us a population made up in a measure of shiftless half-breeds.

I never dared to show this passage to my white friends who had claimed Indian blood, but I often wondered why they were so energetic if they did have some of the bad seed in them.

Those whites who dare not claim Indian blood have an asset of their own. They *understand* Indians.

Understanding Indians is not an esoteric art. All it takes is a trip through Arizona or New Mexico, watching a documentary on TV, having known *one* in the service, or having read a popular book on *them*.

There appears to be some secret osmosis about Indian people by which they can magically and instantaneously communicate complete knowledge about themselves to these interested whites. Rarely is physical contact required. Anyone and everyone who knows an Indian or who is *interested*, immediately and thoroughly understands them.

You can verify this great truth at your next party. Mention Indians and you will find a person who saw some in a gas station in Utah, or who attended the Gallup ceremonial celebration, or whose Uncle Jim hired one to cut logs in Oregon, or whose church had a missionary come to speak last Sunday on the plight of Indians and the mission of the church.

There is no subject on earth so easily understood as that of the American Indian. Each summer, work camps disgorge teenagers on various reservations. Within one month's time the youngsters acquire a knowledge of Indians that would astound a college professor.

Easy knowledge about Indians is a historical tradition. After Columbus "discovered" America he brought back news of a great new world which he assumed to be India and, therefore, filled with Indians. Almost at once European folklore devised a complete explanation of the new land and its inhabitants which featured the Fountain of Youth, the Seven Cities of Gold, and other exotic attractions. The absence of elephants apparently did not tip off the explorers that they weren't in India. By the time they realized their mistake, instant knowledge of Indians was a cherished tradition.

Missionaries, after learning some of the religious myths of tribes they encountered, solemnly declared that the inhabitants of the new continent were the Ten Lost Tribes of Israel. Indians thus received a religious-historical identity far greater than they wanted or deserved. But it was an impossible identity. Their failure to measure up to Old Testament standards doomed them to a fall from grace and they were soon relegated to the status of a picturesque species of wildlife.

Like the deer and the antelope, Indians seemed to play rather than get down to the serious business of piling up treasures upon the earth where thieves break through and steal. Scalping, introduced prior to the French and Indian War by the English,* confirmed the suspicion that Indians were wild animals to be hunted and skinned. Bounties were set and an Indian scalp became more valuable than beaver, otter, marten, and other animal pelts.

---

*Notice, for example the following proclamation:

> Given at the Council Chamber in Boston this third day of November 1755 in the twenty-ninth year of the Reign of our Sovereign Lord George the Second by the Grace of God of Great Britain, France, and Ireland, King Defender of the Faith.

> By His Honour's command
> J. Willard, Secry.
> God Save the King

Whereas the tribe of Penobscot Indians have repeatedly in a perfidious manner acted contrary to their solemn submission unto his Majesty long since made and frequently renewed.

I have, therefore, at the desire of the House of Representatives . . .thought fit to issue this Proclamation and to declare the Penobscot Tribe of Indians to be enemies, rebels and traitors to his Majesty. . . .And I do hereby require his Majesty's subjects of the Province to embrace all opportunities of pursuing, captivating, killing and destroy—all and every of the aforesaid Indians.

And whereas the General Court of this Province have voted that a bounty . . .be granted and allowed to be paid out of the Province Treasury . . .the premiums of bounty following viz:

For every scalp of a male Indian brought in as evidence of their being killed as aforesaid, forty pounds.

For every scalp of such female Indian or male Indian under the age of twelve years that shall be killed and brought in as evidence of their being killed as aforesaid, twenty pounds.

American blacks had become recognized as a species of human being by amendments to the Constitution shortly after the Civil War. Prior to emancipation they had been counted as three-fifths of a person in determining population for representation in the House of Representatives. Early Civil Rights bills nebulously state that other people shall have the same rights as "white people," indicating there *were* "other people." But Civil Rights bills passed during and after the Civil War systematically excluded Indian people. For a long time an Indian was not presumed capable of initiating an action in a court of law, of owning property, or of giving testimony against whites in court. Nor could an Indian vote or leave his reservation. Indians were America's captive people without any defined rights whatsoever.

Then one day the white man discovered that the Indian tribes still owned some 135 million acres of land. To his horror he learned that much of it was very valuable. Some was good grazing land, some was farm land, some mining land, and some covered with timber.

Animals could be herded together on a piece of land, but they could not sell it. Therefore it took no time at all to discover that Indians were really people and should have the right to sell their lands. Land was the means of recognizing the Indian as a human being. It was the method whereby land could be stolen legally and not blatantly.

Once the Indian was thus acknowledged, it was fairly simple to determine what his goals were. If, thinking went, the Indian was just like the white, he must have the same outlook as the white. So the future was planned for the Indian people in public and private life. First in order was allotting them reservations so that they could sell their lands. God's foreordained plan to repopulate the continent fit exactly with the goals of the tribes as they were defined by their white friends.

It is fortunate that we were never slaves. We gave up land instead of life and labor. Because the Negro labored, he was considered a draft animal. Because the Indian occupied large areas of land, he was considered a wild animal. Had we given up anything else, or had anything else to give up, it is certain that we would have been considered some other thing.

Whites have had different attitudes toward the Indians and the blacks since the Republic was founded. Whites have always refused to give non-whites the respect which they have been found to legally possess. Instead there has always been a contemptuous attitude that although the law says one thing, "we all know better."

Thus whites steadfastly refused to allow blacks to enjoy the fruits of full citizenship. They systematically closed schools, churches, stores, restaurants, and public places to blacks or made insulting provisions for them. For one hundred years every program of public and private white America was devoted to the exclusion of the black. It was, perhaps, embarrassing to be rubbing shoulders with one who had not so long before been defined as a field animal.

The Indian suffered the reverse treatment. Law after law was passed requiring him to conform to white institutions. Indian children were kidnapped and forced into boarding schools thousands of miles from their homes to learn the white man's ways. Reservations were turned over to different Christian denominations for governing. Reservations were for a long time church operated. Everything possible was done to ensure that Indians were forced into American life. The wild animal was made into a household pet whether or not he wanted to be one.

Policies for both black and Indian failed completely. Blacks eventually began the Civil Rights movement. In doing so they assured themselves some rights in white society. Indians continued to withdraw from the overtures of white society and tried to maintain their own communities and activities.

Actually both groups had little choice. Blacks, trapped in a world of white symbols, retreated into themselves. And people thought comparable Indian withdrawal unnatural because they expected Indians to behave like whites.

The white world of abstract symbols became a nightmare for Indian people. The words of the treaties, clearly stating that Indians should have "free and undisturbed" use of their lands under the protection of the federal government, were case aside by the whites as if they didn't exist. The Sioux once had a treaty plainly stating that it would take the signatures or marks of three-fourths of the adult males to amend it. Yet through force the government obtained only 10 percent of the required signatures and declared the new agreement valid.

Indian solutions to problems which had been defined by the white society were rejected out of hand and obvious solutions discarded when they called for courses of action that were not proper in white society. When Crow Dog assassinated Spotted Tail the matter was solved under traditional Sioux customs. Yet an outraged public, furious because Crow Dog had not been executed, pressured for the Seven Major Crimes Act for the federal government to assume nearly total criminal jurisdiction over the reservations. Thus foreign laws and customs using the basic concepts of justice came to dominate Indian life. If, Indians reasoned, justice is for society's benefit, why isn't our justice accepted? Indians became convinced they were the world's stupidest people.

Words and situations never seemed to fit together. Always, it seemed, the white man chose a course of action that did not work. The white man preached that it was good to help the poor, yet he did nothing to assist the poor in his society. Instead he put constant pressure on the Indian people to hoard their worldly goods, and when they failed to accumulate capital but freely gave to the poor, the white man reacted violently.

The failure of communication created a void into which poured the white do-gooder, the missionary, the promoter, the scholar, and every conceivable type of person who believed he could help. White society failed to understand the situation because this conglomerate of assistance blurred the real issues beyond recognition.

The legend of the Indian was embellished or tarnished according to the need of the intermediates to gain leverage in their struggle to solve problems that never existed outside of their own minds. The classic example, of course, is the old-time missionary box. People were horrified that Indians continued to dress in their traditional garb. Since whites did not wear buckskin and beads, they equated such dress with savagery. So do-gooders in the East held fantastic clothing drives to supply the Indians with civilized clothes. Soon boxes of discarded evening gowns, tuxedos, tennis shoes, and uniforms flooded the reservations. Indians were made to dress in these remnants so they could be civilized. Then, realizing the ridiculous picture presented by the reservation people, neighboring whites made fun of the Indian people for having the presumption to dress like whites.

But in the East, whites were making great reputations as "Indian experts," as people who devoted their lives to helping the savages. Whenever Indian land was needed, the whites pictured the tribes as wasteful people who refused to develop their natural resources. Because the Indians did not "use" their lands, argued many land promoters, the lands should be taken away and given to people who knew what to do with them.

White society concentrated on the individual Indian to the exclusion of his group, forgetting that any society is merely a composite of individuals. Generalizations by experts universalized "Indianness" to the detriment of unique Indian values. Indians with a common cultural base shared behavior patterns. But they were expected to behave like a similar group of whites and rarely did. Whites, on the other hand, generally came from a multitude of backgrounds and shared only the need for economic subsistence. There was no way, therefore, to combine white values and Indian behavior into a workable program or intelligible subject of discussion.

One of the foremost differences separating white and Indian was simply one of origin. Whites derived predominantly from western Europe. The earliest settlers on the Atlantic seaboard came from England and the low countries. For the most part they shared the common experiences of their peoples and dwelt within the world view which had dominated western Europe for over a millenium.

Conversely Indians had always been in the western hemisphere. Life on this continent and views concerning it were not shaped in a post-Roman atmosphere. The entire outlook of the people was one of simplicity and mystery, not scientific or abstract. The western hemisphere produced wisdom, western Europe produced knowledge.

Perhaps this distinction seems too simple to mention. It is not. Many is the time I have sat in Congressional hearings and heard the chairman of the committee crow about "our" great Anglo-Saxon heritage of law and order. Looking about the hearing room I saw row after row of full-blood Indians with blank expressions on their faces. As far as they were concerned, Sir Walter Raleigh was a brand of pipe tobacco that you got at the trading post.

When we talk about European background, we are talking about feudalism, kings, queens, their divine right to rule their subjects, the Reformation, Christianity, the Magna Charta and all of the events that went to make up European history.

American Indians do not share that heritage. They do not look wistfully back across the seas to the old country. The Apache were not at Runymede to make King John sign the Magna Charta. The Cherokee did not create English common law. The Pima had no experience with the rise of capitalism and industrialism. The Blackfeet had no monasteries. No tribe has an emotional, historical, or political relationship to events of another continent and age.

Indians have had their own political history which has shaped the outlook of the tribes. There were great confederacies throughout the country before the time of the white invader. The eastern Iroquois formed a strong league because as single tribes they had been weak and powerless against larger tribes. The Deep South was controlled by three confederacies: the Creeks with their town system, the Natchez, and the Powhattan confederation which extended into tidelands Virginia. The Pequots and their cousins the Mohicans controlled the area of Connecticut, Massachusetts, Rhode Island, and Long Island.

True democracy was more prevalent among Indian tribes in pre-Columbian days than it has been since. Despotic power was abhorred by tribes that were loose combinations of hunting parties rather than political entities.

Conforming their absolute freedom to fit rigid European political forms has been very difficult for most tribes, but on the whole they have managed extremely well. Under the Indian Reorganization Act Indian people have generally created a modern version of the old tribal political structure and yet have been able to develop comprehensive reservation programs which compare favorably with governmental structures anywhere.

The deep impression made upon American minds by the Indian struggle against the white man in the last century has made the contemporary Indian somewhat invisible compared with his ancestors. Today Indians are not conspicuous by their absence from view. Yet they should be.

In *The Other America,* the classic study of poverty by Michael Harrington, the thesis is developed that the poor are conspicuous by their invisibility. There is no mention of Indians in the book. A century ago, Indians would have dominated such a work.

Indians are probably invisible because of the tremendous amount of misinformation about them. Most books about Indians cover some abstract and esoteric topic of the last century. Contemporary books are predominantly by whites trying to solve the ''Indian problem.'' Between the two extremes lives a dynamic people in a social structure of their own, asking only to be freed from cultural oppression. The future does not look bright for the attainment of such freedom because the white does not understand the Indian and the Indian does not wish to understand the white.

Understanding Indians means understanding so-called Indian Affairs. Indian Affairs, like Gaul, is divided into three parts: the government, the private organizations, and the tribes themselves. Mythological theories about the three sectors are as follows: paternalism exists in the governmental area, assistance is always available in the private sector, and the tribes dwell in primitive splendor. All three myths are false.

The government has responsibility for the Indian estate because of treaty commitments and voluntary assumption of such responsibility. It allegedly cares for Indian lands and resources. Education, health services, and technical assistance are provided to the major tribes by the Bureau of Indian Affairs, which is in the Department of the Interior.

But the smaller tribes get little or nothing from the Interior Department. Since there are some 315 distinct tribal communities and only about 30 get any kind of federal services, there is always a Crisis in Indian Affairs. Interior could solve the problems of 250 small tribes in one year if it wanted to. It doesn't want to.

The name of the game in the government sector is TASK FORCE REPORT. Every two years some reporter causes a great uproar about how Indians are treated by the Bureau of Indian Affairs. This, in turn, causes great consternation among Senators and Congressmen who have to answer mail from citizens concerned about Indians. So a TASK FORCE REPORT is demanded on Indian problems.

The conclusion of every TASK FORCE REPORT is that Congress is not appropriating enough money to do an adequate job of helping Indians. Additionally, these reports find that while Indians are making some progress, the fluctuating policy of Congress is stifling Indian progress. The reports advise that a consistent policy of self-help with adequate loan funds for reservation development be initiated.

Since Congress is not about to appropriate any more money than possible for Indian Affairs, the TASK FORCE REPORT is filed away for future reference. Rumor has it that there is a large government building set aside as a storage bin for TASK FORCE REPORTS.

This last year saw the results of a number of TASK FORCE REPORTS. In 1960, when the New Frontier burst upon the scene, a TASK FORCE REPORT was prepared. It made the recommendations listed above. In 1966 two additional TASK FORCES went abroad in search of the solution to the "Indian problem." One was a secret Presidential TASK FORCE. One was a semi-secret Interior TASK FORCE. In March of 1968 the President asked for a 10 percent increase in funds for Indian programs and after eight years of Democratic rule, a TASK FORCE recommendation was actually carried out.

Government agencies always believe that their TASK FORCES are secret. They believe that anonymous experts can ferret out the esoteric answers to an otherwise insoluble problem. Hence they generally keep secret the names of people serving on their TASK FORCES until after the report is issued. Only they make one mistake. They always have the same people on the TASK FORCE. So when Indians learn there is a TASK FORCE abroad they automatically know who are on it and what they are thinking.

Paternalism is always a favorite subject of the TASK FORCES. They make it one of the basic statements of their preambles. It has therefore become an accepted tenet that paternalism dominates government-Indian relationships.

Congress always wants to do away with paternalism. So it has a policy designed to do away with Indians. If there are no Indians, there cannot be any paternalism.

But governmental paternalism is not a very serious problem. If an employee of the Bureau of Indian Affairs gives any tribe any static the problem is quickly resolved. The tribal chairman gets on the next plane to Washington. The next morning he walks into the Secretary of the Interior's office and raises hell. Soon a number of bureaucrats are working on the problem. The tribal chairman has a good dinner, goes to a movie, and takes the late plane back to his reservation. Paternalism by field men is not very popular in the Department of the Interior in Washington. Consequently, there is very little paternalism in the governmental sector if the tribe knows what it is doing. And most tribes know what they are doing.

In the private sector, however, paternalism is a fact of life. Nay, it is the standard operating procedure. Churches, white interest organizations, universities, and private firms come out to the reservations asking only to be of service IN THEIR OWN INIMITABLE WAY. No one asks them to come out. It is very difficult, therefore, to get them to leave.

Because no chairman has the time to fly into New York weekly and ask the national churches to stop the paternalistic programs of their missionaries, the field is ripe for paternalism. Most of them are not doing much anyway.

But, people in the private area are working very hard to keep Indians happy. When Indians get unhappy they begin to think about kicking out the white do-gooders, paternalism or not. And if the private organizations were kicked out of a reservation, where would they work? What would they claim as their accomplishments at fund-raising time?

Churches, for example, invest great amounts to train white men for Indian missions. If there were ever too great a number of Indian missionaries, Indians might think they should have their own churches. Then there would be no opportunity to convert the pagans. Where, then, would clergy misfits go if not to Indian missions?

So paternalism is very sophisticated in the private sector. It is disguised by a board of "Indian advisors," selected from among the Indians themselves on the reservation. These "advisors" are put to use to make it appear as if all is well. Pronouncements by Indian advisory boards generally commend the private organization for its work. They ask it to do even more work, for only in that way, they declare, can justice be done to their people.

To hear some people talk, Indians are simultaneously rich from oil royalties and poor as church mice. To hear others, Indians have none of the pleasures of the mainstream, like riots, air pollution, snipers, ulcers, and traffic. Consequently, they class Indians among the "underprivileged" in our society.

Primitive purity is sometimes attributed to tribes. Some tribes keep their rituals and others don't. The best characterization of tribes is that they stubbornly hold on to what they feel is important to them and discard what they feel is irrelevant to their current needs. Traditions die hard and innovation comes hard. Indians have survived for thousands of years in all kinds of conditions. They do not fly from fad to fad seeking novelty. That is what makes them Indian.

Three books, to my way of thinking, give a good idea of the intangible sense of reality that pervades the Indian people. *When the Legends Die* by Hal Borland gives a good picture of Indian youth. *Little Big Man* by Thomas Berger gives a good idea of Indian attitudes toward life. *Stay Away, Joe,* by Dan Cushman, the favorite of Indian people, gives a humorous but accurate idea of the problems caused by the intersection of two ways of life. Anyone who can read, appreciate, and understand the spiritual forces brought out in these books will have a good idea of what Indians are all about.

Other books may be nice, accurate, and historical but they are not really about Indians. In general, they twist Indian reality into a picture which is hard to understand and consequently greatly in error.

Statistical information on Indians can easily be found in other books. What is important, for understanding the present state of Indian Affairs, is to know how tribes are organized today, how they work together, and what they anticipate for the future. And there is no easy way to broach the subject. So let us begin.

In 1934 the Indian Reorganization Act was passed. Under the provisions of this act reservation people were enabled to organize for purposes of self-government. Nearly three-quarters of the reservations organized. These reservations are not known as tribes. Often the remnants of larger historical tribal groups that were located on different pieces of land, they became under IRA officially recognized as "tribes."

There are nineteen different Chippewa tribes, fifteen Sioux tribes, four Potawatomi tribes, a number of Paiute tribes, and several consolidated tribes which encompass two different groups that happened to land on the same reservation.

Examples of consolidated tribes are the Salish and Kootenai of Montana, the Cheyenne-Arapaho of Oklahoma, the Kiowa-Comanche-Apache of Oklahoma, and the Mandan, Hidatsa, and Arikara of the Fort Berthold reservation in North Dakota.

Over the past generation tribes have discovered that they must band together to make themselves heard. Consequently most states have inter-tribal councils, composed of the tribes in that state, that meet regularly and exchange ideas. In some areas, particularly in the Northwest, tribal representation is on a regional basis. The Northwest Affiliated Tribes is an organization made up of tribes from Montana, Idaho, Washington, and Oregon. Its counterpart, the Western Washington Inter-tribal Coordinating Council consists of tribes that live in the Puget Sound area.

Rarely do tribes overlap across state boundaries. While there are fifteen Sioux tribes, the United Sioux is an organization of only South Dakota tribes. Sioux groups in North Dakota, Nebraska, or Minnesota are not invited.

Indians have two "mainstream" organizations, the National Congress of American Indians and the National Indian Youth Council. The NCAI is open to tribes, organizations, and individuals, both red and white. Its major emphasis is on strong tribal membership because it works primarily with legislation and legislation is handled on an individual tribal basis.

The NIYC is the SNCC of Indian Affairs. Organized in 1962, it has been active among the post-college group just entering Indian Affairs. Although NIYC has a short history, it has been able to achieve recognition as a force to be reckoned with in national Indian Affairs. Generally more liberal and more excitable than the NCAI, the NIYC inclines to the spectacular short-term project rather than the extended program. The rivalry between the two groups is intense.

Lesser known but with great potential for the future are the traditional organizations. Primary among these is the oldest continuous Indian-run organization: the League of Nations, Pan American Indians. Its President, Alfred Gagne, incorporates the best of traditional Indian life and national problems into a coherent working philosophy. Should this group ever receive sufficient funding to have field workers, it could very well overturn established government procedures in Indian Affairs. It has long fought the Bureau of Indian Affairs and seeks a return to traditional Indian customs.

From the work of the League of Nations has come the alliance of the traditional Indians of each tribe. In June of 1968 they met in Oklahoma to form the National Aborigine Conference. Discussions ranging from religious prophecies to practical politics were held. From this conference is expected to come a strong nationalistic push on the reservations in the next several years.

Another group well worthy of mention is the American Indian Historical Society of San Francisco. Begun by Rupert Costo, a Cauhilla man, the society has become the publishers of the finest contemporary material on Indians. Excellent research and wide knowledge of Indian people makes it an influential voice in Indian Affairs.

Recently, during the Poor People's March, Indian participants formed the Coalition of American Indian Citizens. A loose and perhaps temporary alliance of disgruntled young people, the Coalition brought to Indian Affairs a sense of urgency. Whether it will continue to function depends on the commitment of its members to goals which they originally stated.

Regional groups are occasionally formed around a specific issue. In the Northwest the Survivors of American Indians, Inc., works exclusively on the issue of fishing rights. In Oklahoma the Original Cherokee Community Organization has been formed to defend hunting and treaty rights of the Cherokees.

Most urban areas have urban centers or clubs composed of Indian people. For the most part these centers provide a place where urban Indians can meet and socialize. The best-known centers are in Los Angeles, Oakland, Chicago, and Minneapolis. New centers are always springing up in different cities. There are probably in excess of thirty functioning centers or clubs at any one time. The urban areas show the most potential for strong lasting organizations, however, and once the urban Indians stabilize themselves they will experience phenomenal growth.

All of these groups are primarily interested in issues and policies. The Indian Council Fire of Chicago works primarily in the field of public relations and Indian culture. The American Indian Development, Inc., works in the field of youth work and economic development of Indian communities.

There are a number of white organizations that attempt to help Indian people. Since we would be better off without them I will not mention them, except to comment that they do exist.

Movement occurs easily in Indian Affairs. Tribes are generally quite alert to issues and policies advocated by red and white alike. It is a rare event that goes unnoticed. Careful observation of the effects of the moccasin telegraph indicates a tendency by the Indian people to organize and coalesce around certain issues rather than according to any set pattern.

The National Congress of American Indians is the best example of this tendency. Membership fluctuates in the NCAI according to the urgency of national issues affecting member tribes. The NCAI attracts only those tribes that are interested in its programs. Unity for unity's sake is not yet a concept that has been accepted by the tribes. Nor has unity for future action been understood.

Within the NCAI personal leadership determines policies and programs. In 1954 Congress began the great push to abrogate Indian rights in a series of "termination bills" by which federal services and protections would be denied to tribes. Fortunately the northwestern tribes under the leadership of Joseph Garry, Chairman of the Coeur d'Alenes of Idaho, were then in control of the NCAI. Garry succeeded in uniting enough tribes under his leadership to bring the policy to a stalemate. It has remained in a deadlock ever since, with Congress waiting for the tribes to lose interest and the tribes remaining on the alert against any termination move by Congress.

Garry served as President of the NCAI from 1953-1959. He established a tradition in the Northwest of political cooperation between the tribes. National Indian Affairs has ever since been haunted by the memory of the powerful coalition of that era. Since Garry's days few decisions are made in Indian Affairs without first checking with northwestern tribal leadership. The recent alliance of the Northwest with the Alaskan natives will shortly result in a total takeover of the NCAI by the northwestern tribes as the Indian political balance is once again achieved.

The power of the Northwest has been balanced by the leadership and political ability of the Sioux. During twenty-five years of NCAI existence the Sioux have held the Executive Directorship for fourteen years. The Sioux reign is nearly at an end, however, as other tribes achieve more political sophistication and begin to exert more influence on the total national scene. The rise of the Wisconsin-Minnesota groups of Chippewas as a potent force was noted at the NCAI convention in Omaha in 1968. Since the Chippewa and the Sioux are traditional enemies and the Chippewa are now allied with the northwestern tribes, the Chippewa should be able to take over the entire field of Indian Affairs within a period of three years. They now lack only that charismatic leader who can articulate critical issues to other tribes.

The tribes from California, Kansas, and Nevada have traditionally been slow to rise to the challenge of national Indian political combat. Yet they could unite and take over the organization completely if they were to join it en masse. With the current inroads being made into national Indian Affairs by the Coalition of Indian Citizens and the National Indian Youth Council, California and Nevada may yet exert tremendous influence over other tribes by attending an NCAI convention with full voting power.

The NCAI is important to the Indian people only when it provides a forum in which issues can be discussed. Occasionally it has come to be dominated by a few tribes and then it has rapidly gone downhill. At the Omaha convention of 1968 non-tribal groups attended the meeting hoping to be allowed to participate. Instead they were rebuffed, and during the convention all non-tribal forces became allied outside the normal channels of Indian Affairs. This tragic blunder by the NCAI could cause a great conflict between reservation and non-reservation groups in the future. There is little doubt that urban Indians have more sophistication than do reservation people, and now urban Indians and the National Indian Youth Council have formed together as cooperating organizations to work for urban and young Indian people. It will probably take several years for Indian tribes to absorb the meaning of this new coalition. By then it may be too late for them to survive.

Individual tribes show incredible differences. No single aspect seems to be as important as tribal solidarity. Tribes that can handle their reservation conflicts in traditional Indian fashion generally make more progress and have better programs than do tribes that continually make adaptations to the white value system. The Pueblos of New Mexico have a solid community life and are just now, with the influx of college-educated Pueblos, beginning large development projects. In spite of the vast differences between the generations, the Pueblos have been able to maintain a sense of tribal purpose and solidarity, and developments are undertaken by the consensus of all the people of the community.

Even more spectacular are the Apaches of the Southwest—the Mescalero, San Carlos, White Mountain, and Jicarilla tribes. Numbering probably less than a dozen college graduates among them, the four tribes have remained close to their traditions, holding ancient ceremonies to be of utmost importance to the future of the tribe. Without the benefit of the white man's vaunted education, these four Apache groups have developed their reservations with amazing skill and foresight. Mescalero Apache owns a ski resort worth over one million dollars. Jicarilla has a modern shopping center. White Mountain has a tremendous tourism development of some twenty-six artificial lakes stocked with trout. San Carlos has a fine cattle industry and is presently developing an industrial park.

Contrast the Chippewas with the Apaches and the picture is not as bright. The Chippewas are located in Minnesota, Wisconsin, and Michigan. They have access to the large cities of Chicago, Minneapolis, Milwaukee, and Detroit. The brain drain of leadership from the Chippewa reservations to the cities has been enormous over the years. Migration to the cities has meant an emphasis on land sales, little development of existing resources, and abandonment of tribal traditions. Only among the Red Lake Chippewa has much progress been made. And Red Lake is probably the most traditional of the Chippewa tribes.

The Sioux, my own people, have a great tradition of conflict. We were the only nation ever to annihilate the United States Cavalry three times in succession. And when we find no one else to quarrel with, we often fight each other. The Sioux problem is excessive leadership. During one twenty-year period in the last century the Sioux fought over an area from LaCrosse, Wisconsin, to Sheridan, Wyoming, against the Crow, Arapaho, Cheyenne, Mandan, Arikara, Hidatsa, Ponca, Iowa, Pawnee, Otoe, Omaha, Winnebago, Chippewa, Cree, Assiniboine, Sac and Fox, Potawatomi, Ute, and Gros Ventre. This was, of course, in addition to fighting the U.S. Cavalry continually throughout that period. The United States government had to call a special treaty session merely to settle the argument among the tribes in the eastern half of that vast territory. It was the only treaty between tribes supervised by the federal government.

But the Sioux never quit fighting. Reservation programs are continually disrupted by bickering within the reservations. Each election on a Sioux reservation is generally a fight to the finish. A ten-vote margin of some 1,500 votes cast is a landslide victory in Sioux country. Fortunately strong chairmen have come to have a long tenure on several Sioux reservations and some of the tribes have made a great deal of progress. But the tendency is always present to slug it out at a moment's notice.

The northwestern tribes also have their fierce and gentle side. Over the past two decades there has been continual conflict between the western tribes and the Fish and Game commissions in Oregon and Washington. Violations of treaty fishing rights by the state can bring Yakimas to the riverbanks with guns so quick as to frighten an unsuspecting bystander.

Before anyone conceived of statehood for either state, Isaac Stevens, on behalf of the United States, traveled up the coast signing treaties with all of the Pacific tribes. These treaties promised perpetual hunting and fishing rights for the tribes if they would agree to remain on restricted reservations. After World War II, when the sportsmen began to have leisure time, the states sought to abrogate the treaties. But in the case of Washington there was a specific disclaimer clause in the act admitting Washington into the Union by which the state promised never to disturb the Indian tribes within its borders.

In recent years there have been a number of "fish-ins" by the smaller tribes in Washington in sporadic attempts to raise the fishing-rights issue. Unfortunately the larger tribes have not supported these people. The larger tribes cannot seem to understand that a precedent of law set against a small tribe means one for the larger tribes as well. It may well be that all Indian fishing will eventually be regulated by the states of the Northwest. This would be quite tragic as there is a fundamental difference between Indian and sports fishing. Indian people are fishing for food for their families. Sportsmen are fishing for relaxation and recreation. Indians may have to starve so that whites can have a good time on the weekends if present trends continue.

But the northwestern tribes have taken the lead in pursuing their rights in court in this century. In the last century the Cherokees went to the Supreme Court over and over again and set forth most of Indian law in its developing years. Similarly in this century the tribes of Oregon, Washington, and Idaho have won the more significant cases which have been taken to court. Such landmark cases as *Squire v. Capoeman,* a taxation case which spelled out exemption of individual allotments from income tax, *United States v. Winans,* which defined water rights and fishing rights, *Mason v. Sams,* another fishing-rights case, and *Seymour v. Superintendent,* a jurisdiction case which gave the modern definition of "Indian country"—a concept important for preservation of treaty rights—were all cases initiated by tribes of that area.

In 1967 ABC television began its ill-fated series on Custer. The Tribal Indians Land Rights Association began the national fight to get the series banned. Eventually the NCAI and other groups protested to ABC over the series and a great Indian war was on. Custer, who had never been a very bright character, was tabbed by the NCAI as the "Adolph Eichmann" of the nineteenth century. But not one could figure out the correct strategy by which ABC could be forced to negotiate.

Finally the Yakima tribal lawyer, James Hovis, devised the tactic of getting every tribe to file for equal time against ABC's local affiliate (ABC itself was not subject to FCC regulations). As tribes in the different areas began to move, ABC, through its affiliate board, arranged a trip to California to discuss the program with the NCAI. Several tribes filed against the local affiliates of ABC and did receive some air time to present the Indian side of the Custer story during the brief run of the show. Later we heard that it would have cost ABC some three thousand dollars per complaint if every tribe had gone ahead and demanded FCC hearings on the controversy. Whether this was true or not we never learned, but once again the northwestern Indians had devised a legal strategy by which Indians as a national ethnic group could air their complaints. The series was canceled after nine episodes.

The greatest potential, as yet untapped, lies in Nevada. With a small total population concentrated in Las Vegas and Reno, Nevada is presently on the threshold of development. Some twenty-six tribes, mainly Paiutes and Shoshones, live in Nevada. If these tribes were ever to form a strong political or economic alliance, they would exert tremendous influence within the state. The Nevadan Indian population is fairly young and the possibility of its developing a strong Indian swing vote as it comes of age is excellent.

Perhaps even more spectacular is the pattern by which Indian land is held in that state. In the closing years of the last century there were no large reservations set up in Nevada. Instead, because the groups were so small and scattered, Indians were given public-domain allotments adjoining the larger towns and cities in Nevada. These groups were called colonies and they were simply unorganized groups of Indians living, like the Lone Ranger and Tonto used to do, "not far from town." Today the Nevada tribes have extremely valuable land in areas where development will have to move if the towns in Nevada are going to continue to grow. With few exceptions old desert lands of the last century are now prime prospects for industrial parks and residential subdivisions. If the Nevada tribes were to pursue a careful policy of land exchange, they would soon own great amounts of land and have a respectable bank account as well.

Indian tribes are rapidly becoming accustomed to the manner in which the modern world works. A generation ago most Indians would not have known which way Washington, D.C., lay. Today it is a rare tribe that does not make a visit once a year to talk with its Congressional delegation, tour the government agencies, and bring home a new program or project from the many existing programs being funded by the federal government. Many tribes receive the Congressional Record and a number subscribe to leading national publications such as *The Wall Street Journal, Life, Time,* and *Newsweek.* Few events of much importance pass the eyes of watchful tribal groups without comment.

Tribes are also becoming very skilled at grantsmanship. Among the larger, more experienced tribes, million-dollar programs are commonplace. Some tribes sharpened their teeth on the old Area Redevelopment Administration of the early sixties. When the Office of Economic Opportunity was created they jumped into the competition with incredibly complex programs and got them funded. One housing program on the Rosebud Sioux reservation is a combination of programs offered by some five different government agencies. The Sioux there have melded a winning hand by making each government agency fund a component of the total housing program for the reservation.

Some tribes take home upward of ten million dollars a year in government programs and private grants for their reservation people. Many tribes, combining a variety of sources, have their own development officer to plan and project future programs. The White Mountain Apaches are the first tribe to have their own public relations firm to keep tribal relations with the surrounding towns and cities on an even keel.

With a change in Congressional policy away from termination toward support of tribal self-sufficiency, it is conceivable that Indian tribes will be able to become economically independent of the federal government in the next generation. Most tribes operate under the provisions of their Indian Reorganization Act constitutions and are probably better operated than most towns, certainly more honestly operated than the larger cities.

Tribes lost some ten years during the 1950's when all progress was halted by the drive toward termination. Arbitrary and unreasonable harassment of tribal programs, denial of credit funds for program development, and pressure on tribes to liquidate assets all contributed to waste a decade during which tribes could have continued to develop their resources.

Today the Indian people are in a good position to demonstrate to the nation what can be done in community development in the rural areas. With the overcrowding of the urban areas, rural development should be the coming thing and understanding of tribal programs could indicate methods of resettling the vast spaces of rural America.

With so much happening on reservations and the possibility of a brighter future in store, Indians have started to become livid when they realize the contagious trap the mythology of white America has caught them in. The descendant of Pocahontas is a remote and incomprehensible mystery to us. We are no longer a wild species of animal loping freely across the prairie. We have little in common with the last of the Mohicans. We are TASK FORCED to death.

Some years ago at a Congressional hearing someone asked Alex Chasing Hawk, a council member of the Cheyenne River Sioux for thirty years, "Just what do you Indians want?" Alex replied, "A leave-us-alone law!!"

The primary goal and need of Indians today is not for someone to feel sorry for us and claim descent from Pocahontas to make us feel better. Nor do we need to be classified as semi-white and have programs and policies made to bleach us further. Nor do we need further studies to see if we are feasible. We need a new policy by Congress acknowledging our right to live in peace, free from arbitrary harassment. We need the public at large to drop the myths in which it has clothed us for so long. We need fewer and fewer "experts" on Indians.

What we need is a cultural leave-us-alone agreement, in spirit and in fact.

5 Social Work with Native Americans

Lewis, Ronald G.

Ho, Man Keung

If social workers are to serve Native Americans effectively, they must understand their distinctive characteristics and vary their techniques accordingly.

In the past, the social work profession has failed to serve effectively an important segment of the population—the Native Americans. Although social workers are in sympathy with the social problems and injustices long associated with the Native American people, they have been unable to assist them with their problems. This lack of success on the part of social workers can be attributed to a multitude of reasons but it stems, in general, from the following: (1) lack of understanding of the Native American culture, (2) retention of stereotyped images of Native Americans, (3) use of standard techniques and approaches.

Currently, the majority of social workers attempting to treat Native Americans are whites who have never been exposed to their clients' culture. Even when the social worker is a Native American, if his education and training have been in an environment that has completely neglected the Native American culture, there is still the possibility that he has drifted away from his people's thinking. Social workers with no understanding of the culture may have little or no sympathy for their Native American clients who fail to respond quickly to treatment.

Furthermore, Native Americans continue to be stereotyped by the current news media and often by the educational system. In all likelihood, the social worker will rely on these mistaken stereotypes rather than on facts. As Deloria explained, ''People can tell just by looking at us what we want, what should be done to help us, how we feel, and what a 'real' Indian is like.''[1] If a worker wishes to make progress in helping a Native American, he must begin by learning the facts and discarding stereotypes.

The ineffectiveness of social workers in dealing with Native Americans can often be attributed directly to the methods and techniques they use. Naturally, social workers must work with the tools they have acquired, but these may have a detrimental effect on a Native American. For example, the

© 1975 National Association of Social Workers Inc. Reprinted from *Social Work*, Vol. 20, No. 5 (September 1975), pp 379-382.

concept of "social work intervention" may be consistent with much of the white man's culture, but it diametrically opposes the Native American's cultural concept of noninterference.[2] There is a great need for social workers to examine carefully those techniques they plan to use in treating their Native American clients. If the worker discovers any that might be in conflict with the cultural concepts of the Native American, he should search carefully for an alternative approach. To do this, of course, the social worker must be aware of common Native American cultural traits.

Although there is no monolithic Native American culture—because each tribe's culture is unique to that individual tribe, and no social worker could be expected to be familiar with the cultures of some two hundred tribes—the worker should familiarize himself with those customs that are generally characteristic of all Native Americans. Only after a worker has gained at least an elementary knowledge of Native American customs and culture can he proceed to evaluate the various approaches and techniques and choose the most effective ones.

Native American Traits

The concept of sharing is deeply ingrained among Native Americans who hold it in greater esteem than the white American ethic of saving. Since one's worth is measured by one's willingness and ability to share, the accumulation of material goods for social status is alien to the Native American. Sharing, therefore, is neither a superimposed nor an artificial value, but a genuine and routine way of life.

In contrast to the general belief that they have no concept of time, Native Americans are indeed time conscious. They deal, however, with natural phenomena—mornings, days, nights, months (in terms of moons), and years (in terms of seasons or winters).[3] If a Native American is on his way to a meeting or appointment and meets a friend, that conversation will naturally take precedence over being punctual for the appointment. In his culture, sharing is more important than punctuality.

Nature is the Native American's school, and he is taught to endure all natural happenings that he will encounter during his life. He learns as well to be an independent individual who respects others. The Native American believes that to attain maturity—which is learning to live with life, its evil as well as its good—one must face genuine suffering. The resilience of the Native American way of life is attested to by the fact that the culture has survived and continues to flourish despite the intense onslaught of the white man.

One of the strongest criticisms of the Native American has been that he is pessimistic; he is presented as downtrodden, low-spirited, unhappy, and without hope for the future. However, as one looks deeper into his personality, another perspective is visible. In the midst of abject poverty comes "the courage to be"—to face life as it is, while maintaining a tremendous sense of humor.[4] There exists a thin line between pathos and humor.

The Native American realizes that the world is made up of both good and bad. There are always some people or things that are bad and deceitful. He believes, however, that in the end good people will triumph just because they are good. This belief is seen repeatedly in Native American folktales about Iktomi the spider. He is the tricky fellow who is out to fool, cheat, and take advantage of good people. But Iktomi usually loses in the end, reflecting the Native American view that the good person succeeds while the bad person loses.[5] Therefore, the pessimism of Native Americans should instead be regarded as "optimistic toughness."

Those who are unfamiliar with the culture might mistakenly interpret the quiet Native American as being stoical, unemotional, and vulnerable. He is alone, not only to others but also to himself. He controls his emotions, allowing himself no passionate outbursts over small matters. His habitual mien is one of poise, self-containment, and aloofness, which may result from a fear and mistrust of non-Native Americans. Another facet of Native American thought is the belief that no matter where any individual stands, he is an integral part of the universe. Because every person is fulfilling a purpose, no one should have the power to impose values. For this reason, each man is to be respected, and he can expect the same respect and reverence from others. Hence, the security of this inner fulfillment provides him with an essential serenity that is often mistaken for stoicism.

Native American patience, however, can easily be mistaken for inactivity. For instance, the Kiowa, like other Native American tribes, teach their young people to be patient. Today, when the young Native American has to go out and compete in another society, this quality is often interpreted as laziness. The white man's world is a competitive, aggressive society that bypasses the patient man who stands back and lets the next person go first.

The foregoing are only a few of the cultural traits that are common to most Native American tribes, but they represent important characteristics about which the effective social worker must be informed. The concepts of sharing, of time, acceptance of suffering, and optimism differ significantly from the white man's concepts. In dealing with a Native American client, the social worker must realize this and proceed accordingly. He must be familiar with the Native American view that good will triumph over evil and must recognize that Native Americans are taught to be patient and respectful. If the worker fails to do this, he is liable to make false assumptions, thus weakening his ability to serve his client effectively.

Client-Worker Relations

A social worker's ability to establish a working relationship with a Native American will depend on his genuine respect for his client's cultural background and attributes. A worker should never think that the Native American is primitive or that his culture and background are inferior.

In the beginning, the Native American client might distrust the worker who is from a different race and culture. He might even view the worker as a figure of authority, and as such, the representative of a coercive institution. It is unlikely that he will be impressed with the worker's educational degrees or his professional title. However, this uncompromising attitude should not be interpreted as pugnacity. On the contrary, the Native American is gregarious and benevolent. His willingness and capacity to share depend on mutual consideration, respect, and noncoercion.

Because their culture strongly opposes and precludes interference with another's affairs, Native Americans have tended to regard social work intervention with disfavor. Social workers usually are forced to use culturally biased techniques and skills that are insensitive to the Native American culture and, therefore, are either detrimental to these clients or, at best, ineffective.

In an effort to communicate more fully, a social worker is likely to seat himself facing the client, look him straight in the eye, and insist that the client do likewise. A Native American considers such behavior—covert or overt—to be rude and intimidating; contrary to the white man, he shows respect by not staring directly at others. Similarly, a worker who is excessively concerned with facilitating the display of inner feelings on the part of the client should be aware of another trait. A Native American client will not immediately wish to discuss other members of his family or talk about topics that he finds sensitive or distressing. Before arriving at his immediate concern (the real reason he came to the worker in the first place), the client—particularly the Native American—will test the worker by bringing up peripheral matters. He does this in the hope of getting a better picture of how sincere, interested, and trustworthy the worker actually is. If the worker impatiently confronts the client with accusations, the client will be "turned off."

Techniques of communication that focus on the client—that is, techniques based on restating, clarifying, summarizing, reflecting, and empathizing—may help a worker relate to the client who sometimes needs a new perspective to resolve his problem. It is important that the worker provide him with such information but not coerce him to accept it. The worker's advice should be objective and flexible enough so that its adoption does not become the central issue of a particular interview.

For the Native American, personal matters and emotional breakdown are traditionally handled within the family or extended family system. For this reason, the client will not wish to "burden" the worker with detailed personal information. If the client is estranged from his family and cultural group, he may indirectly share such personal information with the worker. To determine the appropriate techniques for helping a Native American client deal with personal and psychological problems, the worker should carefully observe the client's cultural framework and his degree of defensiveness. The techniques of confrontation traditionally associated with the psychoanalytic approach and the introspective and integrative techniques used by the transactional analysts tend to disregard differences in culture and background between a client and worker.

Family Counseling

In view of the close-knit family structure of Native Americans, along with the cultural emphasis to keep family matters inside the family, it is doubtful that many social workers will have the opportunity to render family counseling services. In the event that a Native American family does seek the worker's help, the family worker should be reminded that his traditional role of active and manipulative go-between must be tempered so that family members can deal with their problems at their own pace.[6] Equally important is the worker's awareness of and respect for the resilience of Native American families, bolstered in crisis by the extended family system. The example of the Redthunder family serves as illustration.

> The Redthunder family was brought to the school social worker's attention when teachers reported that both children had been tardy and absent frequently in the past weeks. Since the worker lived near Mr. Redthunder's neighborhood, she volunteered to transport the children back and forth to school. Through this regular but informal arrangement, the worker became acquainted with the entire family, especially with Mrs. Redthunder who expressed her gratitude to the worker by sharing her homegrown vegetables.
>
> The worker sensed that there was much family discomfort and that a tumultuous relationship existed between Mr. and Mrs. Redthunder. Instead of probing into their personal and marital affairs, the worker let Mrs. Redthunder know that she was willing to listen should the woman need someone to talk to. After a few gifts of homegrown vegetables and Native American handicrafts, Mrs. Redthunder broke into tears one day and told the worker about her husband's problem of alcoholism and their deteriorating marital relationship.
>
> Realizing Mr. Redthunder's position of respect in the family and his resistance to outside interference, the social worker advised Mrs. Redthunder to take her family to visit the minister, a man whom Mr. Redthunder admired. The Littleaxe family, who were mutual friends of the worker and the Redthunder family, agreed to take the initiative in visiting the Redthunders more often. Through such frequent but informal family visits, Mr. Redthunder finally obtained a job, with the recommendation of Mr. Littleaxe, as recordkeeper in a storeroom. Mr. Redthunder enjoyed his work so much that he drank less and spent more time with his family.

Obviously, treating a family more pathogenic than the Redthunders might necessitate that the social worker go beyond the role of mediator. Nevertheless, since Native Americans traditionally favor noninterference, the social worker will not find it feasible to assume the active manipulative role that he might in working with white middle-class families. The social work profession needs new and innovative approaches to family counseling that take into account social and family networks and are sensitive and responsive to the cultural orientation of Native American families.[7]

Group Work

Groups should be a natural and effective medium for Native Americans who esteem the concept of sharing and apply it in their daily lives. Through the group process, members can share their joy, intimacy, problems, and sorrows, and find a means of improving their lives. Today's society tends to foster alienation, anomie, disenfranchisement, dissociation, loneliness, and schizoid coolness.[8] People wish for intimacy but at the same time fear it.[9] The new humanistic approaches to counseling and psychotherapy have developed a wide variety of powerful techniques for facilitating human growth, self-discovery, and interpersonal relations.[10] The effectiveness of these approaches in cutting through resistance, breaking down defenses, releasing creative forces, and promoting the healing process has been amply demonstrated. However, such approaches are highly insensitive to the cultural orientation of Native Americans. These people consider such group behavior to be false; it looks and sounds real but lacks genuineness, depth, and real commitment.

As the worker uses his skills in forming the group, diagnosing the problems, and facilitating group goals, he may inevitably retain certain elements of manipulation. However, if he is committed to recognizing individual potential and to capitalizing on the group model of mutual assistance, he should come close to meeting the needs of Native Americans who value respect and consideration for oneself as well as for others.[11]

To avoid manipulation and coercion, a group worker needs to utilize indirect and extra-group means of influence that will in turn influence the members. Thus the worker may act upon and through the group as a mediating structure, or through program activities, for the benefit of his clients.[12] The success of the worker's influences and activities is related to his knowledge and acceptance of Native American culture, its formal and informal systems and norms.

Regardless of whether the purpose of the group is for effecting interpersonal change or social action, such Native American virtues as mutual respect and consideration should be the essential components of the group process. Using the group to pressure members who are late or silent will not only jeopardize and shorten the group's existence, but will cause alienation and withdrawal from future group activities.

In view of the vast cultural difference between Native Americans and other ethnic groups, especially whites, it is doubtful that a heterogeneous grouping of members will produce good results. Similarly, group activities that are action oriented may be contradictory to Native Americans who view the compulsion to reduce or ignore suffering as immaturity.

Community Work

Because of the Native Americans' experience of oppression and exploitation—along with their emphasis on noninterference and resolute acceptance of suffering—it is doubtful that a social worker, regardless of his racial identity, could bring about any major change in community policies and programs. The only exception might be the social worker who is accepted and "adopted" by the community and who agrees to confine himself to the existing system and norms. A worker's adoption by the Native American community will depend on his sincerity, respect, and genuine concern for the people. This concern can best be displayed through patience in daily contact with the community as well as through his efforts to find positive solutions to problems.

A worker who uses the strategy of trying to resolve conflict as a means of bringing about social change will undoubtedly encounter native resistance and rejection. On the other hand, a worker who shows respect for the system, values, and norms of the Native American eventually places himself in a position of trust and credibility. Only through mutual respect, and not through his professional title and academic degree, can the worker produce meaningful social change.

Obviously, social work with Native Americans requires a new orientation and focus on attitudes and approaches. The term Native American encompasses many tribes, and within these there are intratribal differences; furthermore, individuals within each subtribe may react differently to problems or crises. Therefore, it is impossible for a social worker always to know precisely how to respond to a Native American client or group. The worker must be willing to admit his limitations, to listen carefully, to be less ready to draw conclusions, and to anticipate that his presuppositions will be corrected by the client. The worker must genuinely want to know what the problem or the situation is and be receptive to being taught. Such an unassuming and unobtrusive humanistic attitude is the key to working with Native American people.

The social worker who can deal most effectively with Native Americans will be genuine, respectful of their culture, and empathic with the welfare of the people. By no means does the Native American social worker have a monopoly on this type of attitude. In fact, the Native American social worker who has assimilated the white man's culture to the extent that he no longer values his own culture could do more harm than good.

Recognizing the distinct cultural differences of the Native American people, those who plan social work curricula and training programs must expand them to include specific preparation for workers who will be dealing with Native American clients. Literature on the subject is almost nonexistent, and researchers and educators would do well to devote more study to how social workers can serve Native Americans. More Native Americans should be recruited as students, faculty, and practitioners in the field of social work. All persons, regardless of race, should be encouraged to develop a sensitivity toward Native Americans whom they may have the opportunity to serve. Social work agencies that deal primarily with Native American clients should intensify and refocus their in-service training programs.

A worker has the responsibility of acquiring knowledge that is relevant to the Native American culture so that he is capable of providing this effective treatment. A joint effort on the part of all those involved is required to give the service to Native Americans that they justly deserve.

Notes and References

1. Vine Deloria, Jr., *Custer Died for Your Sins: An Indian Manifesto* (New York: Macmillan Co., 1969), p. 45.
2. For a detailed discussion of noninterference, *see* Rosalie H. Wax and Robert K. Thomas, "Anglo Intervention vs. Native Noninterference," *Phylon,* 22 (Winter 1961), pp. 53-56; and Jimm G. Good Tracks, "Native American Noninterference," *Social Work,* 18 (November 1973), pp. 30-34.
3. Good Tracks, op. cit., p. 33.
4. Clair Huffaker, *Nobody Loves a Drunken Indian* (New York: David McKay Co., 1967).
5. *See* John F. Bryde, *Modern Indian Psychology* (Vermillion, S. Dak.: Institute of Indian Studies, University of South Dakota, 1971), p. 15.
6. *See* Gerald Suk, "The Go-Between Process in Family Therapy," *Family Process,* 6 (April 1966), pp. 162-178.
7. Ross V. Speck and Carolyn L. Attneave, "Social Network Intervention," in Jay Haley, ed., *Changing Families* (New York: Grune & Stratton, 1971), pp. 17-34.
8. Rollo May, "Love and Will," *Psychology Today,* 3 (1969), pp. 17-24.
9. Edward A. Dreyfus, "The Search for Intimacy," *Adolescence,* 2 (March 1967), pp. 25-40.
10. *See* Bernard Gunther, *Sense Relaxation: Below Your Mind* (New York: Macmillan Co., 1968); Abraham Maslow, "Self-Actualization and Beyond," in James F. Bugental, ed., *Challenges of Humanistic Psychology* (New York: McGraw-Hill Book Co., 1967); H. Oho, *Explorations in Human Potentialities* (Springfield, Ill.: Charles C. Thomas, 1966); Carl Rogers, "Process of the Basic Encounter Group," in James F. Bugental, ed., op. cit.
11. For further discussion of a reciprocal model, *see* William Schwartz. "Toward a Strategy of Group Work Practice," *Social Service Review,* 36 (September 1962), pp. 268-279.
12. For further discussion of indirect and extra-group means, *see* Robert Vinter, *Readings in Group Work Practice* (Ann Arbor: Campus Publishers, 1967), pp. 8-38.

6 Counseling the American Indian Child

Youngman, Geraldine
Sandongei, Margaret

"The Indians are coming!" Or so it might be said by those who live in large metropolitan areas. The Indians are moving to the urban areas of the country and are sitting in the classrooms from kindergarten through college. Not all have descriptive last names. There are Browns, Smiths, Gutierrizes, and Johnsons, and they come in various sizes and colors. They come from various tribes—Apache, Pima, Sioux, Hopi, Navajo, Kiowa, Papago, and Pueblo. There are approximately 400 recognized tribes in the United States. Some children are bi-lingual and, depending on tribal background, some speak only English. Contrary to popular belief, there are many different tribal languages. This is why sign language was developed and is still used by the older members of the various tribes, particularly the Plains Indians.

Approximately 400,000 Indians are under 21 years of age today. Of these, 75 to 80 percent will obtain their education on reservations or in the federal boarding schools off reservations. To meet that need, many school systems can be found on one reservation. There are schools operated by the tribe, by churches, by public school districts, or by the Bureau of Indian Affairs. Five percent receive their education from both areas because of moving from reservations to urban areas and back. Another five percent who are handicapped, deaf, or blind receive their education through special institutions.

It is now shown that 10 percent of school-age Indian children are born and reared in cities. These children have never lived on a reservation but they too bring their cultural differences to the school systems, where many counselors are not fully aware of their needs. Many times it is assumed that the urban influence has made the Indian child like all other urban children but in reality they tend to have stronger ties to their own tribe, customs, and languages.

Differences exist in languages—a Papago cannot understand a Kiowa—and in customs: Southwest tribes strive to develop a reserved nature while the Plains Indians strive to develop openness and instant acquaintanceship. There are general characteristics among all Indians that are known as "Indian ways." Some of these are tribal loyalty, respect for elders, reticence, humility, avoidance of personal glory and gain, giving and sharing with as many as three generations of relatives, an abiding love for their own land, attribution of human characteristics to animals and nature, and strong spiritual beliefs. These characteristics are often in direct contrast to a school system based on competitiveness not humbleness, scientific research not social acceptance, verbosity not reticence.

Consequently, we often hear the comment, ''Well, we don't have any problems with our Indian children. We get along fine.'' These ''good Indians,'' as they are dubbed by some educators, are those who fit the concept held by the non-Indian society: All Indian children are slow learners, shy, lack positive identification, are thieves by nature, are undependable, and are potential alcoholics. Indian children who do not care to fit in the mold are labeled incorrigible, hyperactive, brain damaged, and rude.

The Indian child who has been reared with a tribal cultural background faces a difficult task in a non-Indian school, especially if he has no inkling as to what the dominant society expects. He must first learn what is expected and meet those expectations before he can be fully accepted.

One of the most common incidents involving Indian children that confronts teachers and counselors is the taking of things off the teacher's desk. Pencils, markers, tape, etc. from the teacher's desk are often found in an Indian child's desk. When confronted by the teacher, the child will usually admit to taking the objects. In the teacher's eyes the child is a thief, and the child is whisked off to the office.

The Indian child is surprised and hurt when such an act is called stealing, because Indian children know that any person of rank and importance *shares!* The child feels that it is his classroom (actually, it is a compliment to the teacher), and, since he has a sense of belonging, he also has the right to use things off the teacher's desk.

Another incident might involve eye contact, which is considered important and necessary in the non-Indian society. But, in the Indian culture it is (depending on the tribe) an act of rudeness. Indian children are taught to see without looking directly at someone.

In the first incident, a counselor can say to the child, ''Sharing with mother and other family members is wonderful, but sharing with teacher in school is not possible because she is not family. There are too many other children in the room to allow taking things without asking permission first.'' Or, ''I know that you did not steal; I know that you really needed the pencil, and I will try to help you get your own.''

In the second incident, the counselor might say to a concerned teacher, ''These children are taught that to stare or look directly is rude. Try to accept it, but check periodically on attention as you would with any other child. You know, there are many non-Indian children who look but never hear.''

In most Indian cultures it is considered ill-mannered to speak of one's accomplishments. Praise is welcome when earned but is always given by someone else. Yet, in classrooms teachers use ''self-disclosure'' procedures that encourage children to talk about their strengths in front of their classmates. Therefore, most Indian children attempting to meet the teacher's request suffer extreme embarrassment. The child may stand but not talk at all or tell unbelievable stories. Teachers might suggest a general subject rather than talk about self. The Indian child is often aware of his own capabilities and if he sees the need to excel, he does. Last year in the sixth grade Richard sat in class, not doing anything, just sitting. When the reading specialist tested him, she found him capable of reading on the eighth-grade level. Richard knew he could do the work but he didn't see any pressing reason why he should put forth the effort. This year Richard is in the seventh grade, and, through a game, the reading teacher learned how "sharp" he was. The game was fun. Why such an attitude? Perhaps during his first three grades, Richard was told either verbally or nonverbally that he was not teachable or that because he was an Indian he was not quite up to par with non-Indian children.

Indian children are very much involved in decision making at home and are usually given choices. Perhaps they do not always decide wisely, but, nonetheless, they have a part in the decision. Counselors working with Indian children should always present a choice: "Either this or that," "Do you or don't you want to?" For example, in counseling toward more school participation, a counselor could say, "I see that you are a good basketball player; you shoot well and you are fast. We would like to have you join us. Will you play on our team?" It calls for a definite yes or no answer. If the student says no, he will supply the reason.

Indian children are very much aware of nonverbal communication. One of the greatest factors in counseling is the counselor's own individual personality and his perception of people and children around him. If the counselor gives the impression of being busy, communication is broken. The Indian child would not dream of being in the way or taking up anyone's time. The Indian's concept of time is not the number of conferences, the number of minutes, or racing the clock. Rather, it is a relaxed few minutes of listening and talking. This is especially true of Indians who have not spent much time living and working within the urban structure.

As most counselors know, what works for one child may not work for another. This is even more so for Indian children. The key word is patience. Patience and more patience!

The sincerity of a person is a trait that most Indian children are very much aware of. A child brought up in the Indian culture is going to observe how closely the counselor lives with what he says. One of the reasons an Indian is slow to open up is because he is going to watch and observe whether the counselor says one thing and does another. A counselor who shows sincere friendliness, perhaps by visiting the home and developing interest in the entire family, will be more likely to find Indian children confiding in him more often.

Friendly inquisitiveness is considered nosiness by Indians. It can slam doors of communication shut. In counseling a child on being late, one counselor said, "I'm happy you made it to school even though you are late.

Do you have to help clean house or wash dishes before you come to school?'' (Yes) "Let's find ways to help you get your work done on time.'' Some choices were given, such as "You could do more at night; you could talk to your mother to see if you could do more work when you get home from school.'' The problem was handled without embarrassment to the child or family.

There are no set rules for working with Indian children because of different tribal backgrounds. If there are a large number of Indian children in school, the counselor might find out the tribal background and do some research before approaching the child. Use a slow approach: The first session may be all one sided with the counselor doing the talking or it might just be a comfortable silent session. Counselors should have open minds and understand the need for patience and time. Keep in mind that the child's response is apt to be slow. The Indian people have a lot to contribute, but they have learned to be careful in dispensing any knowledge.

Working with Indian children who have different beliefs and values may cause a counselor to question his own beliefs and values. For the young Indians who are caught in the middle, with the dominant society urging them to forge ahead and achieve according to certain standards and the Indian culture saying it is not important to be the "top cheese,'' there can be paths to tragic ends, which must be carefully avoided. Remember—before coming to any conclusion regarding any Indian child try to put yourself in his mocassins.

Selected Readings

American Indian Historical Society. *Indian Voices.* San Francisco: The Indian Historian Press, 1970.

Deloria, V. *Custer Died for Your Sins: An Indian Manifesto.* New York: Macmillan Pub. Co., 1969.

Dinges, N.G., Yazzie, M.L., & Tolletson, G.D. Developmental intervention for Navajo family mental health. *Personnel and Guidance Journal,* 1974, *52* (6), 390-395.

Forbes, J.D. *The Indian in America's Past.* Englewood Cliffs, N.J.: Prentice Hall, Inc. 1964.

Forbes, J.D. *Native Americans of California and Nevada.* Healdsburg, Ca.: Naturegraph Pub., 1969.

Fuchs, E., & Havighurst, R.J. *To Live on this Earth.* Garden City, N.Y.: Doubleday & Co., 1972.

Henry, J. *The American Indian Reader.* San Francisco: American Indian Educational Publishers, 1972.

Tracks, J.G.G. Native American non-interference. *Social Work,* 1973, *18,* 30-34.

The American Indian Client
Cases and Questions

1. Assume you are an elementary school counselor for several rural elementary schools that enroll about twelve American Indian students each year (approximately five percent of the total enrollment). Although the American Indian children perform as well as the Anglo children in kindergarten, by fourth grade it is clear they are less advanced in reading, writing, and computational skills. The district in which these schools are located is quite poor, and you are one of the few specialists available to supplement the resources of the classroom teacher.

   a. Upon entering a teacher's lounge in one school, you hear the English teacher, in conversation with several other teachers, relate the American Indian students' poor performance to their family/cultural background in rather uncomplimentary terms. How would you react?
   b. What responsibility, if any, would you accept for attempting to offset the deficiencies in academic skills these Native American students have?
   c. What response would you expect to receive from American Indian students and their parents to your attempts to improve the students' academic performance (assuming you accept responsibility for doing this)?

2. Assume you are a community social worker employed by the BIA to work with reservation Indian families in which one or both of the parents have a history of chronic alcoholism.

   a. What are some of the factors you believe may contribute to alcoholism among American Indians, and how would this affect your role as a social worker?
   b. What personal and professional qualities which you possess would be helpful in your work with American Indians? What qualities might be detrimental?
   c. Would you attempt to work with several families at once through group counseling? If so, how would you structure the group experience?

3. Assume you are a counselor in an urban high school that enrolls a small number of Native American students whose parents have left reservation

life for the employment opportunities of a big city. Johnny Lonetree, an artistically gifted junior who regularly makes the honor roll, has just informed you that he is contemplating returning to the reservation to live with his grandparents. Johnny knows that for all practical purposes this will mean an end to his scholastic education, but he is intensely interested in being immersed in the tribal culture, specifically tribal art work.

a. How can you best assist Johnny in his decision-making process?
b. How might some of your own values affect how you proceed with Johnny?
c. What are some of the social pressures (exerted by administrators, colleagues, Johnny's parents) that are likely to be exerted upon both you and Johnny if he decides to return to the reservation?

The American Indian Client
Role Playing Exercise

Divide into groups of 4 or 5. Assign each group member to a role and the responsibilities associated with the role as follows:

Role	Responsibilities
1. Counselor	1. Assume role as a counselor or mental health worker who encounters an American Indian. Attempt to build rapport with the client.
2. Client	2. Assume role of an American Indian. To play this role effectively, it will be necessary for the student client to (a) identify cultural values of the American Indian group, (b) identify sociopolitical factors which may interfere with counseling, and (c) portray these aspects in the counseling session. It is best to select a few powerful variables in the role play. You may or may not be initially antagonistic to the counselor, but it is important for you to be sincere in your role and your reactions to the counselor.
3. Observers	3. Observe interaction and offer comments during feedback session.

This exercise is most effective in a racially and ethnically mixed group. For example, an American Indian student can be asked to play the American Indian client role. However, this is probably not possible in most cases. Thus, students who play the client role will need to thoroughly read the articles for the group they are portraying.

Identifying the barriers that could interfere with counseling is an important aspect of this exercise. We recommend that a list be made of the group's cultural values and sociopolitical influences prior to the role playing.

Role playing may go on for a period of 5–15 minutes, but the time limit should be determined prior to the activity. Allow 10–15 minutes for a feedback session in which all participants discuss (within the group) how they felt in their respective roles, how appropriate were the counselor responses, what else they might have done in that situation, etc.

Rotate and role play the same situation with another counselor trainee *or* another American Indian client with different issues, concerns, and problems. In the former case, the group may feel that a particular issue is of sufficient importance to warrant reenactment. This allows students to see the effects of other counseling responses and approaches. In the latter case, the new exposure will allow students to get a broader view of barriers to counseling.

If videotaping equipment is available, we recommend that the sessions be taped and processed in a replay at the end. We have found this to be a powerful means of providing feedbacks to participants.

Part 3
The Asian American Client

Photo by Jean-Claude Lejeune

In contrast to many Third World groups, the contemporary image of Asian Americans is that of a highly successful minority that has "made it" in society. For example, the popular press has often portrayed Asian Americans as a "model" minority, using such headlines as "Success Story: Outwhiting the Whites" and "Success Story of One Minority Group in the U.S." (*U.S. News and World Report*, 1966; *Newsweek*, 1971). A superficial analysis of the 1970 Census seems to support this contention: Chinese, Japanese, and even Philippinos now exceed the median income; Asian Americans complete a higher medium number of grades than all other groups; studies consistently reveal that Asian Americans have low official rates of juvenile delinquency, psychiatric contact, and divorce. The success myth seems also to have been generalized to the Indochinese refugees (Vietnamese, Laotians, and Cambodians) who are viewed as well-educated, middle-to-upper class people who are having little difficulty adapting to U.S. society (*Newsweek*, 1975; *Time*, 1975). The conclusion one can draw from all of these statistics is that Asian Americans and Indochinese refugees have never been victims of prejudice and discrimination.

Yet, a review of the Asian experience in America indicates the massive discrimination directed at them. Assaulted, murdered, denied ownership of land, denied rights of citizenship, and placed in concentration camps during World War II, Asian Americans have been subjected to some of the most flagrant forms of discrimination ever perpetrated against an immigrant group.

A closer analysis of the status of Asian Americans does not support their success story. Reference to the higher median income does not take into account (a) the higher percentage of more than one wage earner in the family, (b) an equal incidence of poverty despite the higher median income, (c) lower poverty assistance and welfare than the general population, and (d) the fact that salaries are not commensurate with the education levels of Asian American workers (lower salaries despite higher educational level). Statistics on educational levels are also misleading. Asian Americans present a picture of extraordinarily high educational attainment for some, while a large number remain uneducated. The impression that Indochinese refugees are a homogeneous, privileged group is also not supported by data. For example, the Vietnamese who evacuated were probably the most heterogeneous group ever to immigrate to the U.S.

There is also recognition that, apart from being tourist attractions, Chinatowns, Manilatowns, and Japantowns in major metropolitan cities represent ghetto areas. Unemployment, poverty, health problems, and juvenile delinquency are major facts of life. For example, San Francisco's Chinatown has the second greatest population density next to Harlem. It not only has a high tuberculosis rate, but a suicide rate three times the national average. Juvenile gangland warfare has also caught the public eye. Under-utilization of mental health facilities by Chinese Americans in San

Francisco is now recognized to be due to cultural factors inhibiting self-referral (shame and disgrace associated with admitting to emotional problems, reliance on the family to prevent it from becoming public, etc.), and/or to inappropriate institutional policies and practices. Furthermore, Indochinese refugees seem to differ from White Americans in what they regard as mental health problems requiring treatment. As a result, we are now beginning to understand why groups like the Vietnamese are reluctant to seek traditional mental health services in the U.S.

In his leadoff article, "Ethnic Identity: The Impact of Two Cultures on the Psychological Development of Asians in America," D. Sue describes the psychological development of two Asian groups with respect to stereotypes, unique cultural values, and the experience of racism. Personality characteristics, academic abilities, and vocational interests of both Chinese and Japanese Americans are described. These descriptions provide important information for counselors who work with Asian Americans and need to look behind the "success myth," and to understand the Asian experience in America.

It is increasingly recognized that traditional counseling approaches must be modified to fit the life experiences of minority clients. In the case of Chinese-Americans, D. Sue and S. Sue in their article "Counseling Chinese-Americans" suggest how such modifications in counseling can be made by taking into account such factors as cultural values and the experience of racism. Specific concrete strategies are presented and discussed. While this article deals only with Chinese American clients, it presents an example of how different approaches might be used for other Asian Americans (Japanese, Philippinos, Koreans, and Hawaiians) as well.

In the last article, Brower provides specific information counselors need to have if they are to be successful when working with one of America's newest immigrant groups, the Vietnamese. Brower suggests that the relationship dynamics of rapport building, interview structure, transference and countertransference, and communication barriers are of particular concern when counseling Vietnamese. She further suggests that counselors need to be sensitive to Vietnamese attitudes toward self-disclosure and sex roles in order to develop a productive counseling relationship. Brower concludes her article by examining mental health problems that counselors who work with Vietnamese are likely to encounter.

Newsweek. Success Story: Outwhiting the whites. June, 1971.

Newsweek. The new Americans. May 12, 1975.

Time Magazine. Future of refugees: The furor and the facts. May 19, 1975.

U.S. News and World Report. Success story of one minority group in the U.S. December, 1966.

7 Ethnic Identity
The Impact of Two Cultures on the Psychological Development of Asians in America
Sue, Derald Wing

Among the many determinants of Asian-American identity, the cultural influences (values, norms, attitudes, and traditions) are of considerable importance. While social scientists agree that psychological development is not an isolated phenomenon apart from socio-cultural forces, most theories of personality are culturally exclusive. Furthermore, empirical studies tend not to deal adequately with the impact of cultural racism on the behavior of ethnic minorities. To understand the psychological development of Chinese- and Japanese-Americans, the cultural and historical forces of racism which serve to shape and define the Asian-American's identity must be examined.

Most studies which focus on the effects of culture on Asian-Americans tend to be highly compartmentalized. For example, one can find research investigating the relationship of culture to (a) personality characteristics (Abbott, 1970; Fong & Peskin, 1969; Meredith, 1966; Arkoff, Meredith & Iswahara, 1964; 1962; Fenz & Arkoff, 1962), (b) child-rearing practices (DeVos & Abbott, 1966; Kitano, 1964), (c) the manifestation of behavior disorders (Marsella, Kinzie, Gordon, 1971; Kitano, 1970; 1969a; Arkoff & Weaver, 1966; Sommers, 1960; Kimmich, 1960), (d) the ineffectiveness of traditional therapy (Sue & Sue, 1972a; 1971; Yamamoto, James & Palley, 1968), (e) acculturation (Matsumoto, Meredith & Masuda, 1970; Meade, 1970; Weiss, 1969; Fong, 1965; Kitano, 1962; Arkoff, 1959), and (f) use of English (Meredith, 1964; Smith & Kasdon, 1961; Smith, 1957). Few attempts integrate these findings into a global description of how cultures influence the socio-psychological functioning of the "whole" person.

Cultural impact is clearly demonstrated in the study of Chinese- and Japanese-Americans, where remnants of Asian cultural values collide with European-American values. The historical meeting of these two cultures and their consequent interaction in a racist society have fundamental importance in understanding the personality characteristics, academic abilities, and vocational interests of Asians in America.

Reprinted by permission of the editors and the publisher from D.W. Sue "Ethnic Identity: The Impact of Two Cultures on the Psychological Development of Asians in America." In S. Sue and N.N. Wagner (Eds.), *Asian-Americans: Psychological Perspectives*. Palo Alto, CA: Science and Behavior Books, 1973.

Asian Cultural Values

Although it is acknowledged that the Asian-American family structure and its subcultural values are in transition, they still retain their many values from the past. Because the primary family is generally the socializing agent for its offspring and because parents interpret appropriate and inappropriate behavior, a description of traditional Asian families will lead to greater understanding of their cultural values.

Chinese and Japanese family interaction patterns have been described as being similar by many social scientists (Sue & Sue, 1971; Abbott, 1970; Kitano, 1969a; 1969b; DeVos & Abbott, 1966; Kimmich, 1960). The Asian family is an ancient, complex institution, the fundamental unit of the culture. In China and Japan, it has long been more or less independent of political alliances; its form has survived political upheavals and invasions of foreigners.

The roles of family members are highly interdependent. Deviations from traditional norms governing behavior are suppressed to keep the family intact. Independent behavior which might upset the orderly functioning of the family is discouraged. The family structure is so arranged that conflicts within the family are minimized; each member has his own role to play which does not interfere with that of another. If a person has feelings which might disrupt family peace and harmony, he is expected to hide them. Restraint of potentially disruptive emotions is strongly emphasized in the development of the Asian character; the lack of outward signs of emotions has given rise to the prevalent opinion among Westerners that Asians are "inscrutable."

The Chinese and Japanese families are traditionally patriarchal with communication and authority flowing vertically from top to bottom. The father's behavior in relationship to other family members is generally dignified, authoritative, remote, and aloof. Sons are generally highly valued over daughters. The primary allegiance of the son is to the family, and obligations as a good father or husband are secondary. Asian women are expected to carry on the domestic duties, to marry, to become obedient helpers of their mothers-in-law, and to bear children, especially males.

The inculcation of guilt and shame are the principal techniques used to control the behavior of family members. Parents emphasize their children's obligation to the family. If a child acts independently (contrary to the wishes of his parents), he is told that he is selfish and inconsiderate and that he is not showing gratitude for all his parents have done for him. The behavior of individual members of an Asian family is expected to reflect credit on the whole family. Problems that arise among Asian-Americans such as failure in school, disobedience, juvenile delinquency, mental illness, etc., are sources of great shame. Such problems are generally kept hidden from public view and handled within the family. This fact may explain why there are low *official* rates of juvenile delinquency (Abbott & Abbott, 1969; Kitano, 1967) and low utilization of mental health facilities among Asians (Sue & Sue, 1972a;

Kitano, 1969a; Yamamoto, James & Palley, 1968; K
other hand, outstanding achievement in some aspec'
educational and occupational success) is a source r
family. Thus, each family member has much at '
others.

In summary, traditional Asian values em'
interpersonal relations, restraint and inhibition o.
authority, obligations to the family, high academic an
achievement, and use of shame and guilt to control behaviv.
values have a significant impact on the psychological characterisu.
in America.

Historical Experience: Cultural Racism

Kovel (1970) believes that White racism in America is no aberration but an
ingredient of our culture which serves as a stabilizing influence and a source
of gratification to Whites. In defining cultural racism, Jones (1972) states that
it is "...the individual and institutional expression of the superiority of one
race's cultural heritage over that of another race. Racism is appropriate to the
extent that racial and cultural factors are highly correlated and are a
systematic basis for inferior treatment." (p. 6) Any discussion concerning the
effects of racism on the psychological characteristics of minorities is
necessarily fraught with hazards. It is difficult to distinguish the relevant
variables which affect the individual and to impute cause-effect relations.
However, a historical analysis of Asians in America suggests that cultural
racism has done great harm to this ethnic group.

Unknown to the general public, Asian-Americans have been the object
of much prejudice and discrimination. Ironically, the American public is
unaware that no higher walls of prejudice have been raised, historically,
around any other ethnic minority than those around the Chinese and Japanese.
Asians have generally attempted to function in the existing society without
loud, strong, or public protest (Sue & Sue, 1972a).

The first Chinese immigrants came to the United States during the
1840s. Their immigration from China was encouraged by the social and
economic unrest in China at that time and by overpopulation in certain
provinces (DeVos & Abbott, 1966). During this period, there was a demand
for Chinese to help build the transcontinental railroad. Because of the need
for cheap labor, they were welcomed into the labor force (Daniels, 1971).
However, a diminishing labor market and fear of the "yellow peril" made the
Chinese immigrants no longer welcome. Their pronounced racial and cultural
differences from the White majority made them conspicuous, and they served
as scapegoats for the resentment of White workers. Although Daniels (1971)
mainly discusses the economic aspect for the hostility expressed against the
Chinese, he points out that the anti-Chinese movement soon developed into
an ideology of White supremacy which was compatible with the mainstream
of American racism. Chinese were seen as "subhuman" or "heathens," and
their mode of living was seen as undesirable and detrimental to the well-being

s which were passed to harass the Chinese denied them the
ship, ownership of land, the right of marriage, etc. At the
anti-Chinese movement, when prejudice and discrimination
Chinese flourished, many Chinese were assaulted and killed by
Whites. This anti-Chinese sentiment culminated in the passing of the
Chinese Exclusion Act of 1882 which was the first exclusion act
any ethnic group. This racist immigration law, justified by the alleged
to exclude masses of "cheap Chinese labor" from the United States,
not repealed until 1943 as a gesture of friendship toward China, an ally
f the United States during World War II.

Likewise, the Japanese in America faced severe hostility and
discrimination from White citizens. Japanese began immigrating to the United
States during the 1890s when anti-Chinese sentiment was great. As a result,
they shared in the pervasive anti-Oriental feeling. Originally brought in to fill
the demand for cheap agricultural labor and coming from an agrarian
background, many Japanese became engaged in these fields (Kitano, 1969b).
Their fantastic success in the agricultural occupations, coupled with a racist
climate, enraged many White citizens. Legislation similar to the anti-Chinese
acts was passed against the Japanese, and individual-mob violence repeated
itself. Such cries as "The Japs must go" were frequently echoed by the mass
media and labor and political leaders. In response to hostility toward members
of their race, both Chinese and Japanese formed their own communities to
isolate and protect themselves from a threatening racist society.

Within this background of White racism, it became relatively easy for
White society to accept the relocation of 110,000 Japanese-Americans into
camps during World War II. Their pronounced racial and cultural
characteristics were enough justification for the atrocious actions taken against
the Japanese. The dangerous precedent created by American reaction to the
Japanese is an ever-present threat that racial strains can again result in a
repeat of history.

There can be no doubt that cultural racism has been practiced against the
Chinese and Japanese. Many people would argue that, today,
Asian-Americans face no such obstacles as their ancestors. The myth that
Asians represent a "model minority" and are successful and functioning well
in society is a popular belief often played up by the press (Newsweek, 1971;
U.S. News & World Report, 1966). The 1960 Census reveals that Chinese
and Japanese, indeed, have higher incomes and lower unemployment rates
than their *non-White* counterparts. A further analysis, however, reveals that
Chinese and Japanese are lower in income and higher in unemployment rates
than the *White* population. This disparity is even greater when one considers
that, generally, Chinese and Japanese achieve higher educational levels than
Whites. It can only be concluded that social and economic discrimination are
still flagrantly practiced against Asian-Americans.

Thus far, the fact that cultural racism has and is being practiced against
Asian minorities has been documented. Attention now will be focused on the
psychological costs of culture conflict.

Culture Conflict

Jones (1972) believes that many forms of culture conflict are really manifestations of cultural racism. Although there is nothing inherently wrong in acculturation and assimilation, he believes that "...when it is forced by a powerful group on a less powerful one, it constitutes a restriction of choice; hence, it is no longer subject to the values of natural order." (p. 166)

When an ethnic minority becomes increasingly exposed to the values and standards of the dominant host culture, there is progressive inculcation of those norms. This has been found for both the Chinese (Abbott, 1970; Meade, 1970; Fong & Peskin, 1969; Fong, 1965) and Japanese (Matsumoto, Meredith & Masuda, 1970; Kitano, 1962; Arkoff, 1959). However, assimilation and acculturation are not always smooth transitions without their pitfalls. As they become Westernized, many Asian-Americans come to view Western personality characteristics as more admirable qualities than Asian characteristics. Constantly bombarded with what constitutes desirable traits by a society that has low tolerance for differing life styles, many Asian males and females begin to find members of their own race undesirable social partners. For example, Weiss (1969) found many Chinese-American girls coming to expect the boys they date to behave boldly and aggressively in the traditional Western manner. They could be quite vehement in their denunciation of Asian-male traits. Unfortunately, hostility to a person's minority cultural background may cause Asians to turn their hostility inward. Such is the case when Japanese-American females express greater dissatisfaction with their body image than Caucasian females (Arkoff & Weaver, 1966). The individual may develop a kind of racial self-hatred that leads to lowered self-esteem and intense conflicts (Sue & Sue, 1971; Sommers, 1960). Among individuals of minority cultural background, we find many instances of culture conflict; the individual finds that he is heir to two different cultural traditions, and he may have difficulty in reconciling their effects on his own personality; he may find it difficult to decide to which culture he owes primary loyalty. Such a person has been called a Marginal Man. Because of his marginal status, he often experiences an identity crisis and feels isolated and alienated from both cultures.

In previous articles (Sue & Sue, 1972a; 1971), three different reactions to this stress were described. A person may remain allied to the values of his own culture; he may attempt to become over-Westernized and reject Asian ways; or he may attempt to integrate aspects of both cultures which he believes are functional to his own self-esteem and identity. The latter mode of adjustment is being advocated by the ethnically conscious Asians on many college campuses. In an attempt to raise group esteem and pride, Asian-Americans are actively exploring and challenging the forces in White society which have served to unfairly shape and define their identity (Sue & Sue, 1972b). No longer are they content to be a "banana," a derogatory term used to designate a person of Asian descent who is "Yellow on the outside but White on the inside."

Psychological Characteristics of Chinese- and Japanese-American Students

The cultural background of both the Japanese and Chinese, the historical and continuing forces of White racism, and the cultural conflicts experienced in the United States have left their mark on the current life styles of Asian-Americans. Although it is difficult to impute a direct cause-effect relationship between these forces and the psychological characteristics of Asian-Americans, the following description, certainly, seems consistent with their past background. The remaining sections will focus upon the personality traits, academic abilities, and vocational interests of Chinese- and Japanese-American college students. Findings presented in these sections will rely heavily on research conducted at the University of California, Berkeley (Sue & Kirk, in press; forthcoming). Three tests consisting of the Omnibus Personality Inventory, the School and College Ability Tests, and the Strong Vocational Interest Blank were administered to an entire entering Freshman class. Chinese-American, Japanese-American, and all other students were compared to one another on these three instruments.

Personality Characteristics

The studies conducted at Berkeley reveal that Chinese- and Japanese-American college students tend to exhibit similar characteristics. This is not surprising in view of their similar cultural and historical backgrounds. Asian-Americans of both sexes tend to evaluate ideas on the basis of their immediate practical application and to avoid an abstract, reflective, theoretical orientation. Because of their practical and applied approach to life problems, they tend to be more intolerant of ambiguities and to feel much more comfortable in well-structured situations. Asian-Americans also appear less autonomous and less independent from parental controls and authority figures. They are more obedient, conservative, conforming, and inhibited. In interpersonal relationships, they tend to be cautious in directly expressing their impulses and feelings. In comparison to Caucasian norms, both Chinese- and Japanese-American students appear more socially introverted and will more often withdraw from social contacts and responsibilities. Other investigators have found similar results for the Chinese (Abbott, 1970; Fong & Peskin, 1969; DeVos & Abbott, 1966) and Japanese (Meredith, 1966; Fenz & Arkoff, 1962; Arkoff, 1959).

Asian cultural values, emphasizing restraint of strong feelings, obedience, dependence upon the family, and formality in interpersonal relations, are being exhibited by these students. These values are in sharp contrast to Western emphasis on spontaneity, assertiveness, and informality. Because of socialization in well-defined roles, there is a tendency for Asian students to feel more comfortable in structured situations and to feel uncomfortable in ambiguous ones. As a result, they may tend to withdraw from social contacts with those outside their ethnic group or family. As discussed later, their minority status and sensitivity to actual and potential discrimination from White society may make them suspicious of people. It is possible, also, that their concrete and pragmatic approach was reinforced because it possessed social and economic survival value.

The socio-emotional adjustment characteristics of Asian-Americans also seem to reflect their cultural background and experiences as minorities in America. Meredith (1966), in testing Sansei students at the University of Hawaii, found them to be more tense, apprehensive, and suspicious than their Caucasian counterparts. A study by Fenz & Arkoff (1962) revealed that senior high school students of Chinese and Japanese ancestry possessed significantly higher needs for abasement. This trait indicates a need to feel guilty when things go wrong and to accept personal blame for failure. The Berkeley studies also support the fact that Asian-Americans seem to be experiencing more stress than their Caucasian controls. Both Chinese- and Japanese-American students exhibited attitudes and behaviors that characterize alienated persons. They were more likely to possess feelings of isolation, loneliness, and rejection. They also appeared more anxious, worried, and nervous.

Three factors seem to be operating in these findings. First, cultural elements are obviously affecting these tests. For example, Asian values emphasizing modesty and the tendency to accept blame (guilt and shame) would naturally elevate their abasement score. However, clinical observations and the consistency of personality measures revealing higher experienced stress point to real problems. Second, past and present discrimination and the isolation imposed by a racist society would affect feelings of loneliness, alienation, and anxiety. Last, the earlier discussion of culture conflict leading to a negative self-image could be a strong component of these findings.

Academic Abilities

Using the School and College Ability Tests, the Berkeley studies revealed that Chinese- and Japanese-Americans of both sexes scored significantly lower on the verbal section of the test than their control counterparts. In addition, Chinese-Americans of both sexes scored significantly higher on the quantitative section of the test. Although Japanese-American students tended to obtain higher quantitative scores, the differences were not significant.

Although the possibility of inherited racial characteristics cannot be eliminated, greater explanatory power seems to lie in a sociocultural analysis. The Asian-American's lowered verbal performance probably reflects his bilingual background (Smith & Kasdon, 1961; Smith, 1957). The nature of Asian society also stresses filial piety and unquestioning respect for authority. Limited communication patterns in the home (parent to child) and the isolation imposed by a dominant society (one that rewarded silence and inconspicuousness and punished outspoken behavior from minorities) greatly restricted verbal interaction (Watanabe, 1971). The higher quantitative scores may represent compensatory modes of expression. Quantitative activities also tend to be more concrete, impersonal, and structured. These attributes are highly attractive to Asian-Americans.

Vocational Interests

Most educators, pupil personnel workers, and counselors throughout the West and East Coasts have frequently remarked on the abundance of Asian students entering the physical sciences. Surveys undertaken at the University of California, Berkeley, (Chu, 1971; Takayama, 1971) reveal that approximately 75 percent of Chinese and 68 percent of Japanese males enter the physical sciences. Using the Strong Vocational Interest Blank, the Berkeley studies compared the interests of Chinese-Americans, Japanese-Americans, and all other students. Chinese-American men expressed more interest in the physical sciences (Mathematician, Physicist, Engineer, Chemist, etc.) than all other students. Although not statistically significant, Japanese-American men also tended to express more interest in these occupations. Males from both ethnic groups appeared more interested in occupations comprising the skilled-technical trades (Farmer, Aviator, Carpenter, Printer, Vocational-Agricultural Teacher, Forest Service Man, etc.) and less interested in sales (Sales Manager, Real Estate Salesman, Life Insurance Salesman) and the verbal-linguistic occupations (Advertising Man, Lawyer, Author-Journalist). Although Chinese-American males exhibited less interest in the social sciences, this was not true for the Japanese-American males. Generally, both groups expressed more interest in the business fields, especially the detail (Senior Certified Public Accountant, Accounting and Office Man) as opposed to the business contact vocations. They tended to be less interested in the aesthetic-cultural fields (Musician and Artist). Although they did not differ significantly in the biological sciences as a group, they did express more interest in the clinically applied ones (Dentist and Veterinarian).

The Asian-American females had a profile similar to their male counterparts. Both ethnic groups exhibited more interest in business occupations, applied-technical fields, biological and physical sciences and less interest in verbal-linguistic fields, social service, and aesthetic-cultural occupations. Although Chinese- and Japanese-American females tended to express more interest in the domestically oriented occupations (Housewife, Elementary Teacher, Office Worker, and Stenographer-Secretary), only the Chinese-American females scored significantly higher.

An analysis of the relationship between personality traits, academic abilities, and vocational interests for Asian-Americans reveals a logical consistency among all three variables. Greater interest in the physical sciences and lower interest in sales, social sciences, and verbal-linguistic fields are consistent with the Asian-American's higher quantitative and lower verbal skills. Furthermore, the people-contact professions call for some degree of forceful self-expression. These traits are antagonistic to the Asian-American's greater inhibition, reserve in interpersonal relations, and lower social extroversion. Physical sciences and skilled-technical trades, also, are characterized by more of a structured, impersonal, and concrete approach.

The Asian-American's restricted choice of vocations can be explained by two factors. First, early immigrants came from a strongly agricultural and peasant background. This is especially true of the Japanese who, according to the 1960 Census, were over-represented in agricultural fields. Second, early immigrants may have encouraged their sons and daughters into occupations with potentially greater social and economic survival value. Thus, their concern with evaluating choice of vocations on the basis of pragmatism was reinforced by a racist society. Agricultural fields, skilled-technical trades, and physical sciences can be perceived as possessing specific concrete skills that were functional in American society. Discrimination and prejudice were minimized in these occupations while people-contact professions were wrought with hazards of discrimination. Even though the Chinese and Japanese expressed more interest in the businesses, most of the fields were accounting and bookkeeping activities. Furthermore, business occupations which they have historically chosen tended to be within their ethnic community (import-export, family-owned businesses, restaurants, etc.) rather than within the larger society.

Differences Between Chinese- and Japanese-Americans

The discussion thus far has revealed many similarities between Chinese- and Japanese-American students. In light of their many common cultural values and experiences in America, this is not surprising. However, differences certainly exist. On all three measures (personality, abilities, and interests) administered at the University of California, Berkeley, Japanese-American students consistently fell into an intermediate position between the Chinese-American and the control students. In other words, Japanese-Americans are more similar to the controls than are the Chinese-Americans. This finding suggests two possibilities. It might be assumed that Japanese values are much more similar to European-American values than are those of the Chinese. An analysis of Japanese and Chinese cultural values would dictate against this as the sole interpretation. Additionally, the high rate of industrialization in Japan is a relatively recent phenomenon that may have minimal impact at this time. A more plausible explanation lies in the differential acculturation of both groups.

Arkoff, Meredith, & Iswahara (1962) conclude that Japanese-American females appear to be acculturating faster than their male counterparts. Weiss (1969) feels that Chinese females are much better accepted by American society than males. This leads to greater social contact with members of the host society and acculturation is fostered. If differential acculturation occurs between sexes of the same ethnic group, it might be possible that a similar phenomenon has and/or is affecting both the Chinese and Japanese. An answer to this question may lie in the historical past of both the Chinese and Japanese in America.

Prior to the outbreak of World War II, relations between Japan and the United States became noticeably strained. Many Japanese in America feared that their loyalty would be questioned. Fearing that war would break out between the two nations and bring retaliation against Japanese-Americans, many Japanese-American organizations such as the Japanese-American Citizens League emphasized the need to appear as American as possible. Pro-American proclamations were common, and offspring were encouraged to acculturate and identify themselves with the American people.

With the bombing of Pearl Harbor, war was declared on Japan and the relocation experience of 110,000 Japanese-Americans did much to foster acculturation (Umemoto, 1970; Kitano, 1969b). First, it broke up Japanese-American communities by uprooting their residents. Homes and properties of the Japanese were confiscated and lost. Even today, the Japanese communities (Japantowns) are not comparable to the cohesive Chinatowns in San Francisco and New York, which serve as visible symbols of ethnic identity for the Chinese. Second, the camp experience disrupted the traditional family structure and lines of authority. Elderly males no longer had a functional value as household heads. Control and discipline of children and women became noticeably weakened under these circumstances. Third, many Japanese-Americans chose to migrate to the East Coast and Midwest rather than suffer the humiliation of internment. Even after the termination of the relocation centers, some Japanese-Americans chose not to return to the West Coast because of the strong anti-Japanese feeling there. Their greater physical dispersal increased contact with members of the host society and probably aided acculturation.

Conclusions

The psychological characteristics exhibited by Asian-Americans are related to their culture and the Asian-American's interaction with Western society. Any study of ethnic minorities in America must necessarily deal with the forces of racism inherent in American culture. Since there are no Asian-Americans untouched by racism in the United States to use as a control group, the relationship of racism to psychological development becomes a complex issue that cannot easily be resolved. If an attempt is made to use control groups in Taiwan, Hong Kong, or China, the problem becomes clouded by a whole complex of other social and cultural differences. For these reasons, the analyses presented in this article must be seen as somewhat tentative and speculative. Hopefully, further research will help clarify this issue.

References

Abbott, K.A. *Harmony and Individualism,* Taipei: Orient Cultural Press, 1970.
Abbott, K., and Abbott, E. "Juvenile Delinquency in San Francisco's Chinese-American Community." *Journal of Sociology* 4, 1968, 45-56.

Arkoff, A. "Need Patterns of Two Generations of Japanese-Americans in Hawaii." *Journal of Social Psychology* 50, 1959, 75-79.

———; Meredith, G.; and Iswahara, S. "Dominance-Deference Patterning in Motherland-Japanese, Japanese-American, and Caucasian-American Students." *Journal of Social Psychology* 58, 1962, 61-63.

———; Meredith, G.; and Iswahara, S. "Male-Dominant and Equalitarian Attitudes in Japanese, Japanese-American, and Caucasian-American Students." *Journal of Social Psychology* 64, 1964, 225-229.

———, and H. Weaver. "Body Image and Body Dissatisfaction in Japanese-Americans." *Journal of Social Psychology* 68, 1966, 323-330.

Chu, Robert. "Majors of Chinese and Japanese Students at the University of California, Berkeley, for the Past 20 Years." Project report, AS 150, Asian Studies Division, University of California, Berkeley, Winter, 1971.

Daniels, R. *Concentration Camps USA: Japanese-Americans and World War II.* New York: Holt, Rinehart, and Winston, Inc., 1971.

DeVos, G., and Abbott, K. "The Chinese Family in San Francisco." MSW dissertation, University of California, Berkeley, 1966.

Fenz, W., and Arkoff, A. "Comparative Need Patterns of Five Ancestry Groups in Hawaii." *Journal of Social Psychology* 58, 1962, 67-89.

Fong, S.L.M. "Assimilation of Chinese in America: Changes in Orientation and Social Perception." *American Journal of Sociology* 71, 1965, 265-273.

———, and Peskin, H. "Sex-Role Strain and Personality Adjustment of China-born Students in America: A Pilot Study." *Journal of Abnormal Psychology* 74, 1969, 563-567.

Jones, J.M. *Prejudice and Racism.* Massachusetts: Addison-Wesley Publishing Company, 1972.

Kimmich, R.A. "Ethnic Aspects of Schizophrenia in Hawaii." *Psychiatry* 23, 1960, 97-102.

Kitano, H.H.L. "Changing Achievement Patterns of the Japanese in the United States." *Journal of Social Psychology* 58, 1962, 257-264.

———. "Inter and Intra-Generational Differences in Maternal Attitudes Toward Child Rearing." *Journal of Social Psychology* 63, 1964, 215-220.

———. "Japanese-American Crime and Delinquency." *Journal of Psychology* 66, 1967, 253-263.

———. "Japanese-American Mental Illness." In S.C. Plog and R.B. Edgerton (eds.), *Changing Perspectives in Mental Illness.* New York: Holt, Rinehart, and Winston, 1969a.

———. *Japanese-Americans: The Evolution of a Subculture.* New Jersey: Prentice-Hall, 1969b.

———. "Mental Illness in Four Cultures." *Journal of Social Psychology* 80, 1970, 121-134.

Kovel, J. *White Racism: A Psychohistory.* New York: Vintage Books, 1971.

Marsella, A.J.; Kinzie, D.; and Gordon, P. "Depression Patterns among American College Students of Caucasian, Chinese, and Japanese Ancestry." Paper presented at the Conference on Culture and Mental Health in Asia and the Pacific. March, 1971.

Matsumoto, G.M.; Meredith, G.; and Masuda, M. "Ethnic Identification: Honolulu and Seattle Japanese-Americans." *Journal of Cross-Cultural Psychology* 1, 1970, 63-76.

Meade, R.D. "Leadership Studies of Chinese and Chinese-Americans." *Journal of Cross-Cultural Psychology* 1, 1970, 325-332.

Meredith, G.M. "Personality Correlates of Pidgin English Usage among Japanese-American College Students in Hawaii." *Japanese Psychological Research* 6, 1964.

———. "Amae and Acculturation among Japanese-American College Students in Hawaii. *Journal of Social Psychology* 70, 1966, 171-180.

Smith, M.E. "Progress in the Use of English after Twenty-Two Years by Children of Chinese Ancestry in Honolulu." *Journal of Genetic Psychology* 90, 1957, 255-258.

———, and Kasdon, L.M. "Progress in the Use of English after Twenty Years by Children of Filipino and Japanese Ancestry in Hawaii." *Journal of Genetic Psychology* 99, 1961, 129-138.

Sommers, V.S. "Identity Conflict and Acculturation Problems in Oriental-Americans." *American Journal of Orthopsychiatry* 30, 1960, 637-644.

Success Story: "Out-Whiting the Whites." *Newsweek,* June, 1971.

Success Story of One Minority Group in the U.S. *US News and World Report,* December, 1966.

Sue, D.W., and Sue, S. "Counseling Chinese-Americans." *Personnel and Guidance Journal* 50, 1972a, 637-644.

———, and Sue, S. "Ethnic Minorities: Resistance to Being Researched." *Professional Psychology* 2, 1972b, 11-17.

———, and Kirk, B.A. "Psychological Characteristics of Chinese-American College Students." *Journal of Counseling Psychology* in press [1972].

———, and Kirk, B.A. "Differential Characteristics of Japanese- and Chinese-American College Students." Research in progress at the University of California, Berkeley.

Sue, S., and Sue, D.W. "Chinese-American Personality and Mental Health." *Amerasia Journal* 1, 1971, 36-49.

Takayama, G. "Analysis of Data on Asian Students at UC Berkeley, 1971." Project report, AS 150, Asian Studies Division, University of California, Berkeley, Winter, 1971.

Unemoto, A. "Crisis in the Japanese-American Family." In *Asian Women.* Berkeley: 1971.

Watanabe, C. "A College Level Reading and Composition Program for Students of Asian Descent: Diagnosis and Design." Asian Studies Division, University of California, Berkeley, 1971.

Weiss, M.S. "Selective Acculturation and the Dating Process: The Patterning of Chinese-Caucasian Interracial Dating." *Journal of Marriage and the Family* 32, 1970.

Yamamoto, J.; James, Q.C.; and Palley, N. "Cultural Problems in Psychiatric Therapy." *General Archives of Psychiatry* 19, 1968, 45-49.

8 Counseling Chinese Americans

Sue, Derald Wing
Sue, Stanley

The Chinese-American student's cultural background plays an important part in his expression of personality traits and the manifestation of his problems. This article presents an analysis of Chinese values and suggests that the counseling situation may arouse intense conflicts for many Chinese-American students. It also suggests a modified counseling approach that can be used in working with these students.

Many people believe that the Chinese in America represent a model minority group. Unlike the blacks and Chicanos, the Chinese have tried to function in the existing social structure with a minimum of visible conflict with members of the host society. Historically, they have accepted much prejudice and discrimination without voicing strong public protest (DeVos & Abbott, 1966). Their traditional nonthreatening stance and the public's lack of knowledge about Chinese people have masked their problems of poverty, unemployment, and juvenile delinquency. The notion that Chinese people experience few problems in American society is also shared by many educators, counselors, and mental health workers. The Chinese-Americans' strong emphasis on educational achievement (DeVos & Abbott, 1966), their custom of handling problems within the family, and their limited use of mental health facilities (Kimmich, 1960; Kitano, 1969) have reinforced this misconception.

Since many Chinese-American college students find it difficult to label themselves as having emotional problems, they tend to under-use psychiatric facilities on campuses when they encounter personal problems (Sue & Sue, 1971). Rather, they often seek the less threatening services of campus counseling centers with an educational-vocational orientation, because they feel that less social stigma is involved. It is especially important for guidance workers to understand the Chinese-American students' cultural background and the conflicts they experience. These cultural influences may, in fact, hinder the development of a therapeutic relationship between counselor and client. However, very few counselors know enough about the Chinese-Americans' background to understand their reaction to the counseling-therapy situation. An examination of Chinese culture and family interaction patterns suggests that the counseling situation may cause a great deal of conflict for many Chinese-American students.

Chinese Culture and Personality

Although the Chinese family in America is changing, it still retains many of the cultural values from its past (DeVos & Abbott, 1966). The Chinese family is an ancient and complex institution, and the roles of family members have long been rigidly defined. Chinese are taught to obey parents, to respect elders, and to create a good family name by outstanding achievement in some aspect of life, for example, by academic or occupational success. Since misbehaviors (juvenile delinquency, academic failure, and mental disorders) reflect upon the entire family, an individual learns that his behavior has great significance. If he has feelings whose expression might disrupt family harmony, he is expected to restrain himself. Indeed, the Chinese culture highly values self-control and inhibition of strong feelings (Abbott, 1970).

Sue and Kirk (1972, in press) found that the personality traits of Chinese-American students reflect this family and cultural background. The investigators studied the entire entering freshman class in the fall of 1966, at the University of California in Berkeley. Chinese-American students seemed to be more conforming to authority, inhibited, and introverted than the general student body. They also tended to be more practical in their approach to tasks and to be less tolerant of ambiguity, preferring to deal with concrete facts and events. Although their quantitative skills appeared high, their verbal scores were lower than that of the general student body, perhaps reflecting a bilingual background and limited communication patterns in the home.

The Acculturation Process

The Chinese individual in America is in a position of conflict between the pulls of both his cultural background and the Western values he is exposed to in school and by the mass media. American values emphasizing spontaneity, assertiveness, and independence are often at odds with many Chinese values. As Chinese people progressively adopt more of the values and standards of the larger community as their own, the transition is not always smooth. Indeed, culture conflict seems to be an intimate part of the Asian-American experience.

It is our impression that Chinese students do not react in any stereotyped manner to culture conflict (Sue & Sue, 1971), but we have most frequently observed three main types of reaction. Some tend to resist assimilation by maintaining traditional values and by associating predominantly with other Chinese. Others try to become assimilated into the dominant culture by rejecting their Chinese culture. The Asian-American movement on college campuses has attracted yet another group of students by stressing pride in racial identity.

Obviously, each Chinese student does not fall neatly into one of the three groups, and there are quantitative differences in the types of conflicts exhibited in counseling situations, depending upon the cultural orientation of individuals. To illustrate the many conflicts experienced by Chinese-American students in their personal life and in their reactions to counseling, in this article we will use case descriptions of clients we have seen for counseling. We have taken care to insure the anonymity of all case materials.

Maintaining Traditional Values

John C. is a 21-year-old student majoring in electrical engineering. He first sought counseling because he was having increasing study problems and was receiving failing grades. These academic difficulties became apparent during the first quarter of his senior year and were accompanied by headaches, indigestion, and insomnia. Since he had been an excellent student in the past, John felt that his lowered academic performance was caused by illness. However, a medical examination failed to reveal any organic disorder.

During the initial interview, John seemed depressed and anxious. He was difficult to counsel because he would respond to inquiries with short but polite statements and would seldom volunteer information about himself. He avoided any statements that involved feelings and presented his problem as a strictly educational one. Although he never expressed it directly, John seemed to doubt the value of counseling and needed much reassurance and feedback about his performance in the interview. In view of John's reluctance to open up, it seemed unwise to probe immediately into areas that aroused much anxiety in him.

As the sessions progressed, John became less anxious and more trusting of the counselor. Much of his earlier difficulties in opening up were caused by his feelings of shame and guilt at having come to a counselor. He was concerned that his family might discover his seeking of help and that it would be a disgrace to them. This anxiety was compounded by his strong feelings of failure in school. However, when the counselor informed him that many Chinese students experienced similar problems and that these sessions were completely confidential, John seemed quite relieved. As he became increasingly able to open up, he revealed problems such as we have found are typical of Chinese students who have strongly internalized traditional cultural values and whose self-worth and identity are defined within the family nexus.

John's parents had always had high expectations of him and constantly pressured him to do well in school. They seemed to equate his personal worth with his ability to obtain good grades. This pressure caused him to spend endless hours studying, and generally he remained isolated from social activities. This isolation did not help him to learn the social skills required in peer relationships. In addition, John's more formalized training was in sharp contrast to the informality and spontaneity demanded in Caucasian interpersonal relationships. Therefore, his circle of friends was small, and he was never really able to enjoy himself with others.

John experienced a lot of conflict, because he was beginning to resent the pressure his parents put on him, and also their demands. For example, they stated that it would be nice if he would help his brothers through school after graduation. This statement aroused a great amount of unexpressed anger in John toward them. He felt unable to lead his own life. Furthermore, his lack of interest in engineering was intensified as graduation approached. He had always harbored secret wishes about becoming an artist but was pressured into engineering by his parents. His deep-seated feelings of anger toward his parents resulted in his passive-aggressive responses of failure in school and in his physical symptoms.

The case of John C. illustrates some of the following conflicts encountered by many Chinese students attempting to maintain traditional Chinese values: (a) there is often a conflict between loyalty to the family and personal desires for independence; (b) the learned patterns of self-restraint and formality in interpersonal relationships often result in a lack of social experience and subsequent feelings of loneliness, and furthermore, they can act as impediments to counseling; (c) the family pressure to achieve academically accentuates feelings of shame and depression when the student fails.

Rejecting Chinese Customs

Many Chinese-Americans attempt to become Westernized and reject traditional Chinese customs. Vontress (1970) points out that many blacks develop a hatred of their own group and culture, and many Chinese counselees experience a similar type of conflict, especially in their social life. It is typified in the following counseling interchange.

Counselor: You seem to prefer dating Caucasians . . .

Client: Well . . . It's so stupid for my parents to think that they can keep all their customs and values. I really resent being Chinese and having to date all those Chinese guys. They're so passive, and I can make them do almost anything I want. Others [Chinese] are on a big ego trip and expect me to be passive and do whatever they say. Yes . . . I do prefer Caucasians.

Counselor: Is that an alternative open to you?

Client: Yes . . . but my parents would feel hurt . . . they'd probably disown me. They keep on telling me to go out with Chinese guys. A few months ago they got me to go out with this guy—I must have been the first girl he ever dated—I wasn't even polite to him.

Counselor: I guess things were doubly bad. You didn't like the guy and you didn't like your parents pushing him on you.

Client: Well . . . actually I felt a little sorry for him. I don't like to hurt my parents or those [Chinese] guys, but things always work out that way.

The client's last statement reflected some feelings of guilt over her rudeness toward her date. Although she was open and honest, her desire to be independent was confused with a constant rejection of her parents' attempts to influence her life. During a later session, she was able to express her conflict:

Client: I used to think that I was being independent if I went out with guys that my parents disapproved of. But that isn't really being independent. I just did that to spite them. I guess I should feel guilty if I purposely hurt them, but not if I *really* want to do something for myself.

Although the rejection of Chinese culture is often a developmental phase adequately resolved by most Chinese-Americans, many come to look upon Western personality characteristics as more admirable. For example, some Chinese-American girls come to expect the boys they date to behave boldly and aggressively in the Western manner. Weiss (1969) found that many Chinese-American college females were quite vehement in their denunciation of their male counterparts as dating partners. They frequently described the Chinese male as immature, inept, and sexually unattractive. Although the males denied the more derogatory accusations about themselves, they tended to agree that they were more inhibited and unassertive than Caucasians.

The Asian-American Movement

Recently, a growing number of Chinese students on college campuses throughout the nation are, like the blacks and Chicanos, emphasizing their own heritage, pride, and self-identity. They feel that the role of a conforming "banana" (a derogatory term used to describe a person of Asian ancestry who is "yellow on the outside but white on the inside") is too degrading. In an attempt to gain the self-respect they feel has been denied them by white society, they have banded together in an attempt to reverse the negative trend of bananaism among their own group. This group of individuals seem much more aware of political, economic, and social forces that have shaped their identity. They feel that society is to blame for their present dilemma and are actively challenging the establishment. They are openly suspicious of institutions, such as counseling services, because they view them as agents of the establishment. Very few of the more ethnically conscious and militant Asians will use counseling—because of its identification with the status quo. When they do, they are usually suspicious and hostile toward the counselor. Before counseling can proceed effectively, the counselor will have to deal with certain challenges from these students, such as the following:

Client: First of all . . . I don't believe in psychology . . . I think it's a lot of bullshit. People in psychology are always trying to adjust people to a *sick* society, and what is needed is to overthrow this goddamned establishment. . . .I feel the same way about those stupid tests. Cultural bias . . .they aren't applicable to minorities. The only reason I came in here was . . .well, I heard your lecture in Psychology 160 [a lecture on Asian-Americans], and I think I can work with you.

The counselee in this case happened to be hostile and depressed over the recent death of his father. Although he realized he had some need for help, he still did not trust the counseling process.

Client: Psychologists see the problem inside of people when the problem is in society. Don't you think white society has made all minorities feel inferior and degraded?
Counselor: I know that. White society has done great harm to minorities.

The client was posing a direct challenge to the counselor. Any defense of white society or explanations of the value of counseling might have aroused greater hostility and mistrust. It would have been extremely difficult to establish rapport without some honest agreement on the racist nature of American society. Later, the counselee revealed that his father had just died. He was beginning to realize that there was no contradiction in viewing society as being racist and in having personal problems.

Often, growing pride in self-identity makes it difficult for students who are having emotional problems to accept their personal difficulties. This is not to say that militance and group pride are signs of maladjustment. On the contrary, the Asian-American movement is a healthy attempt to resolve feelings of inferiority and degradation fostered by discrimination and prejudice.

The Counseling Process as a Source of Conflict

Chinese students are often caught between the demands of two cultures, but individuals react differently to this conflict. The counseling situation reflects the cultural conflicts encountered by Chinese students in their everyday life.

First, counselors and other mental health professionals are often at a loss to explain why Chinese counselees do not actively participate in the counseling process. Our colleagues have remarked that Chinese students are difficult to counsel because they repress emotional conflicts. These remarks indicate that counselors expect their counselees to exhibit some degree of openness, psychological-mindedness, or sophistication. Such characteristics are often beneficial in counseling. However, openness is quite difficult for many Chinese students who have learned to inhibit emotional expression, and direct or subtle demands by the counselor for openness may be quite threatening to them.

Second, Chinese students frequently find it difficult to admit they have emotional difficulties, because such problems arouse a great deal of shame and a sense of having failed one's family. Often, Chinese students may indirectly ask for help with personal difficulties by presenting educational problems or somantic complaints. Some investigators (Abbott, 1970; Marsella, Kinzie, & Gordon, 1971) feel that Chinese frequently express psychological distress through indirect routes, such as bodily complaints and passive-aggressive responses. Since emotional problems are felt to reflect shamefully on family upbringing, somatization could represent a more acceptable means of expressing psychological disturbance. Such was the case of John C.

Third, the counseling or therapy situation is often an ambiguous one. The counselee is encouraged to discuss any problems; the counselor listens and responds. Many Chinese students prefer concrete and well-structured situations, and the well-defined role expectations in the Chinese family are in sharp contrast to the ambiguity of the counseling process.

Implications for the Counseling Process

Just as it is unwise to suggest definite guidelines in dealing with all Chinese-Americans in counseling, it seems equally unwise to ignore cultural factors that might affect the counseling process. The counselor's inability to recognize these factors may make the Chinese counselee terminate prematurely. The difficulty in admitting social and emotional problems despite a need for help places the Chinese-American in an intense conflict. A too-confrontive and emotionally intense approach at the onset of counseling can frequently increase the level of shame. The counselor may facilitate counseling by responding to what may be viewed as superficial problems, such as the educational difficulties and somatic complaints that may mask more serious emotional conflicts. The counselee is then in a position to move at his own rate in exploring more threatening material.

In addition, the counselor can often facilitate self-disclosure by referring to psychological material relevant to vocational choice or job demands. For example, test interpretation can be threatening to the Chinese student, especially when psychological problems are involved. Many students are able to talk more freely about their difficulties if test interpretations are related concretely to their vocational future. Therefore, counselors involved in vocational decision-making may be in an advantageous position not shared by other mental health professionals, as the following case illustrates.

Pat. H. was a 19-year-old pre-pharmacy major who came for vocational counseling. Since he was the eldest of three boys, his parents had high expectations of him. He was expected to set a good example for his younger brothers and enhance the good name of the family. Because his grades were mediocre, he was beginning to doubt his ability to handle pharmacy. However, results of his interest and ability tests and his counselor's impressions supported his choice of the pharmacy major. The counselor felt that his difficulty in courses reflected passive resistance to his parents' high expectations of him for being the oldest son.

On his Edwards Personal Preference Schedule, Pat showed high achievement, change, and abasement scores. Earlier attempts to explore his feelings dealing with parental expectations proved fruitless. However, the following transcript demonstrates how testing was used to open up exploration in a nonthreatening manner.

Counselor: Let's explore the meaning of your scores in greater detail as they relate to future vocations. All right?
Client: Okay.

Counselor: Your high score on achievement indicates that whatever you undertake you would like to excel and do well in. For example, if you enter pharmacy, you'd like to do well in that field [*client nods head*]. However, your high change score indicates that you like variety and change. . . .You may tend to get restless at times . . .maybe feel trapped in activities that bore you.

Client: Yeah.

Counselor: Do you see this score [abasement score]?

Client: Yeah, I blew the scale on that one. . . . What is it? [*some anxiety observable*]

Counselor: Well, it indicates you tend to be hard on yourself . .For example, if you were to do poorly in pharmacy school . . .you would blame yourself for the failure . . .

Client: Yea, yeah . . .I'm always doing that . .I feel that . . .it's probably exaggerated.

Counselor: Exaggerated?

Client: I mean . . .being the oldest son.

Counselor: What's it like to be the oldest son?

Client: Well . . .there's a lot of pressure and you can feel immobilized. Maybe this score [*points to change scale*] is why I feel so restless.

This progression marked a major breakthrough in Pat's case and led to an increasingly personalized discussion.

The difficulty in self-disclosure for Chinese-American students indicates that assurances of confidentiality between counselor and counselee are of utmost importance. A frequent concern of many Chinese-American students is that their friends, and especially their parents, will find out that they are seeing a counselor. For this reason, group counseling or therapy is very threatening. It is difficult enough to share their thoughts with one individual, let alone an entire group. Chinese students frequently refuse to participate in groups, and when in a group, they are often quiet and withdrawn. It may be wise to discuss the issue of confidentiality, the feelings of trust and mistrust in one another, and the cultural barriers in talking about feelings. We have found that many Chinese-American counselees are able to open up and express feelings quite directly once they develop trust of the counselor.

Since many Chinese-American students tend to feel more comfortable in well-structured and unambiguous situations, counseling by providing guidelines in the form of explanations and suggestions may be helpful. Such guidelines might include an explanation of the counseling process. In addition, the Chinese-American's emotional inhibition and lower verbal participation may also indicate the need for a more active approach on the part of the counselor. The following case description is an example of an active structuring of interviews.

Anne W. was quite uncomfortable and anxious during the first interview dealing with vocational counseling. This anxiety seemed more related to the ambiguity of the situation than anything else. She appeared confused about the direction of the counselor's comments and questions. At this point the counselor felt that an explanation of vocational counseling would facilitate the process.

Counselor: Let me take some time to explain to you how we usually proceed in vocational counseling. Vocational counseling is an attempt to understand the whole person. Therefore, we are interested in your interests, likes and dislikes, and specific abilities or skills as they relate to different possible vocations. The first interview is usually an attempt to get to know you...especially your past experiences and reactions to different courses you've taken, jobs you've worked at, and so forth. Especially important are the hopes and aspirations that you have. If testing seems indicated, as in your case, you'll be asked to complete a battery of tests. After testing we'll sit down and interpret them together. When we arrive at possible vocations, we'll use the vocational library and find out what these jobs entail in terms of background, training, etc.

Client: Oh! I see . . .

Counselor: That's why we've been exploring your high school experiences. . . . Sometimes the hopes and dreams in your younger years can tell us much about your interests.

After this explanation, Anne participated much more in the interviews.

Culture and Counseling

Since guidance workers may lack understanding of cultural influences, they frequently encounter difficulty in working with minority groups. Because there are cultural determinants of behavior, and counseling is essentially a white middle class activity, it may be necessary to modify counseling approaches. This is especially true in working with many Chinese-American counselees. The suggestions we have offered are primarily directed to the establishment of a working relationship of rapport and trust. Once a strong relationship has been established, the counselor has greater freedom in varying his therapeutic approach. To avoid oversimplification and the creation of an artificial situation, we have purposely kept our discussion of techniques somewhat general. The use of counseling techniques should be evaluated on the basis of the client's needs and their compatibility with the counselor's style and personality. Perhaps the most important tool a counselor could possess is knowledge of the Asian-American experience and its relationship to counseling. The counselor must address himself to problems of guilt and shame and lack of openness in the case of the traditionalist, to problems of independence and self-hate in the marginal man, and to racism in society with the Asian-American.

Finally, a word of caution must be noted. Most Chinese-Americans are able to handle cultural conflicts and adequately resolve them. This article has been mainly concerned with that relatively small number who seek counseling help when they feel that they cannot resolve their conflicts.

References

Abbott, K.A. *Harmony and individualism*. Taipei: Orient Cultural Service, 1970.

DeVos, G., & Abbott, K. The Chinese family in San Francisco. Unpublished master's thesis, University of California, Berkeley, 1966.

Kimmich, R.A. Ethnic aspects of schizophrenia in Hawaii. *Psychiatry*, 1960, *23*, 97-102.

Kitano, H.H.L. Japanese-American mental illness. In S.C. Plog and R.B. Edgerton (Eds.), *Changing perspectives in mental illness*. New York: Holt, Rinehart & Winston, 1969.

Marsella, A.J., Kinzie, D., & Gordon, P. Depression patterns among American college students of Caucasian, Chinese, and Japanese ancestry. Paper presented at the Conference on Culture and Mental Health in Asia and the Pacific, March 1971.

Sue, D.W., & Kirk, B.A. Psychological characteristics of Chinese-American students. *Journal of Counseling Psychology*, 1972 in press.

Sue, S., & Sue, D.W. Chinese-American personality and mental health. *Amerasia Journal*, 1971, *1*(2), 36-49.

Vontress, C.E. Counseling blacks. *Personnel and Guidance Journal*, 1970, *48*, 713-719.

Weiss, M.S. Inter-racial romance: The Chinese-Caucasian dating game. Paper presented at the Southwestern Anthropological Association. Las Vegas, Nevada, April 1969.

Selected Readings

Atkinson, D.R., Maruyama, M. & Matsui, S. Effects of Counselor race and counseling approach on Asian Americans' perceptions of counselor credibility and utility. *Journal of Counseling Psychology*, 1978, *25* (1), 76-83.

Fong, S.L.M. Assimilation and changing social roles of Chinese-Americans. *Journal of Social Issues*, 1973, *29* (2), 115-127.

Hayasaka, P. The Asian experience in White America. *Journal of Intergroup Relations*, 1973, *2*, 67-73.

Kim, B.C. Asian-Americans: no model minority. *Social Work*, 1973, *18* (1), 44-53.

Kitano, H.H.L., & Sue, S. The model minorities. *Journal of Social Issues*, 1973, *29* (2), 1-9.

Levine, G.N., & Montero, D.M. Socioeconomic mobility among three generations of Japanese Americans. *Journal of Social Issues*, 1973, *29* (2), 33-48.

Maykovich, M.F. Political activation of Japanese-American youth. *Journal of Social Issues*, 1973, *29* (2), 167-185.

Sue, D.W., & Kirk, B.A. Differential characteristics of Japanese-American and Chinese-American college students. *Journal of Counseling Psychology*, 1973, *20* (2), 142-148.

Sue, D.W., & Sue, D. Understanding Asian-Americans: The neglected minority. *Personnel and Guidance Journal*, 1973, *51*, 386-389.

Sue, S., & McKinney, H. Asian Americans in the community mental health care system. *American Journal of Orthopsychiatry*, 1975, *45* (1), 111-118.

Sue, S., & Wagner, N.N. *Asian Americans: Psychological Perspectives*. Ben Lomand, California: Science and Behavior Books, Inc., 1973.

Watanabe, C. Self-expression and the Asian-American experience. *Personnel and Guidance Journal*, 1973, *51*, 390-396.

9 Counseling Vietnamese

Imogene C. Brower

The continuing influx of Vietnamese refugees means that increasing numbers of counselors unfamiliar with Vietnamese culture will be called on to build helping relationships with refugee children and their families. This article provides specific information to help the counselor establish rapport, avoid misunderstandings in explicit and implicit communication, minimize transference dangers, and deal with Vietnamese attitudes toward sex roles and the individual/family relationship. It also discusses relevant socioeconomic and ethnic differences among the Vietnamese themselves, as well as some war-related mental health problems. Practical matters, such as the proper use of Vietnamese names, are explained.

The United States has historically been a haven for immigrants seeking a brighter future and freedom from oppression. Since 1975 waves of Indochinese refugees, principally Vietnamese, have added a new thread to the rich tapestry of American society. Totaling approximately 304,000 by January 1980, the refugees continue to arrive at a rate of many thousands each month.

As newcomers, the culturally different Vietnamese are not always understood by either the dominant culture or other minorities. A special issue of the *Personnel and Guidance Journal* (March 1973) devoted to Asian Americans makes many general points that can apply to Vietnamese culture. But the Asian Americans discussed in the special issue have been here for generations, and the newly arrived Vietnamese have suffered 30 years of war and often traumatic refugee experiences.

A goal of counseling is to assist recipients in adjusting to or otherwise negotiating various environments (Vontress, 1976). Increasing numbers of Vietnamese "boat people" are encountering adjustment problems after resettling in the United States. This article suggests ways for counselors to build positive relationships—based on understanding of psychosocial differences and war-related traumas—to help Vietnamese students and their families adjust to American environments.

The Relationship

Because of their very different backgrounds, experiences, and value systems, developing a helping relationship between a Vietnamese and an American is not easy. It may take persistent efforts to establish rapport, to structure the relationship to gain understanding, to overcome communication barriers, and to eliminate possible interference from unconscious negative feelings. By far the most important ingredient in the counseling relationship is rapport or mutual trust. When a Vietnamese trusts someone, other barriers become less important (Nguyen Ngoc Bich, 1979).

Rapport

Vontress (1980) defines *rapport* as a "mutual bond" or "emotional bridge." How does the counselor establish rapport with a Vietnamese client? Because the Vietnamese are family-oriented, the counseling process should begin with parents or older family members. Sensitivity to the family and its reactions—particularly in the initial interview, which is likely to be the introduction to the school system and the concept of counseling—will lay a foundation for building trust with the student. The basis of this sensitivity is understanding and respect for Vietnamese customs and values.

The first possibility for misunderstanding or showing "ethnic superiority" often arises in the use of Vietnamese names. These names may be difficult for the counselor to pronounce, and they are often confusing to Americans because the family name is seldom used, and when it is written it appears first. In the case of a male teacher named Nguyen Hung Dung, for example, *Nguyen* is the family name, *Hung* the middle name, and *Dung* the given name. His close friends would call him Dung; others would call him Mr. Dung or simply "teacher" (*thay,* an honorific title). A married woman does not take her husband's family name. Instead, she will prefix the title of *Mrs.* to her husband's given name or to her own given name. Children, however, do use the father's family name. Compounding the difficulty, no more than 200 or 300 family names are in use, so that unrelated persons often have the same one. In contrast to family names (which are mostly those of ancient royal dynasties), given and middle names have precise meanings (e.g., *Dung*—brave; *Hung*—powerful; *Ngoc Bich*—blue pearl). For this reason, and because the Vietnamese expect formality in the use of names, nicknames or anglicized pronunciations may be unintentionally offensive. The expectation of formality, moreover, may make it difficult at first for a Vietnamese to call a counselor by a first name.

The Vietnamese family is patriarchal. Therefore, in interviews with the student and family the counselor should remember that according to Vietnamese custom, the father, not the student, is the important person. This will be true even if the meeting concerns decisions that mainstream American children are usually expected to make for themselves, such as what electives to take in school (rare in Vietnam except in experimental schools). In such a case, a direct request to the child to choose from among several subjects might only embarrass the child, who would feel that such decisions should be made by the school or the father. It might also upset the father, who would feel his authority was being questioned. In some conferences the mother may participate alone, because traditionally she supervises the house and children. However, decisions about placement, curriculum, or other school matters are best deferred to enable her to consult the father (or in the absence of a father, perhaps an older son). Older students, especially those who have been in the United States several years, may wish to make their own decisions, but family approval is often sought.

Establishing rapport with Vietnamese is a dynamic process of building respect and understanding between the counselor on the one hand and the client and family on the other. Because the process is mutual, the counselor should be not only sensitive to Vietnamese customs, but also ready to help the Vietnamese learn about American ones. A good place to begin is with the concept of counseling itself.

Structure

Many minority groups have had limited experience with counseling and are more accustomed to authorities teaching or telling them what to do (Vontress, 1974). Thus, in counseling minorities there is greater need for structure than with the culturally dominant (Sue & Sue, 1972; Vontress, 1974). Counseling and psychotherapy are nearly unknown in Vietnam (Nguyen Duy San, 1969). Vietnamese culture is highly structured, with definite roles ascribed; the school is part of the Confucian authority hierarchy; and officials, including counselors, are expected to be authoritative and directive. Vietnamese clients may perceive counselors who are not authoritative as unconcerned (Alexander, Workneh, Klein, & Miller, 1976).

Many American psychotherapeutic theories stress the client's self-disclosure, active participation, openness, decision making, and growth in independence (Frank, 1961). Although these are dominant American cultural ideals, they are not necessarily appropriate goals in counseling Asian Americans (Sue & Sue, 1977). The ideals are even less appropriate for newly arrived Vietnamese, who are accustomed to a concrete, well-structured society.

Referring to the role of counselor as "school parent" may help both counselor and student focus their expectations in a Vietnamese context. According to Trinh Ngoc Dung (1979), school authorities in Vietnam are perceived as school parents. Although such a perception suggests danger of overdependence, it is important to recognize that in Vietnam the student is primarily a passive receiver of knowledge, dispensed by a wise and superior teacher. Learning by rote with few textbooks for individual students (Nguyen Ngoc Bich & Dao Thi Hoi, 1978), young children are taught to listen but not encouraged to ask questions in class (Duong Thanh Binh,

1975). Therefore, it is not surprising that newly arrived Vietnamese students may participate less actively in class, need more direction, and expect more help than typical American students. As acculturation progresses, however, this dependence is likely to change. Any initial overdependence on the counselor or teacher can gradually be lessened as the student develops new support systems.

By encouraging the Vietnamese to discuss their view of the school and their educational expectations and by contrasting these with American educational theory and practice, the counselor can help bridge differences. For example, the traditional Vietnamese view of learning as the way to succeed and bring honor to one's family may result in family pressure for a child's academic success, to the extent of discouraging extracurricular activities (National Indochinese Clearinghouse, 1977). The counselor may have to help the family understand that some nonacademic activities provide excellent opportunities to learn more English and adjust to school. Another difference is that in Vietnam, PTAs and parent-teacher conferences are less common, and active parent participation in school affairs is rare. In the United States, therefore, Vietnamese parents may seem to lack interest—they are actually reluctant to intrude on what they regard as the school's perogative (Trinh Ngoc Dung, 1979). The counselor will need to clarify the American view that education is every parent's responsibility.

Transference and Countertransference

The highly visible United States presence and involvement in the Vietnam war left a residue of strong feelings in many Vietnamese and Americans. In striving to develop a good relationship, the counselor should be aware of possible interference from such feelings, either negative or positive.

Transference, or projecting feelings that stem from former experiences onto the counselor or counseling relationship, is common. Some Vietnamese clients may have had unpleasant war or refugee experience that may impinge on the counseling relationship (Dinh Phuc Van, 1976). Sullivan (1979) reports that during an initial interview, a Vietnamese male adolescent interpreted the counselor's forward lean as highly threatening. He hypothesizes that negative transference may have triggered this response.

Counselors are usually aware of the danger of countertransference, especially when working with those of a different culture. When counseling Vietnamese, counselors should check their personal feelings about clients, particularly because of the residues of strong and deeply divided emotions that the United States involvement in the Vietnam war created in American public opinion. These residual feelings range from contempt and antagonism to guilt and deep sympathy. Recent media reports of the sufferings of the boat people have created a new wave of sympathy. One possible result is preferential treatment—real or merely perceived—which in turn breeds resentment in other groups. Such resentment has already been voiced by some Blacks and Hispanics. Counselors should remember that an overly protective attitude can create barriers as easily as a latently hostile one. If, in addition, being overprotective gives an impression of favoritism, such an attitude also invites difficulties with other minorities.

Communication Barriers

Explicit Communication. We expect "talk" in a counseling interview. Unfortunately, basic language barriers are great for the newly arrived Vietnamese. The difficult Vietnamese language was rarely studied here before United States' involvement in the war, and there were few Vietnamese college students here. French was the preferred second language for most educated Vietnamese. The refugees of 1975 found no preexistent ethnic community to help with language problems (Vuong Gia Thuy, 1976). Until the student and family learn English, finding an interpreter for basic communication can present difficulties.

The counselor may be tempted to use a Vietnamese student who speaks some English as an interpreter. Nguyen Ngoc Bich (1979) points out, however, that it is a mistake to use a young person for that purpose in a school setting, where the Vietnamese expect adult authority. It is desirable to obtain the help of an older man or woman, especially in an initial parent interview. When this is not possible, it is best to write, asking the new student and parents to bring someone if they wish, or for the counselor to use simple, slow, and, if necessary, written English. If the adults are secondary school or university educated, they will have studied either English, French, or both. But classes were so large (60 to 70 pupils) that conversation practice was not feasible; as a consequence, many Vietnamese can read or write some English but not speak it (Duong Thanh Binh, 1975). In communication with parents, the telephone should be avoided if possible. Except in larger Vietnamese cities, the telephone was rarely used and may be a source of anxiety for many older Vietnamese. The anxiety results not only from unfamiliarity with the equipment, but from difficulty of English comprehension, which is intensified by the absence of visual clues.

When an interpreter is used, two pitfalls must be avoided. First, the counselor must be careful to pay attention to the principal parties, not to the interpreter. Otherwise it will be difficult to note reactions, convey warmth, and create rapport. Second, the interpreter must not be allowed to encroach on the counselor's role by offering amplification or clarification. The interview should remain a dialogue between the principal party or parties and the counselor.

Even when an interpreter is unnecessary, explicit communication can be frustrating because the responses may not be as expected. *Yes* in reply to a question may not be an affirmative but merely a polite acknowledgment. Also, Vietnamese often will say *yes* simply because they believe this is the answer desired or fear a negative reply would be rude (Parsons, 1968). Accordingly, it is wise to avoid direct questions when possible. Later on, the counselor may help the student understand that in English a person may say *no* and still be polite. Until this has been learned, the counselor should be aware that a Vietnamese *yes* may mean *no* or *maybe*.

Implicit Communication. Nonverbal responses amplify explicit communication, sometimes reinforcing and sometimes contradicting it (e.g., Argyle, 1972; Sielski, 1979). One's culture provides specific interpretations for variations in speech and for nonverbal cues. The Vietnamese have several implicit communication patterns that can lead to misunderstandings by one who does not share them. For example, a loud voice and a warm, hearty greeting are often ways in which Americans communicate welcome. To the Vietnamese, however, these actions are rude and unseemly in a person of authority. A quiet, dignified, and restrained voice and manner are expected, and, when confronted with the opposite, the Vietnamese will often lapse into embarrassed silence. The counselor may feel rebuffed, and the relationship will suffer.

A smile in American culture usually means happiness, often assent. For the Vietnamese it may communicate not only these sentiments, but anger, embarrassment, rejection, and other emotions as well (Duong Thanh Binh, 1975). In certain situations a Vietnamese smile may seem inappropriate to Americans. For the Vietnamese, smiling may reflect stoic behavior in adversity, which is admired, or cover hostile or angry impulses (Bourne, 1970).

Eye contact also sends different messges to the two cultural groups. In general, Americans think of "shifty eyes" or unwillingness to look someone in the face as a negative, even suspicious trait. For the Vietnamese adults and children, to look directly at a person with whom they are speaking is a sign of disrespect and rudeness (Nguyen Van Thuan, 1962). When speaking to an older person or one in authority, Vietnamese will glance up occasionally, but usually keep their eyes down. Eye avoidance is especially noticeable in girls and in the lower class.

Socially acceptable body contact is another area in which the two cultures differ. For example, although an affectionate pat on a small child's arm would generally be understood by the Vietnamese, touching a young person on the head is offensive to them. Also, social touching of the opposite sex is usually not done in the Vietnamese culture except sometimes to family members (Nguyen Van Thuan, 1962). A male counselor's handshake to a Vietnamese male would be better received than a handshake to a female. In fact, the male counselor should be aware that the Vietnamese consider his touching females older than age 12 as threatening or insulting. For the adolescent or older Vietnamese woman, even sitting in a room with a nonfamily male with the door closed creates discomfort. In some cases counselors will have to sacrifice privacy to put a student or parent at ease.

In contrast to opposite-sex touching, touching between persons of the same sex, especially age cohorts, is common in Vietnam. Adolescents of the same sex, and even persons in their early twenties, often walk together holding hands or arm in arm. This is merely a show of friendship and has no sexual meaning. Counselors should instruct the student in acceptable and unacceptable American social behavior, because adhering to social expectations enhances acceptance and adjustment.

Psychosocial Differences

Human beings, Sundberg (1976) points out, comprise similarities and differences—sharing univerals with all, sharing specific socializations with their own group, and having individual uniqueness. Counselors aware of the universals and individual uniqueness can still be blocked by those specific socializations that make someone "different from us." Only by understanding these differences can we hope to overcome any barriers they may present.

Unwillingness to Self-disclose and Humility

Most therapists would agree that in a counseling interview, frank discussion of feelings, problems, and concerns is desirable. This can be inhibited by two Vietnamese traits: unwillingness to disclose problems and feelings, and extreme humility. Vietnamese find it difficult to discuss problems and reveal emotions. As children they were taught to conceal antisocial emotions such as anger and hostility. This helped preserve domestic harmony, which was essential because the family was large, with several generations living together in close quarters. It also helped prevent tension between the family and the community, where individual actions tended to involve the family or reflect on its honor. In addition, children were taught not to question authority, especially the father's. According to Bourne (1970), it is almost impossible for a Vietnamese to express anger, resentment, or frustration toward a parent or authority figure. Suppression—refusal to recognize conflict or anger—or withdrawal, either physical or emotional, are the usual ways of coping with authority conflicts (Nguyen Duy San, 1969). Although an emotional explosion can result from unresolved conflicts, such outbursts are usually turned inward, sometimes by committing suicide or running away (Nguyen Duy San, 1969).

The Vietnamese are taught to adopt a humble, self-depreciating attitude toward their accomplishments and those of their family. They are reluctant to complain to authority for fear of being disrespectful, even when injustice has been done or a mistake made. Because a braggart or an overly assertive person is consisered rude, the Vietnamese may find it hard to speak of their own accomplishments, to ask questions in class, to volunteer to answer questions, or to express opinions, lest they appear to be showing off. In America, where assertiveness is valued, Vietnamese who exhibit extreme humility will often find it difficult to sell themselves. The counselor may need to help Vietnamese understand American expectations, and assertiveness training may be indicated to aid in future employment or education.

Vietnamese upbringing also teaches young persons to conceal stress as a matter of stoic pride. Although Nguyen Ngoc Bich (1979) suggests that the threshold of pain (physical and mental) may be higher for Vietnamese than for Americans, it is more likely that the Vietnamese simply conceal pain better. Personal matters that embarrass or cause hurt or stress are not usually discussed with anyone except family and very close friends. Openness as a basis of understanding and "talking out problems" in a counseling dyad will not be possible to the same extent as with an American, and accuracy in diagnosis may be affected. Group therapy, which Kaneshige (1973) says presents problems for Asian Americans, would also be difficult for Vietnamese because of their reluctance to verbalize their feelings or confront others.

Sex Roles and Attitudes

Male and female roles and expectations were viewed differently in Vietnam. Both sexes had obligations to bring honor to the family, avoid shame, and be obedient (Hammer, 1966)—however, the male led and the female followed. Beginning in childhood, the boy had more freedom of action and fewer specific tasks. To be male was desirable in itself; to be female was desirable only in the context of how well duties or tasks were performed.

The Vietnamese woman thus tends to be less concerned with equal rights than American women and more inclined to value obedience (Penner & Anh Tran, 1977). On the other hand, she controls the family finances and is responsible for the children. She is thus competent and, although theoretically subservient, actually powerful within her sphere. She has also learned to adapt, adjusting to the requirements of obedience—first to her father, then to her husband, and if widowed, to her sons. Therefore Vietnamese girls in school here may hesitate to assert themselves, particularly with boys and male authorities. Because of their adaptibility, however, they and their mothers may adjust more easily than the male members of the family (Trinh Ngoc Dung, 1979).

Another Vietnamese female trait contributing to adjustment problems is extreme physical modesty. Vietnamese girls in school find showering in locker rooms with other girls, attending a class on human reproduction, or participating in a mixed group discussion of personal matters highly embarrassing. (Information and previous discussion with the girl's family about such activities would be an important step in lessening embarrassment.) Girls also find it difficult to associate with boys. Although boys and girls went to school and had classes together in Vietnam, they sat in separate sections, not even sharing lab partnerships, and their social contacts were minimal; American-style dating was not practiced.

The obverse of female subservience in nondomestic matters is male dominance. This intensifies the problems many Vietnamese men face as a result of war and refugee experiences. Defeat in the war often has undermined male self-esteem (Bourne, 1970). Also, Vietnamese are highly status conscious; for example, a study (Kelly, 1978) of male Vietnamese college students noted their unwillingness to accept janitorial jobs acceptable to American students in the same college. According to the U.S. Department of Health, Education, and Welfare (HEW) (1978), Vietnamese immigration to the United States has usually meant loss of occupational status; 68% of former white-collar workers hold blue-collar jobs here. The resulting tension—especially in families in which the women are also working, often in equivalent jobs—leads to an increase in divorce, a virtually unknown phenomenon in Vietnam.

The counselor working with Vietnamese males may have to help them rebuild their confidence and self-esteem. This can be done by acknowledging traditional male authority in the home, and if a low status job must be suggested, by giving reassurances that as English is learned and skills mastered, higher status employment can be found (Sullivan, 1979). Career suggestions for either sex should always consider the status of the occupation, particularly for the first-born child.

The Family and the Individual

It is not easy for an American to grasp fully the extent of Vietnamese family involvement in the person's past, present, and future plans. In Vietnam, the family—a community in miniature—was the source of financial and personal support, old-age and child care, the keeper of all rituals, and the home of the ancestors. Transplanted to America, the family still provides security and order in an alien world (Vuong Gia Thuy, 1976). By including the entire Vietnamese family in school activities, the American school helps to reinforce this support system.

For the Vietnamese, the family's honor, pride, and traditions are more important than the individual's, and any appeal to self alone tends to fail (McAlister & Mus, 1970). If an individual's wishes for a career or goal are counter to the family's desires, the latter will usually prevail. Discussion of educational or career goals will, therefore, involve more parent consultation and active approval than would be expected or desired for the average American.

The American ideal of independence—its lack viewed as maladjustment—is not a Vietnamese ideal. Unmarried Vietnamese men and women in their twenties with advanced degrees usually continue to live with their parents. Even marriage, while no longer arranged, is still a family concern. The American custom of dating creates problems; a "good" Vietnamese family strongly disapproves of a child's going out, especially with an American, partly for fear that marriage may result.

Differences among Vietnamese

Vietnamese society is heterogeneous, and some of its variations are significant to the adjustment of refugees in the United States. The counselor should be aware of a refugee family's former socioeconomic status (often related to educational level, previous cross-cultural experience, and degree of urbanization) and possible membership in the ethnic Chinese subculture.

Many of the 1975–76 refugees were from the upper or upper-middle class, were well-educated, had urban backgrounds, and had worked with French or Americans. They were prepared to meld portions of Vietnamese and American cultures, and their adjustment progressed well (Montero, 1978). On the other hand, those who came to the United States later encompass a much broader social spectrum, and for many the culture shock has been severe. A female refugee's ignorance of how to use a simple mechanical can opener, described in *Newsweek* (Conrad, 1979), may seem an extreme example but warns effectively against assuming too much sophistication.

To "emphasize with differences, to learn the latent messages in intercultural communications" (Alexander et al., 1976, p. 91), the counselor needs to learn as much as possible about the culturally different client. Were the Vietnamese city or rural dwellers? Were they used to western culture, French, or American? What was the father's former occupation? What is the parents' educational background? The answers to such questions will suggest the probable degree of culture shock and will yield valuable insights into potential adjustment problems.

Many of the current refugees are ethnic Chinese. Residents of Vietnam for generations, they have survived in an often hostile environment by sticking together, and have developed a unique subculture bridging the Chinese and Vietnamese cultures. Most of them speak one of three Chinese dialects: Hakka, Fukinese, or Cantonese. The Chinese in Vietnam maintain their own schools, so that their school placement in America may be different from that of other Vietnamese and their schooling may have been interrupted. They tend to live apart, concentrating in the Cholon section of Saigon. They have more group identification than other Vietnamese, may be more suspicious of strangers, may fear "officials," and may fear forms and written documents. (Forms were often used for tax collection by anti-Chinese authorities.) Because it is very difficult for someone who is not Vietnamese to distinguish the two groups by name or appearance, the counselor should ask whether the family is ethnic Chinese. If so, local Chinese-American organizations may be able to help in language and cultural matters, as there is some feeling of community among overseas Chinese.

If a family is not ethnic Chinese, it is important that the counselor avoid mistakenly referring to them as such. Although indebted to Chinese culture, the Vietnamese tend to be anti-Chinese—a feeling that extends, subtly or blatantly, to their own ethnic Chinese minority (Foreign Area Studies of the American University, 1967).

Where concern is with the overall socialization patterns of the two cultures, these distinctions among Vietnamese may seem oversubtle. They will serve to remind the counselor, however, that there is no stereotypical Vietnamese.

Mental Health Problems

Because the Vietnamese are generally unfamiliar with psychotherapy and mental health facilities (Nguyen Duy San, 1969), an individual with problems usually goes to someone older, preferably in the family. In Vietnam the person might go to a "healer" or Buddhist monk known to be adept in such matters. Many believe that mental or nervous difficulties, and problems in general, are caused by evil spirits and are solved by religious means (Hickey, 1964).

Thirty years of war brought dislocation, loss of loved ones and property, and great stress to the Vietnamese people. For the refugees, this stress has been prolonged in dangerous escapes, often in crowded, leaky boats, followed by many months in squalid refugee camps where rape and robbery were common. Because the Vietnamese lack familiarity with mental health and are hesitant in approaching strangers, counselors need to be alert to evidence of stress and the emotional scars of war and refugee experiences.

Depression and Anxiety

Costello (1976) believes that depression is often caused by a loss of structure and meaning in life. According to an HEW report (1978), severe depression and other mental health problems may be three times more frequent among the refugees than in the population as a whole. This report resulted in the funding of a project to train Indochinese paraprofessionals for community health services; so far only six have been trained.

A Vietnamese suffering from severe depression or anxiety has two special problems: Early diagnosis is made difficult because the Vietnamese are unwilling to self-disclose (noted above), and qualified professionals are few. American psychiatrists have had little success with Vietnamese patients because of the language barrier and unfamiliarity with Vietnamese culture (Trinh Ngoc Dung, 1979). Tom That Toai (1979), one of the few Vietnamese psychologists, points out that a Vietnamese child, confronted by a tall stranger speaking English, is very frightened and finds it difficult to respond, even through an interpreter.

A school counselor is in a good position to observe changes in behavior or appearance that may indicate anxiety or the onset of depression. Also, Vietnamese tend to manifest their emotional disturbances in physical symptoms (Nguyen Duy San, 1969); thus, the counselor, teacher, and school nurse should be especially concerned about the child who displays physical symptoms (e.g., frequent stomach upsets, or unexplained aches and pains). Because of the lack of professionals familiar with Vietnamese language or culture, referrals will be difficult and counselors may find themselves working with problems that they might not have otherwise attempted to solve.

Sullivan (1979) notes that counselors have reported students who are preoccupied with blood, guns, and fears of death and dying. These anxieties are particularly true of children who were in the active war zone and also had terrifying escapes. Dinh Phuc Van (1976) writes that many children from the active war zone "do not believe in anyone or anything" (p. 87). *Newsweek* (Deming, Copeland, Buckley, & Coppola, 1979) quotes one refugee as saying about those who had harrowing escapes: "They are maimed. Despair and frustration saturate their minds" (p. 52). The counselor may wish, as the students' English progresses, to help them talk, write, or perhaps draw pictures about experiences that need to be brought into present focus.

Family Conflicts and School Adjustment Problems

According to Ton That Toai (1979), poor adjustment and low achievement at school, especially after a satisfactory start, may reflect conflict within the family. The child who comes home eager to show off English learned or American ways copied from peers may be rebuffed by a formal, traditional family; a passive, indifferent family; or a family that views adaptation to American culture as a positive threat to its solidarity and eventual return to Vietnam.

Various factors contribute to these family attitudes. To a traditional Vietnamese family, becoming "like an American" may mean loudness, disobedience, disrespect, and lack of concern for the elderly. Too often, students who want to be more like Americans but do not have experience in discriminating between behavioral levels fulfill their parent's fears by modeling themselves after peers whose extreme behavior is unacceptable, even to most Americans. To prevent this, a counselor may need to model acceptable behavior for school, social events, and other situations (Sullivan, 1979). Also, the insecurity they have known in the past makes many Vietnamese reluctant to plan for a future in the United States. The Buddhist philosophy, to which 80% of Vietnamese adhere, instills a passive fatalism rather than active striving to shape the future (Nguyen Thanh Liem, 1976). There is also a widespread belief among some refugees that they are here temporarily. Many fled to the United States only to save their lives, and if the Communist regime adopted different policies, they would return to Vietnam. For all these reasons, some older adults have made only minimal efforts to learn English or adjust to American culture and they may actually resist doing so. The result may be conflict with younger family members who seek to be more bicultural, adopt a more "western" attitude toward the future, and lean increasingly toward permanent residence in the United States.

The family's adjustment to life in America may improve as its socioeconomic status rises and it can begin to look to a more secure future. Less successful adults, however, may prefer to live in the past, which can cause problems for their children. The counselor working with a young person may find that all family members need help in adjusting to their environments.

Summary

In dealing with Vietnamese clients, good relations with the family as well as the student are especially necessary. Rapport may be difficult to establish because of the language barrier or conflicting nonverbal cues, Vietnamese humility and unwillingness to self-disclose may inhibit frank discussion, and transference or countertransference may hinder counseling. The counselor may have to structure the relationship more concretely and adopt a more directive approach than is normal with Americans. Differing attitudes toward sex roles and the family may contribute to adjustment problems, as may the emotional scars of war and refugee experiences. Socioeconomic and ethnic differences among the Vietnamese themselves will also have a bearing on adjustment.

But if the counselor is able to convey a respect for cultural differences, a desire to understand and help, and a flexible approach, a positive helping relationship can be established despite these barriers. The rescue of the boat people is not complete when they reach American shores. Problems often follow, and the counselor can help the Vietnamese overcome them.

Acknowledgment

The author wishes to thank Clemmont E. Vontress, Professor of Education, The George Washington University, for his help and encouragement.

References

Alexander, A. A.; Workneh, F.; Klein, M. H.; & Miller, M. H. Psychotherapy and the foreign student. In P. Pederson, W. J. Lonner, & J. G. Draguns (Eds.), *Counseling across cultures*, pp. 82–97. Honolulu: University Press of Hawaii, 1976.

Argyle, M. Non-verbal communication in human social interaction. In R. A. Hinde (Ed.), *Non-verbal communication*, pp. 243–269. Cambridge, Mass.: Harvard University Press, 1972.

Bourne, P. G. *Men, stress and Vietnam.* Boston: Little, Brown, 1970.

Conrad, P. Living with refugees. *Newsweek,* 13 August 1979, p. 15.

Costello, C. G. *Anxiety and depression.* Montreal: McGill-Queen's University Press, 1976.

Deming, A.; Copeland, J. B.; Buckley, J.; & Coppola, V. Home of brave. *Newsweek,* 2 July 1979, p. 52.

Dinh Phuc Van. A Vietnamese child in your classroom. *Instructor,* 1976, *85,* 86–92.

Duong Thanh Binh. *Vietnamese in the U.S.* Arlington, Va.: Center for Applied Linguistics, 1975.

Foreign Area Studies of the American University. *Area handbook for South Vietnam.* Washington, D.C.: U.S. Government Printing Office, 1967.

Frank, J. *Persuasions and healing.* Baltimore: The John Hopkins University Press, 1961.

Hammer, E. *Vietnam yesterday and today.* New York: Holt, Rinehart & Winston, 1966.

Hickey, G. C. *Village in Vietnam.* New Haven, Conn.: Yale University Press, 1964.

Kaneshige, E. Cultural factors in group counseling. *Personnel and Guidance Journal,* 1973, *51,* 407–412.

Kelly, P. L. *Vietnamese students on a small college campus: Observations and analysis.* Paper presented at the meeting of the National Association of Foreign Student Affairs, Iowa State University, Ames, 1978.

McAlister, J. T., & Mus, P. *The Vietnamese and their revolution.* New York: Harper & Row, 1970.

Montero, D. *The Vietnamese refugees in America: Patterns of socioeconomic adaptation and assimilation.* Paper prepared for the Institute of Urban Studies, University of Maryland, College Park, 1978.

National Indochinese Clearinghouse and Technical Assistance Center. *A manual for Indochinese refugee education 1976–1977.* Arlington, Va.: Center for Applied Linguistics, 1977.

Nguyen Duy San. Psychiatry in the army of the Republic of Viet Nam. In P. G. Bourne (Ed.), *The psychology and physiology of stress,* pp. 45–73. New York: Academic, 1969.

Nguyen Ngoc Bich. Personal communications, Arlington County, Virginia, Public Schools Intake Center. June, August, & September 1979.

Nguyen Ngoc Bich & Dao Thi Hoi. *The Vietnamese learner: Hints for the American teacher.* Unpublished manuscript, Arlington County, Virginia, Public Schools, 1978.

Nguyen Thanh Liem. *Vietnamese culture kit.* Iowa City: Research Institute for Studies in Education, University of Iowa, 1976. (ERIC Document Reproduction Service No. ED 149 602)

Nguyen Van Thuan. *An approach to better understanding of Vietnamese society.* Saigon: Michigan State University Advisory Group, 1962.

Parsons, J. S. *Americans and Vietnamese: A comparison of values in two cultures.* Arlington, Va.: Human Science Research, Inc., 1968.

Penner, L. A., & Anh Tran. A comparison of American and Vietnamese values system. *Journal of Social Psychology,* 1977, *101,* 187–204.

Sielski, L. M. Understanding body language. *Personnel and Guidance Journal,* 1979, *57,* 238–242.

Sue, D. W., & Sue, D. Barriers to effective cross-cultural counseling. *Journal of Counseling Psychology,* 1977, *24,* 420–429.

Sue, D. W., & Sue, S. Counseling Chinese-Americans. *Personnel and Guidance Journal,* 1972, *50,* 637–644.

Sullivan, W. Personal communication, student advisor, Arlington County, Virginia, Public Schools Career Center. 20 September 1979.

Sundberg, N. D. Toward research evaluating intercultural counseling. In P. Pederson, W. J. Lonner, & J. G. Draguns (Eds.), *Counseling across cultures,* pp. 139–169. Honolulu: University Press of Hawaii, 1976.

Ton That Toai. Personal communication, psychologist, Arlington County, Virginia, Public Schools. 4 October 1979.

Trinh Ngoc Dung. Personal communication, HEW Indochinese Refugee Task Force. June & September, 1979.

U.S. Department of Health, Education, and Welfare. *Report to the Congress, Indochinese Refugee Assistance Program.* Washington, D.C.: U.S. Government Printing Office, 31 December 1978.

Vontress, C. E. Barriers in cross-cultural counseling. *Counseling and Values,* 1974, *18,* 160–165.

Vontress, C. E. Racial and ethnic barriers in counseling. In P. Pederson, W. J. Lonner, & J. G. Draguns (Eds.), *Counseling across cultures,* pp. 42–64. Honolulu: University Press of Hawaii, 1976.

Vontress, C. E. Racial and ethnic barriers in counseling. In P. Pederson, W. J. Lonner, & J. G. Draguns (Eds.), *Counseling across cultures* (Rev. ed.). Honolulu: University Press of Hawaii, 1980. (In press).

Vuong Gia Thuy. *Getting to know the Vietnamese and their culture.* New York: Frederick Unger, 1976.

The Asian American Client
Cases and Questions

1. Assume you are a high school counselor in a large suburban high school. A Japanese American student whom you have seen for academic advising on several occasions has just shared with you his involvement as a marijuana dealer. Although attempting to hide his emotions, the student is clearly distraught. He is particularly concerned that a recent arrest of a marijuana supplier will eventually lead authorities to him.

   a. How *might* the student's cultural background affect his feelings as he shares this problem?
   b. What kind of input from you as a counselor do you think this student wants/needs most?
   c. Can you anticipate any prejudicial reaction on the part of the school administration (if the student's behavior is uncovered) as a result of the student's racial/ethnic background?

2. Assume you are a community psychologist employed by a community agency which provides psychological services to a population of middle class Japanese American families, among others. A Young Buddhist Association (YBA) has asked you to speak on, "resolving inter-generational conflict" at their next meeting. (Your agency is aware that generational conflict has become a major problem in this community in recent years.)

   a. What do you think are some of the causes of the inter-generational conflict being experienced by these young people and their parents?
   b. Other than your talk, what services do you feel qualified to render these young Japanese Americans and their families?
   c. How do you think these services will be received by the YBA members and their families?

3. Assume you are a high school counselor who has been asked by the Dean of Guidance to organize and moderate a number of value clarification groups. You plan to set up six groups of eight students each from a list of volunteers, although seven students were referred by

teachers because they are non-participators in class. Six of the seven students referred by teachers are Asian Americans.

a. Will the composition of your six groups be determined by the fact six of seven teacher referrals are Asian American?
b. What goals do you have for your six groups and for the individual members of these groups?
c. How will your own cultural/educational background affect the way in which you relate to the six Asian American students?

The Asian American Client
Role Playing Exercise

Divide into groups of 4 or 5. Assign each group member to a role and the responsibilities associated with the role as follows:

Role	Responsibilities
1. Counselor	1. Assume role as a counselor or mental health worker who encounters an Asian client. Depending on the client role, the person may be Chinese, Japanese, or Indochinese. Attempt to build rapport with the client.
2. Client	2. Assume role of an Asian client (Chinese, Japanese, or Indochinese refugee). To play this role effectively, it will be necessary for the student client to (a) identify cultural values of the Asian group, (b) identify sociopolitical factors which may interfere with counseling, and (c) portray these aspects in the counseling session. It is best to select a few powerful variables in the role play. You may or may not be initially antagonistic to the client, but it is important for you to be sincere in your role and your reactions to the counselor trainee.
3. Observers	3. Observe interaction and offer comments during feedback session.

This exercise is most effective in a racially and ethnically mixed group. For example, an Asian American student can be asked to play the Asian client role. However, this is probably not possible in most cases. Thus, students who play the client role will need to thoroughly read the articles for the group they are portraying.

Identifying the barriers that could interfere with counseling is an important aspect of this exercise. We recommend that a list be made of the group's cultural values and sociopolitical influences prior to the role playing. For example, how might restraint of strong feelings, preference for structure and activity, and trust/mistrust be manifested in the client?

Role playing may go on for a period of 5–15 minutes, but the time limit should be determined prior to the activity. Allow 10–15 minutes for a feedback session in which all participants discuss (within the group) how they felt in their respective roles, how appropriate were the counselor responses, what else they might have done in that situation, etc.

Rotate and role play the same situation with another counselor trainee *or* another Asian client with different issues, concerns, and problems. In the former case, the group may feel that a particular issue is of sufficient importance to warrant reenactment. This allows students to see the effects of other counseling responses and approaches. In the latter case, the new exposure will allow students to get a broader view of barriers to counseling.

If videotaping equipment is available, we recommend that the sessions be taped and processed in a replay at the end. We have found this to be a powerful means of providing feedbacks to participants.

Part 4
The Black Client

Photo by Jean-Claude Lejeune / EKM-Nepenthe

"It's Great to Be a Problem"

It's great to be a problem,
A problem just like me;
To have the world inquiring
And asking what you be.
You must be this,
You can't be that,
Examined through and through;
So different from all other men,
The world is studying you.
(J. D. Work)

Black Americans have been researched, analyzed, and critiqued throughout their history. As the late Whitney Young noted, "the 'Negro-studying business' has become so big that I'm afraid if we just end it quickly, too many people will be thrown out of work . . ." (Young, 1968). Yet despite the energy expended in prolific research efforts, relatively little change has taken place in the popular image or perceptions held of this group. For example, little difference is found in the doctrine posited by Dr. Van Evrie, a physician, during the 1800s and that recently proposed by Nobel Prize winner William Shockley. Dr. Van Evrie asserted that, the "Negro is a man, but a different and inferior species of man who could no more originate from the same source as the White man, than the owl could have from the eagle . . ." (Van Evrie, 1863). Nearly 150 years later, Professor Shockley suggested in his Theory of Dysgenics that, "the major cause of American Negroes intellectual and social deficits is hereditary and racially genetic in origin and is not remediable to major degree by improvements in environment" (Jones, 1980).

Evidence is also found which suggests that Americans are constantly bombarded with stereotyped images of Blacks. Americans watch an average of 29.25 hours of television per week and, according to a report released by the U.S. Commission on Civil Rights (1979), the popular image portrayed of Blacks in this medium is clearly stereotyped. It cites as a prime example the popular television comedy *Good Times*. The Commission strongly endorsed *Time* magazine's (Morrow, 1978) appraisal of this show which asserted that:

> It was a strange and destructive message that *Good Times* sent out when its producers eliminated not only the family's strong, if frustrated father (John Amos) but also, later, its mother (Esther Rolle), who abandoned her three children in their Chicago housing project to move to Arizona to be with her new man. Says Rolle, who quit the show because of her differences with the producers over the way the characters were portrayed: 'It was an outrage, an insult.' (p. 101–02)

Time magazine concluded that, "Whites who know relatively little about Blacks are receiving a brutalized, stupid, or stereotyped image of Blacks through television" (p. 102).

Many of these stereotypes have become a common part of American perceptions and treatment of Blacks (Smith, 1977). Despite volumes of research and empirical evidence to the contrary, these misconceptions persist in the minds of both laymen and professionals (Swick, 1974).

Until recently, few helping professionals would accept that racial biases and stereotyping existed in counseling and even fewer would acknowledge that these attitudes could have meaningful effects on the services offered Black clients. Szasz (1971), for instance, points out that as far back as 1851, Dr. Samuel A. Cartwright, a prominent psychiatrist, proposed that the efforts of the Negro slave to gain his freedom by running away were merely symptomatic of serious mental diseases. Such statements are found throughout the psychiatric literature (Thomas & Sillen, 1972). As Sattler (1977) points out, many of the characterizations were crude and blatant, involving statements that Negroes are at a much lower cultural level than Caucasians, with a simple dream life and an inability to grasp subjective ideas (Lind, 1914); that Negroes are superstitious, changeable in impulse and emotion, and lacking in the ability to comprehend abstractions (O'Malley, 1914); that they are irresponsible, unthinking, easily aroused to happiness, and happy-go-lucky (Green, 1914); and show a comparative lack of self-consciousness, drawing a fainter line of demarcation between will and destiny, illusion and knowledge, and dreams and facts, and make less distinction between hallucinations and objective existences than do more civilized races (Lewis & Hubbard, 1931).

Unfortunately, many of these misconceptions are still around. Their impact on various aspects of counseling has been substantially documented. In the first article in this section, "The Emergence of Black Perspective in Counseling," Jackson looks at some of these effects from a historical viewpoint. He asserts that a more comprehensive perspective on Black behavior has begun to emerge, one in which the focus is on maintaining awareness of psychosocial factors which determine Black behavior, the effects of racism on ego development, and self-perception of the counselee.

In the second article, "Dimensions of the Relationship between the Black Client and the White Therapist," Jones and Seagull focus on "self-perception" as it relates to the White counselor working with the Black client. They emphasize the importance of the White counselor becoming familiar with his or her own racial values and attitudes as well as those of the client. Concepts such as countertransference and the detrimental effects of counselor guilt are also explored.

In the final article in this section, "Counseling Black Clients Effectively: The Eclectic Approach," McDavis reviews several methods that have previously been proposed for counseling Black clients and provides an eclectic approach for working with these clients. He also proffers ways in which this approach can be effectively applied.

To paraphrase Sattler (1977), if the counselor is to be effective in working with the Black client, he or she will need special awareness of the client and their own feelings about Blackness and Whiteness, in addition to an understanding of counseling theories and techniques proven effective with members of this group.

Green, E. M. Psychoses among Negroes: A comparative study. *Journal of Nervous and Mental Disease*, 1914, *41*, 697–708.

Jones, S. Playboy Interview: William Shockley. *Playboy Magazine,* August, 1980, pp. 69–102.

Lewis, N. D. & Hubbard, L. D. Manic depressive reactions in Negroes. In Association for Research in Nervous and Mental Disease, *Manic-depressive Psychosis*. Baltimore: Williams & Wilkins, 1931.

Lind, J. E. The color complex in the Negro. *Psychoanalytic Review,* 1914, *1*, 404–414.

Morrow, L. Blacks on TV: A Disturbing Image. *Time* March 27, 1978, pp. 101–102.

O'Malley, M. Psychosis in the colored race: A study in comparative psychiatry. *American Journal of Insanity,* 1914, *71*, 309–337.

Sattler, J. M. The effects of therapist-client racial similarity. In A. S. Gurman & A. M. Razin (Eds.), *Effective Psychotherapy*. New York: Pergamon Press, 1977.

Smith, E. J. Counseling Black Individuals: Some stereotypes. *Personnel and Guidance Journal,* 1977, *55,* 390–396.

Swick, J. J. Challenging Preservice and inservice teachers' perceptions of minority group children: A review of research. *Journal of Negro Education,* 1974, *43,* 194–201.

Szasz, T. S. The Negro in psychiatry: An historical note on psychiatric rhetoric. *American Journal of Psychotherapy,* 1971, *25,* 228–239.

Thomas, A. P. & Sillen, S. *Racism and Psychiatry*. New York: Brunner/Mazel, 1972.

Van Evrie, J. *Negroes and Negro Slavery: The First, and Inferior Race—the Latter, Its Normal Condition* (3rd. Ed.) New York: Van Evrie, Horton & Co., 1863.

Young, W. M. Why We Should Suspend The Studies of Negroes. *National Observer,* April 1, 1968, p. 17.

10 The Emergence of a Black Perspective in Counseling
Gerald Gregory Jackson

Scholarly concern with the process of counseling the Black client can be traced readily to the 1940s when, for example, workers in the field were disturbed and uncertain about specific aspects of counseling Black youth and adults (Williams, 1949). Specifically, need was expressed for special information in counseling such youth. Today, concerned counselors have expressed a similar need for special techniques to use with minorities or asked if it is better for minorities to be counselors to other minorities, since racial and ethnic barriers are so threatening and difficult to penetrate (Vontress, 1973). The difference today, however, is that the volume of data on counseling Blacks is greater, as is the tolerance for discussion of those related issues, such as racism. This increase in attention was predicted by one researcher who found three studies on the subject at the time of his review but asserted that in the ensuing years considerably more research would be reported (Island, 1969). The plethora of publications since the initial review tends to confirm the prediction. Ironically though, while the quantity and quality of articles waxed, the number of reviews remained conspicuously low. To illustrate, using the term "review of the literature" in the most liberal sense, only six such "reviews" could be uncovered (Island, 1969; Sattler, 1970; McGrew, 1971; Banks, 1971; Carkhuff, 1972; Denmark & Trachtman, 1973). This finding is particularly striking when one considers both the attacks on the profession in terms of the practices of its professionals toward Black clients (Williams, 1949; Barney & Hall, 1965; Washington & Anderson, 1974) and Black professionals (Jones, M. C. & Jones, M. H.; Smith, 1970; Smith 1971a; Daley, 1972) and the perennial admonishments by Black people that they are not receiving adequate services (Himes, 1948; Manley & Himes, 1948; Russell, 1949; Waters, 1953; Brazziel, 1958; Hypps, 1959; Record, 1966; Russell, 1970; Tolson, 1972).

As limited as the number of reviews may be, the genuine need is not for still another summation of contemporary publications but, more importantly, a synthesis of the emerging Black perspective in counseling. Briefly stated, this outlook is derived from a sense of Black culture and focuses on means of liberating Black people. This acknowledgment and ensuing description does not suggest, however, that a concern by Black professionals with their profession has not been historically manifested; this viewpoint suggests a new genre of expression, one that emerged from the civil rights throes of the 1960s which exposed many of the shibboleths of the profession. For example, one long-standing barrier to innovation was the notion that everyone should be regarded as the same. More specifically, the individuality of the counselor should not affect the techniques used and the psychosociological background of the client, though probably different, should not affect the techniques which he will use or his role (Trueblood, 1960). Under the aegis of this notion, which has been referred to ironically as the doctrine of color-blindness (Fibush, 1965), consideration of the differential services rendered to Black clients, problems basic to Blacks because of racial discrimination and changes in the training of personnel based upon the preceding were kept at an ineffectual minimum.

Conversely, the Black perspective demands that the construction of counseling theories take into account the factor of culture (Strikes, 1972) and that the ultimate objective of counseling entail more than the development of academic skills. Counseling, from this point of view, should give instruction in Black ideology and cultural identity which embraces the social and political realities involved in existing symbiotically with the larger culture (Toldson & Pasteur, 1972). Any other posture, it is viewed, is merely another means of perpetuating the slavery of both Blacks and whites—Blacks to their victimized status, and whites to their illusions of superiority (Barnes, 1972). Similarly, training institutions located at colleges and universities, it was felt, should transfer experiential learning activities from their academic settings to indigenous community centers, street academies, or store front schools so that students can gain practical skills in assisting Black clients (Smith, 1971b). To grasp the meaning of the roles, techniques, and stances advocated by this new perspective, one has to be cognizant of the historical struggle preceding its development, and its clash with traditional outlooks.

Struggle for Positive Recognition

Tolson's (1972) charge, "We try so hard not to see black or poor that we end up seeing nothing," suggests that recognition of the Black client and professional may apparently be the crux of the problem, but upon closer inspection it is evidently only a symptom. Acts, for example, which are now a part of history cogently demonstrate how both groups were dissected from the benefits to be accrued American citizens. Frank Parsons, one of the founders of the guidance movement, who was paradoxically concerned with matching people with their appropriate job, favored European immigrants, over native born Blacks, in allocating his services (Smith, 1971b). Similarly, Black professionals found little kinship with the professional organization of the American Personnel and Guidance Association until the inception of the National Defense Act and its training institutes. Moreover, Black professionals were denied a modicum of political prominence in the professional organization until the 1970s, after over twenty years of its existence as a body (Daley, 1972). These forms of discrimination could not have transpired without acknowledgment of a separate racial group and as a consequence, support the contention that Black people were not only seen but viewed in a negative light.

This negative perception of Black people is largely the result of the conceptual framework employed by the vast majority of professional counselors who unwittingly subscribe to the deficit hypothesis (Hayes and Banks, 1972). To elaborate, rather than searching in the environment for causal explanations of observed behavior, it is postulated that Black people have underlying deficiencies which are attributable to genetic and/or social pathology, which in the context of this reality, limits the probability of achieving successful academic and/or social adjustment. The implications for practitioners are facile; rather than critically observing their own behavior, the assumption of the hypothesis eliminates such a need and minimizes the likelihood of counselors considering important psychosocial factors which determine Black behavior. More importantly, since the onus of the problem is on the client, the professional's mission is oppressively one of getting the client to adjust to the status quo, while the behavior of those in power and the role they perform in creating and maintaining psychologically oppressive environments, in which Blacks must function, are ignored. In short, professionals alternately espouse the doctrine of color-blindness on the one hand, but practice discrimination on the other because acknowledgment of the latter implicitly demands affirmation of racial difference and discrimination which is too painful for many of them to bear. Clearly, it is the recognition of their passivity in the face of manifestations of racism, coupled with the guise of the notion of a melting pot, which instinctively encouraged them to adhere to certain reactionary principles. To illustrate, Williams (1949), in reaction to the cry for special information in counseling Blacks, responded that there was no need for special information. Deceptively for some, Rousseve (1965) added that while the environment of Blacks and whites can be differentiated because of racist patterns still prevalent in America, no essential distinction exists as far as behavioral or adjustive processes are concerned. Myopically, educators have interpreted such statements as meaning that the white middle-class can therefore serve as a model. Frequently overlooked or repressed is the condition of racism resulting from skin color differences. Williams added, for example, that while Blacks have the same basic needs, the frustrations, defeats, and conflicts are intensified and faced more frequently because of their color. She observed that in counseling Black students, counselors too often, either directly or indirectly, have discouraged vocational interests and choices and added that counseling for maximum adjustment does not attempt to adjust them to accept barriers of the status quo, but prepares them to cope with the barriers, find ways around them, and even to master techniques for removing them. This belief that Black clients should be assisted in learning how to negotiate in all senses of the term is one of the pillars of the Black perspective which is frequently minimized in the general literature and often overlooked in counseling contacts with such individuals. To return again to the significance of color, Boykins (1959) asserted that to counsel the Black college student effectively, one had to proceed on the assumption that the personality development of the youth was affected both by participation in the culture of the larger society and by membership in the caste to which Blacks in the U.S. are subjected by their minority position and status. Being a Black, she noted, had many implications for ego development that were not inherent in lower class membership. Here again is another important point which is frequently misconstrued by researchers and professionals in their haste to disregard how Black people are treated because of their color. Lumping Black with lower-class whites is a more convenient and face-saving alternative than understanding and dealing with the American contradiction of discrimination. More recently, Siegel (1970) expressed the view that in counseling the non-white student today, counselors must be aware of that student's identity because in her estimation, there lies the key to a proper approach to him, that is, does he see himself as a Negro American or an American Negro, colored person or Black man? White counselors in particular it has been shown are uniquely vulnerable in this regard (Vontress, 1971; Jackson & Kirschner, 1973); and Cross (1971) postulated five identifiable psychological stages black people undergo in moving from a self perception of Negro to a more liberated one of Black. Yet, the professional band continues to play the tune of "see no evil."

It is apparent from the references alluded to that the case for viewing Blacks in unique ways is not a recent issue and the same holds true for proposals to correct the problems engendered by the profession. Trueblood (1960), as others have similarly reported, felt that a counselor should explore the personality adjustment of the Black student and the possible influence that being Black, with the attendant social, educational, and economic restrictions has on his personality adjustment. He based his belief on the idea that there are possible problems of behavior and attitude which are related to the fact that the student is Black. Where he, in addition, digressed appreciably from conventional wisdom was in his view that while the process or techniques employed in assisting the student remained basically the same as those used for other population groups, the role of the counselor must be affected by his special knowledge of the student's needs. This special knowledge, he felt, could be gained only by studying the psychological and sociological background of Blacks. Presumably, such a professional understanding would be gained in graduate training where, theoretically, the opportunities are given and the insights gained. Yet, those who are trained in counseling, those who teach it and those who write it, do not have the instinctive, internalized knowledge of the ghetto culture, nor has a realistic opportunity to learn been provided them (Jones, M. C. & Jones, M. H., 1970). The student of counselor who wished such knowledge had to find his own way of acquiring it, which took unusual determination and initiative. To illustrate, Mickelson and Stevic (1967) also felt that counselor educators were not meeting the special needs of trainees in preparing them for work with the disadvantaged. They even conceded that many times the fault may reside within the counselor; however, in the opinion of these authors, "in all too many cases the root of the problem may well be traced to the preparation program of the counselor" (p. 77). Similarly, the Lewises (1970) noted that present programs of counselor education did not provide the basis for inner-city counselors to understand their students and their culture, or provide them with knowledge of the processes of social change and their potential contribution. Finally, Boxley and Wagner in their 1971 publication of a survey of APA approved psychology training programs reported that while many of the schools responding indicated an interest in recruiting more minority students, the available sites (clinics and counseling centers) were centered on the white middle-class client and minority faculty members at these schools were underrepresented. In their replicative study reported in 1973, they found no significant changes in the representation of minority group faculty, significant changes in the representation of minority peoples in the graduate student population but training programs which remained limited in breadth. Proposals to correct this deficit in training have been largely ignored. Vontress (1969a) for one, proposed pre-professional training which was undergirded in anthropology, sociology, and psychology, and the removal of counselor training from educational settings. He saw it within the purview of training programs to also provide opportunities for trainees to explore their feelings about the culturally different, live in the ghetto, and have a representative from the community be employed by the training institute to help counselors relate to the culturally different (Vontress, 1969b). Rousseve (1965) proposed that such trainees be exposed more extensively to updated scientific findings in cultural anthropology and related fields as these findings relate to intergroup prejudice and discrimination. Moreover, he felt that they should be required to sample and analyze some of the recent literary expressions of minority group authors.

In spite of these proposals, training programs in general showed little imagination in practice or in developing attitudes toward the preparation of counselors to work in settings focused primarily on urban Blacks (Smith, 1971a). Even those programs, however, which have been designed, in theory at least, with the preceding recommendations in mind still err because the Black perspective demands even greater allegiance. A brief description of some of these programs will illustrate the significant difference between the two points of view. Mickelson and Stevic (1970) recommended that counselor educators think beyond the rather traditional approach which had been taken in preparation programs and think in terms of a two-year integrated program. The first year of such a program would entail an introduction to the various theoretical, cultural, and philosophical foundations of the profession. The second year would involve placement in a ghetto school or in a federally sponsored program such as the Neighborhood Youth Corps. In addition, the second year would include courses in Black sociology and psychology and seminars which would bring in prominent local Black leaders and students at the university. This curriculum they believed would enable counselors to be of service to teachers which would further the rights of the pupil since the counselor would be promoting appropriate classroom behavior and understanding. They concluded that counselor educators could continue to ignore the need, but if they did others would institute programs to replace the school counselor "who is now charged with various guidance and counseling responsibilities, but who because of lack of preparation and/or commitment had fallen far short of the goal of providing assistance to all youth (p. 77)." The Lewises (1970) proposed that students be paired with an experienced counselor and placed full-time for a year in an inner-city school. During this stay he would be expected to provide direct counseling with students, attempt to involve the community in the operation of the school and the school in the operation of the community and spend a good deal of time working in a consultative capacity with teachers. Didactic course work was viewed as a bridge between theory and practice and included courses designed to enhance the trainees' awareness of the school's total milieu and the sociology of the school and the community. Their model counselor would be recognized as a consultant and an agent of change; however, they envisioned a training program that would specifically prepare the counselor for the role rather than assuming "that he will learn these functions later in some mystic manner" (p. 37). In terms of criticisms, George Banks (1971), after reviewing the literature in counseling, psychotherapy, testing, information-gathering, social casework, and education regarding the effects of race on the outcome of the interview situation, concluded that the task was no longer to analyze the Black man, but to reexamine the training and experiences of those involved in working with Blacks. He advocated that professionals should be concerned with selection and training based on the set of facilitative and action-oriented variables found to make a constructive difference in one-to-one relationships in general. One step further, the argument was advanced that even training programs which encouraged the perception of differences still may produce helpers who are a part of the problem rather than the solution. Accordingly, the comprehension of alienation divorced from a Black perspective, was deemed insufficient because the propensity of the formidable majority of professionals constrained them to center on what they considered as problems of personal disorganization within the Black client (Banks, W. 1972a), that is, the deficit hypothesis. More specifically, others cautioned against the use of certain approaches. Counselors were cautioned against subscribing to psychoanalytic models in general and classical psychoanalysis in particular when providing assistance to Black counselees (Harper, 1973a). The criticism was that the original theory of Freud was based upon middle- and upper-class white Europeans of the 1800s which had little, if anything, to do with a Black ghetto child. In addition, it was viewed as a post-dictive therapeutic approach which explained the why of behavior and not how to get food to quell hunger. As a more appropriate objective, it was felt to be the moral duty of the counselor to recondition the behavior of the counselee in helping him to learn new ways of meeting his needs and new ways of relating to the world, since he had been conditioned not to achieve such an end or even predestined by the dehumanizing conditions into which he is born. In contrast with the psychoanalytical approach, the use of behavioral principles was advanced as being progressive since they went beyond the deficit hypothesis (Hayes & Banks, 1972). Once again, from the Black vantage point, it was added that behavioral theory would be useless if the counselor did not understand what constitutes reward or punishment for a Black client, or if he failed to perceive the particular environmental conditions that effect a reward or punishment to his client (Banks, 1972a). This is an extremely important consideration, but an even more important one is that the counselor using such an approach should not confine himself to remedying the individual's lack of skill or inappropriate response repertoire because to do so is to inherently accept the notion that the problem is solely within the individual and encourages one to lose sight of the parameters of the problem.

The Alternatives

To counteract the unrelenting negative view of Black people, the Black perspective reordered some fundamental tenets. First, the locus of problems was shifted from the individual to society. Termed systemic counseling, this model assumed that most of the problems that had heretofore been labeled client problems were in actuality system problems. The role of the counselor in such an arrangement would be to treat the system for its problems which, when appropriate, would ultimately bring about a corresponding change in individuals (Gunnings & Simpkins, 1972). A word of caution must be added because of the tendency of some to use the concept of the culpability of the system as a justification for doing absolutely nothing. They ascribe all problems to the operation of the system and postulate that since they cannot correct the system through their individual assistance they cannot assist the Black client (Thomas, 1962). Such an approach is not systemic counseling but systemic racism and should not be confused with the view that Blacks are not disadvantaged but are placed in situations where they are at a disadvantage (Simpkins, Gunnings & Kearney, 1973).

Second, techniques and approaches evolved which were based upon Black culture. Mitchell (1971), for one, attacked what he perceived as the traditional posture of counselors to attempt to be nice guys by just listening. He felt that such a stance was not enough because Black students needed tools for dealing with their problems. The counseling process itself, in his estimation, should deal with the present as well as with the "hereafter." Those counselors, he charged, who dwelled only on early childhood experience often turned off Black students, because the latter do not see how such early experiences are relevant to their current crises. Moreover, the Rogerian trilogy of congruence, empathy and positive regard had to be combined with definite techniques through which the student could acquire desirable skills or attitudinal change. Toldson and Pasteur (1972) saw the use of soul music as an appropriate way of achieving positive counseling ends when working with Black students. Stikes (1972) advocated the use of modeling and simulation techniques, verbal reinforcement and contracts as culturally specific counseling devices for assisting Black clients. In addition, he felt that advising Black students was appropriate because they expected authority figures to do so and did not result in expected dependency, and he suggested the use of the environment as a means of teaching the client appropriate attitudes and skills for dealing with the environment. In line with this approach, the counselor would provide psychologically safe experiences by reducing threat and removing barriers and helping the client understand and actualize his personal perspective in the Black social movement. Tolson (1973) analyzed the human potential movement and concluded that all Black groups were the most appropriate vehicle for Black liberation. Finally, Edmund Gordon (1970) not only challenged the individual psychological model still regnant today, he proposed as a substitute a developmental-ecological model which incorporates the preceding culturally specific recommendations. His model envisioned a shift from the study of clients to the study of systems, i.e., the family, the school, or office, and their development as social processes. Adherents to this model would no longer assess behavioral products, but would instead assess behavioral processes and as a consequence examine the nature of intellectual and social functioning for the individual and describe those functions qualitatively—in short, a movement away from prediction to prescription or from identification and placement in available opportunities to the creation of, and placement in, appropriate situations. In addition, the subscriber would no longer rely upon didactic exhortation, but on discovery and modeling as vehicles for learning and give more attention to the use of naturally occurring or contrived environments to provide interactions supportive of learning and development in specified directions. Gordon further suggests that counseling, which he said should be abandoned as a field, should be shifted from interpretation to environmental orientation as its principle focus. Greater emphasis, he imagined, should be given to consultation. Finally, but not inclusive of all his points, he felt there should be a shift from primary concern with socialization to a major concern with politicalization, that is, systems maneuvering skills which would be skills that were not only essential to adequate concept of self but also to future survival.

Third, the Black perspective gave new interpretations of Black behavior and posited new images based upon strengths to supplant the old images based upon weakness. To illustrate, while most counselors subscribe to the notion advanced by Freud that a counselor should be a blank screen or a reflector of the client's problems, it was acknowledged finally that such an approach registered to Black students as indifference, remoteness and superiority (Scheffler, 1969). In lieu of the blank screen idea was the acclamation that a willingness to reveal something personal is a key to reaching Black students (Lefkowitz & Baker, 1971) and can build strong bonds of trust and rapport (Stikes, 1972). In a similar vein, the notion that Black people are somehow innately non-verbal was exposed on a number of fronts. It was found, for example, that they disclosed less than whites to certain target persons (Braithwaite, 1973). More importantly, this reservation to reveal oneself is based upon their minority status (English, 1957) and the need to maintain a facade in order to survive in a land that metes out rewards and punishments according to skin color (Phillips, 1961). Again, failure to recognize the genesis of observed behavior is not only an indictment of the training of the professional but the institutions which provide such training and the profession which proposes inclusion in such programs. What is suggested, also, is complicity in the scheme where Black people are not viewed in terms of how they are generally mistreated but in terms of their resistance to becoming totally assimilated into American society. In short, the phenomena is a classical instance of the self-fulfilling prophecy (Rosenthal & Jacobson, 1968) in operation by a profession avowing humanistic principles. This ambiguity, as well as other discrepancies, is clearly seen by adherents of the Black perspective and has served as one of its motivational forces. Another dimly grasped reality, based upon cultural difference, were the fact that Blacks and whites have different ways of communicating and the implication of this lack of recognition by the professional. Dr. Scheffler (1969), for example, reported that her expectation of verbal proficiency was a middle-class bias rooted in her experience in college and psychiatric settings where articulateness was often used as a convenient "hallmark of intelligence or potential" (p. 114). She discovered that ghetto residents were less fluent than middle-class people in vocabulary and form of middle-class English and were inhibited in using street language with those in authority, but only because the precise use of English she was accustomed to was less important to them. More important for communicating was observing gestures, intonations, facial expressions, or a variety of uses for a single word or phrase. From a Black point of view, if professionals such as Dr. Scheffler had been familiar with the life-style of inhabitants of the ghetto, they would know also that ghetto residents, too, give prestige and power to the fast talker, so that non-verbal really translates to "non-verbal in white terms" (Sager, Brayboy & Waxenberg, 1972). It is, therefore, as Scheffler indicated, the expectation of a certain way of being fluent verbally and a lack of cognition of non-verbal messages which result in the label of "uncommunicative," "silent" or "non-verbal" (Barnes, 1972). The real problem, then, from the Black perspective, is that the so-called non-verbal client is the one who usually receives the little help from the counselor who, in turn, often gets frustrated and gives up his attempt to establish contact, especially when the lure of heavy case loads can be used as a rationalization (Patterson, 1973). Another example of the disadvantage of the designation "non-verbal" is the case of the clinical and counseling psychology students who were provided with a practicum experience with Black trainees (Payne & Mills, 1970). The graduate students reported that the subjects were "non-verbal," and as a consequence, they discovered that they had to abandon the traditional interviewing format which depended upon high verbal interactions and focus greater attention on the non-verbal cues. Two shortcomings are illustrated by the observations made by students: first, that the subjects were defined as non-verbal as a label when the behavior manifested could merely have been a reflection of the appropriate tact to take under the circumstances and had nothing to do with the subject's verbal proficiency. Second, the assumption by such persons that Black clients enjoy such roles as professional examinee and should be cooperative, energetic and enthusiastic is naive and illustrative of how a well intentioned learning experience can be undermined by a lack of knowledge of the culture and history of Black people.

Beyond the challenges to the old notions held of Black people as indolent, recalcitrant and, in general, without singular distinctions, is a new view of them as initiators, problem-solvers and competent. For instance, in one setting a peer counseling program utilizing disadvantaged high school students found that it bettered classroom skills, improved grades, and raised levels of vocational and educational aspirations among the students (Vriend, 1969). In another case, Black students demonstrated competencies in counseling peers in a variety of settings, initiating guidance programs, and assessing how an educational system operates to the detriment of Black students (Jackson, 1972a). Critical to the point that Black people possess unusual strengths are the reports that Black students have been trained to serve in a counseling capacity where professionally trained counselors were found to be inadequate (Sue, 1973); initiated and conducted programs on drug abuse (Jones, 1970); and conducted programs on career guidance (Amsterdam News, 1972). Finally, a program was developed to convert minority school teachers into qualified school counselors. The program had as one of its premises the fact that skin color, language or inner-city social origin were advantages in counseling minority students (Lindberg &

Wrenn, 1972). It was reported also that one of the indirect benefits of the program was the positive reaction of the inner-city community to it and, as a consequence, a greater support for the total counseling program. In addition to the struggle for positive recognition is the concomitant struggle to gain personnel who will not only have a Black philosophical orientation, but a commitment to the new role carved out of this perspective as well. What follows is a description of the struggle for personnel, followed by a consideration of the roles evolving from the struggles.

Struggle for Services

One of the earliest studies on guidance services for Black students which reported some of the problems entailed found that Black high schools in the southeast region of the United States suffered from: (1) inadequately trained personnel, (2) inadequate facilities, and (3) inadequate programs and personnel (Himes, 1948). It was noted further that, in some instances, the community was an additional hindrance. For example, some officials pointed to parental indifference, poor school-community relations, and lack of cooperation from community leaders. Even though the facilities were manned by Black people which suggests that guidance problems may be independent from the factor of race, racial prejudice was blamed in part for the inadequacies cited. In a similar study, poor training of teachers was cited as the number one cause for the problem in guidance and the conclusion drawn from the data that it was probable that the expansion of guidance was making little positive contribution to the success of the total school program (Manley & Himes, 1948). Guidance programs at Black colleges started during the 1940s (Russell, 1949) and a report by Patterson (1947) indicated that Black students were in need of this form of assistance since the close guidance relationship between student and faculty was no longer a significant practice. A study of Black rural high school students found the guidance services were inadequate and the recommendation made that more attention should be devoted to this area (Waters, 1953).

Integrated Settings

In a study which focused on the relative guidance services given in a segregated surrounding, white schools had greater services (Brazziel, 1958). It has been noted similarly that even in cities where Black students are not segregated on the basis of race, they are still under-serviced (Hypps, 1959). To amplify, in a study conducted in an integrated high school which sought to determine if students felt Black youth were discriminated against in educational counseling (Barney & Hall, 1965), no statistical difference was found. However, a review of individual cases revealed that counselors tended to be a little less willing to advise Black marginal students to apply for college admission.

Attitudes toward Services Given

Civil rights organizations frequently saw counselors who indirectly encouraged Black students to drop-out or to aspire to low level occupations or to form poor self-images (Record, 1966) as an integral part of the whole apparatus of discrimination. Brazziel (1970) noted that in 1940 ten per cent of Black students went to college in comparison to twenty per cent for whites. However, in 1969 twenty per cent of Black students went to college whereas forty per cent of whites did so.

In terms of the Black community, Tolson (1972) observed that Blacks were angry and impatient with the traditional role of the counselor which was seen as maintaining the status quo rather than improving the condition of any individual or group. She noted that they were becoming increasingly suspicious of counselors and counseling bodies, to the point that suspicion often becomes rejection. In her view, a counselor was good for working with the powerless only when he had proven in their eyes his effectiveness in working toward a real change in their behalf. Corroborating her belief, Russell (1970) interviewed Black residents of one community who were unskilled and seasonal workers and found them to be unanimous in their belief that all guidance did for Black children was to put them in special classes, punish them for infractions, and get rid of them as soon as possible. Patterson (1973) noted two extreme and inappropriate practices of many counselors. They either encouraged Black clients to accept, in the name of reality testing, menial "Black" jobs which required little education or, after 1960 and the realization of new opportunities, they encouraged Black clients to aspire to any imaginable goal regardless of apparent qualifications or abilities. This erratic behavior on the part of counselors often stems from their inability to sort out inappropriate behavior on the part of the counselee from the inappropriate behavior of society in engendering such behavior. For example, in a training program for drop-outs in which Southern reared females were transplanted from the South to the North and then released to work in northern urban settings, one white employer complained that he was disappointed that prospective candidates from the program would not look him in the eye. He interpreted such behavior as a lack of confidence. The Black counselor, on the other hand, informed the employer that the students had been conditioned to respond to whites in power in that manner and that it was his responsibility to give the students the security to be themselves. The counselor went a step further, however, and used behavioral rehearsal and role-playing techniques to assist the students in being more assertive in the job interview situation (Jackson, 1972b). In short, he worked on both aspects of the problem and indicated to the students that they did not have to accept the offer of appointment. This counselor also had some of his clients enroll in a local college even though the program was not designed to have its graduates seek further education (Bates College newspaper, 1969).

Failure in Counselor Orientation

The implications of the preceding are apparent. First, the remarkable number and variety of college placement programs that developed outside the schools, with or without federal support, suggest that there is a crisis in guidance services in the school (Kendrick, 1970). Second, this crisis or failure, from a Black perspective, can be traced to the application of traditional middle-class pre-college guidance techniques to Black youth which are inappropriate (Kadota & Menacker, 1971).

Another means of delimiting the services given to Black clients is the traditional way in which counselors arrange to be seen and how they structure such interviews. Irvine (1968), for example, asserted that a counselor interested in serving such individuals may have to "permit himself to establish contacts in what appears to be inappropriate places at inappropriate times with the most inappropriate people" (p. 177). This is a point supported by Mitchell's (1970) observation that, "The counselor must also be willing to leave the security of his office in order to deal with some of the situational factors in white institutions which cause problems for Black students. He should be willing to make a personal contact for the student who is overwhelmed by the bureaucracy" (p. 36). Banks (1973) and Gordon (1965) both support this approach to counseling.

In short, the Black perspective castigates counselors for administering services solely from their offices (Washington, B., 1970) or waiting for Black youth to seek them out first (Kadota & Menacker, 1971; Smith, 1971a; Banks, 1973). Specifically, Brown (1973) observed that a counseling center, staffed primarily by whites, is generally perceived as a potentially hostile agency whose structure and office atmosphere projects to the Black student a sense of "going to see the Man." The problem with changing the situation, he indicated, was the tradition in higher education that often blocks the modification of programs and structures even when adult members of ethnic minority groups are involved in establishing the program or designing the structure. In fact, he was struck by his finding that programs set up on college campuses specifically for ethnic minority students have more often than not been structured in almost identical ways to similar programs offered by the institution for the general student body. By traditional he meant being assigned office space, given a desk, and expected to maintain regular posted office hours. As a consequence, he noted: "I have not been surprised that many students will not come for assistance under these conditions even when they are in serious academic or personal difficulty, but I have been bewildered that nonwhite administrators would expect ethnic minority students to feel comfortable and to relate to counselors under these conditions" (p. 169). This point is not difficult to understand, however, if one considers who trained the administrators and the bulk of their staff, and from what framework the institution operates.

Selection of Staff

Another dilemma encountered, then, in the administration of services is the problem of selecting suitable staff. Russell (1970), for example, suggested that the demand for Black counselors by Black students was the result of the latter's dissatisfaction with the present functioning of guidance which they considered to be "irrelevant" to their needs and an instrument of repression which was controlled by counselors who constituted roadblocks that they had to somehow manage to get around, particularly if their ambitions did not coincide with those which their counselors considered appropriate for them.

Feelings vary, however, on the subject of the significance of the race of the counselor who attempts to counsel Blacks. Taylor (1973) expressed a consensus that it is generally undesirable for whites to be involved in mental health research and treatment with Black people because of the former's racist proclivities; and, others have concurred. White counselors have been charged with lacking awareness of the problems, feelings and outlook of Blacks (Hypps, 1959; Brown, 1973), the ability to identify with Black counselees (Rousseve, 1965) and the inability to assist when the decision entails rejecting society (Kincaid, 1969). Moreover, white counselors have been viewed in general as being discouraging and defeatist (Smith, 1967), and young white females, in particular, as anxiety-ridden when attempting to assist Black males of comparable age (Vontress, 1969b). Smith (1971a) saw one of the major problems as that of overcoming a sense of superiority. In terms of student perceptions, Lewis (1969) reported that most Black youth doubted the sincerity of a "helping" white counselor. Similarly, Russell (1970) conveyed that Black students' belief that racial bias existed in interracial counseling thwarted them from believing that a white counselor could regard them as individuals who possessed the same emotions, aspirations and potentials as whites. It was observed that a white skin automatically placed one strike against the counselor (Mitchell, 1970).

On the opposite side of the pendulum, it has been stressed that some Black counselors who were born and bred in the ghetto have negative attitudes toward relating to Black youth (Smith, 1968). In the same vein, one writer speculated that Black militant counselors would reject clients who termed themselves colored (Vontress, 1972). In more specific terms, Hypps (1959) expressed the view that because most Black counselors have been limited traditionally in the United States as a consequence of their race in their vocational, social, and political experiences they would not be able to impart the full evaluation of the business, industrial, and political life in a free society to their counselees. McDaniel (1968) felt that in a Black-Black relationship there was the persistent danger that the counselor will have difficulty with the counselee because he perceives the counselor as being a person who is a member of the establishment and, as a consequence, a threat to his existence. McDaniel noted that he found it easier to work with white clients because the prejudiced ones did not seek his assistance, whereas Black students did and wondered whether or not he had been a traitor. Personally, he found greater success with juniors and seniors in college because they had the opportunity to observe his behavior and had at least come to the tentative conclusion that maybe he was not an Uncle Tom and, therefore, was able to relate to them in a meaningful way. Mitchell (1970) saw two distinct problems for the Black counselor. First, if he had not examined himself, Mitchell felt, there would be a tendency to project his attitudes and feelings onto other Blacks and as a consequence he would be just as "uptight" as the white counselor. Second, if he works in a white institution, he will have to demonstrate his legitimacy to Black students who need to feel that he is someone who is honestly interested in them and not an "Uncle Tom" or an unqualified showpiece. Finally, Lindberg and Wrenn reported (1972) that one criticism occasionally registered about minority counselors was that they tended to be militant at times and push minority causes. Interestingly enough though, as counselor educators these authors did not see such behavior as a criticism but rather an indication of success because they wanted their counselors to be in the front line of the current ethnic-social struggles and fully involved with students who were experiencing these struggles.

Research studies conducted on the race of the counselor point to the employment of Black counselors to assist Black counselees. To illustrate, a number of reports demonstrate either the efficacy of Black counselors over white ones (Phillips, 1960; Stranges & Riccio, 1970; Heffernon & Bruehl, 1971; Gardner, 1972; Grantham, 1973) or that Black counselees found comparatively less satisfaction with white counselors than white counselees (Burrell & Rayder, 1971); Brown, Frey & Crapo, 1972). In the same vein, trained Black adults were preferred over white professional counselors (Carkhuff, 1970) and white counselors were found to have low linguistic compatibility with Black students (Schumacher & Banikiotes, 1972). Other studies on the subject found that race was relatively insignificant (Backner, 1970; Barrett & Perlmutter, 1972, Cimbolic, 1972; Cimbolic, 1973) and in only one instance favored white counselors over Black ones (Bryson & Cody, 1972).

From the Black perspective, the rhetoric on the subject and even the mounting research which favors the employment of Black counselors are embellishments of two central concerns. First, as Barnes (1972) has indicated, if we take seriously what we know about the process of psychological identification, we must inevitably conclude that the white counselor contributes to the identity crisis of the Black student. In his view, identification in this instance was simultaneously denying self and identifying with the symbol of the oppressive system. A Black Counselor, on the other hand, who shares a common experience with his counselee and who has not rejected his own personal history, presents an appropriate figure for identification and is most able to inspire a feeling of confidence and a sense of hope in his Black counselees. Second, Banks (1971) argued that in light of the Black man's struggle to establish that Black people can do something for themselves, proving that they can establish an effective helping program for themselves will give them some additional sense of identity and manhood. In a Black context then, the encompassing consideration is the general plight of Black people and not solely the advancement of one individual who happens to be Black.

The Interim

Today, a number of Black students are pleading that skin color be noticed and ask that they not be expected to find their heritage in a counter-part of white society (Siegel, 1970). Black professionals, too, have rejected the notion that a student is a student whether he is Black, white, red or polka dot (Banks, 1970). These developments partially account for why the belief that students are students and that all they need is to be listened to, appreciated, guided, given moral and social examples, and given alternatives has not worked (Charnofsky, 1971). What is posed as a substitute for the doctrine of color-blindness is a view which recognizes that skin color has an enormous consequence in the U.S. and that if one is defined as Black, then such a person's condition is significantly different from that of any white immigrant or native (Tucker, 1973). Given this perspective, the traditional role of the counselor is no longer acceptable as an aid to Black people. In fact, one writer (Adams, 1973) went so far as to suggest that if counselors were to be helpful in the struggle for fundamental change requisite to assist minorities, they would have to abandon the following traditional activities: (1) vocational guidance, because it made an unfair and inadequate job market more acceptable and also helped to fill "manpower" needs of an economy based on exploitation; (2) large-scale achievement and intelligence testing, because it performed a stratification function; (3) crisis intervention counseling, because it served to keep the lid on potentially explosive situations; and, (4) personal adjustment counseling, because it served to convince clients that the source of their alienation was within the self. As an alternative, counselors would use their skills to help people realize the source of their alienation and organize them to take action. A more general consensus seems to be the abandonment of the individualistic orientation of the profession and movement towards the assumption of responsibility for addressing societal issues which bear upon the effectiveness of counseling. To illustrate, Anderson and Love (1973) advocated that counselors help Black clients to develop a sense of pride and white clients an increased racial understanding. To bolster this goal, they developed a program of exercises to increase racial awareness by enhancing relations for the school. Similar in thrust, Sedlacek and Brooks (1973a) reported how research could be employed to lessen the practice of institutional racism. Similar to Love and Anderson, these writers also reported a model for solving the problem of racism in educational settings (Sedlacek & Brooks, 1973b) and viewed as a whole, this model can be interpreted as implying two poorly recognized needs: first, that racism does not only exist in the larger society but the framework of educational settings as well; and second, that it is the responsibility of counselors to not only be cognizant of the phenomena but to actually initiate programs to ameliorate its occurrence. This approach, by the way, is not an autonomous function but is an integral part of the broader role of consultant which Gordon (1970) felt should replace the counseling function. In general, the role of consultant includes work with the faculty (Proctor, 1970), administration, staff, and community (Banks, 1973) and, in effect, catapults the counselor from the role of individual ministration to environmental manipulator (Harper, 1973b). It has been further defined as entailing the demonstration to teachers of the power of their expectations (Coffin, Dietz & Thompson, 1970), the translation of the needs of students to teachers (Bolden, 1970), the presentation of culturally oriented programs in the school, (Charnofsiy, 1971) and curriculum adviser (Washington, 1968). In terms of the community, this new role includes seeking employment opportunities and financial aid for Black students (Trueblood, 1960), introducing the school to the home (Rousseve, 1965), and giving talks at churches, social organizations and schools (Jones, M. C. & Jones, M. H., 1970).

Another role emanating from the Black perspective is that of innovator. Examples of this role would be the work of Tolson and Pasteur (1972) who developed techniques for therapeutic intervention based upon a synthesis of Rogerian principles and Black spirituality, and Stikes's (1972) eclectic use of behavioral and analytical techniques based upon a unified concept of Black culture. An additional case of an innovative advance is the movement by Black professionals to make the professional association more responsive to the needs of the Black client. Jones and Jones (1970) recommended that Black counselors form their own association so they would have a forum to exchange methods and ideology regarding the "neglected" client. Historically though, at the 1969 national convention in Las Vegas, a minority caucus presented a resolution to establish a salaried National Office of Non-White Concerns within the executive structure of the American Personnel and Guidance Association (APGA). These caucus members, according to Daley (1972), were: "tired of aquiesence; they were tired of an 'acceptable' existence; they were tired of all the rhetoric about warmth, acceptance, and development of each one's maximum potential" (p. 495). Each year until 1972 when a separate division within APGA was formed, caucuses met and presented grievances. At present the separate division has its own journal which projects the Black perspective in counseling, conducts programs related to minority interests both during conventions and throughout the year, and has moved from the smallest division out of eleven to the seventh in size.

Given the historical roots of the Black perspective and the continuation of conditions in the environment which gave rise to this outlook, one may infer that in the ensuing years this perspective will probably grow in substance and acquire a firmer shape. Schools employing counselors and counselor educators who train these counselors will have to adjust their policies and procedures to embrace this expanding point of view. In the absence of such resources, counseling may transpire outside of traditional institutions and training relegated to other agents.

Bibliography

Adams, H. J. The Progressive Heritage of Guidance: A View From the Left. *Personnel and Guidance Journal,* 1973, 50, 531–538.

Amsterdam News (N.Y.), "School Program Studies Local Community Role," December 30, 1972, p. 8.

Anderson, N. J. & Love, B. Psychological Education for Racial Awareness. *Personnel and Guidance Journal,* 1973, 51, 666–670.

Backner, B. L. Counseling Black Students: Any Place for Whitey. *Journal of Higher Education,* 1970, 41, 630–637.

Banks, G.; Berenson, G. G.; & Carkhuff, R. R. The Effects of a Counselor Race and Training Upon Counseling Process With Negro Clients in Initial Interviews. *Journal of Clinical Psychology,* 1967, 23, 70–72.

Banks, G. P. The Effects of Race on One-to-One Helping Interviews. *Social Service Review,* 1971, 45, 137–146.

Banks, W. M. The Changing Attitudes of Black Students. *Personnel and Guidance Journal,* 1970, 48, 739–745.

Banks, W. M. The Black Client and the Helping Professional. In Reginald L. Jones (ed.), *Black Psychology.* New York: Harper & Row, 1972 (a)

Banks, W. M. Militant Counselors: Riffraff or Vanguard? *Personnel and Guidance Journal,* 1972, 50, 575, 581–584. (b)

Banks, W. M.; & Martens, K. Counseling: The Reactionary Profession. *Personnel and Guidance Journal,* 1973, 51, 457–462.

Barnes, E. J. Counseling and the Black Student: The Need for a New View. In Reginald L. Jones (ed.), *Black Psychology.* New York: Harper & Row, 1972.

Barney, O. P.; & Hall, L. D. A Study in Discrimination. *Personnel and Guidance Journal,* 1965, 43, 707–709.

Barrett, F. T.; & Perlmutter, F. Black Clients and White Workers: A Report From the Field. *Child Welfare,* 1972, 51, 19–24.

Bolden, J. A. Black Students and the School Counselor. *The School Counselor,* 1970, 17, 204–207.

Boxley, R. & Wagner, N. Clinical Psychology Training Programs and Minority Groups: A Survey. *Professional Psychology,* 1971, 2, 75–81.

Boxley, R.; Padilla, E.; & Wagner, N. The Desegregation of Clinical Psychology Training. *Professional Psychology,* 1973, 4, 259–264.

Boykins, L. Personality Aspects of Counseling the Negro College Student. *Quarterly Review of Higher Education Among Negroes,* 1959, 27, 64–73.

Braithwaite, R. A. A Paired Study of Self-Disclosure of Black and White Inmates. *Journal of Non-White Concerns,* 1973, 1, 87–94.

Brazziel, W. F. Meeting the Psychosocial Crisis of Negro Youth Through a Coordinated Guidance Service. *Journal of Negro Education,* 1958, 27, 79–83.

Brazziel, W. F. Getting Black Kids into College. *Personnel and Guidance Journal,* 1970, 48, 747–751.

Brown, R. D.; Frey, D. H.; & Crapo, S. E. Attitudes of Black Junior College Students Towards Counseling Services. *Journal of College Student Personnel,* 1972, 13, 420–424.

Brown, R. A. Counseling Blacks: Abstractions and Reality. In Charles F. Warnath (ed.) *New Directions for College Counselors.* San Francisco: Jossey-Bass, 1973.

Bryson, S.; & Cody, J. Relationship of Race and Level of Understanding Between Counselor and Client, *Journal of Counseling Psychology,* 1973, 20, 495–498.

Burrell, L.; & Rayder, N. Black and White Students' Attitudes Toward White Counselors. *Journal of Negro Education,* 1971, 40, 48–52.

Carkhuff, R. R. The Development of Effective Courses of Action for Ghetto School Children. *Psychology in the Schools,* 1970, 7, 272–274.

Carkhuff, R. R. Black and White in Helping. *Professional Psychology,* 1972, 3, 18–22.

Charnofsky, S. Counseling for Power. *Personnel and Guidance Journal,* 1971, 49, 351–357.

Cimbolic, P. Counselor Race and Experience Effects on Black Clients. *Journal of Consulting and Clinical Psychology,* 1972, 39, 328–332.

Cimbolic, P. T. Group Effects on Black Clients' Perceptions of Counselors. *Journal of College Student Personnel,* 1973, 14, 296–302.

Coffin, B.; Dietz, S.; & Thompson, C. Academic Achievement in a Poverty Area High School: Implications for Counseling. *Journal of Negro Education,* 1971, 40, 365–368.

Cross, W. The Negro-to-Black Conversion Experience. *Black World,* 1971, 20, 13–27.

Daley, T. T. Life Ain't Been No Crystal Stair. *Personnel and Guidance Journal,* 1972, 50, 491–496.

Denmark, F.; & Trachtman, J. The Psychologist as Counselor in College 'High Risk' Programs. *The Counseling Psychologist,* 1973, 4, 87–92.

English, W. H. Minority Group Attitudes of Negroes and Implications for Guidance. *Journal of Negro Education,* 1957, 26, 99–107.

Fibush, E. The White Worker and the Negro Client. *Social Casework,* 1965, 36, 271–277.

Gardner, W. E. The Differential Effects of Race, Education and Experience. *Journal of Clinical Psychology,* 1972, 28, 87–89.

Gordon, J. E. Project Cause, the Federal Anti-Poverty Program, and Some Implications of Sub-professional Training. *American Psychologist,* 1965, 20, 334–343.

Gordon, J. E. Counseling the Disadvantaged Boy. In William E. Amos and Jean Dresden Grambs (eds.), *Counseling the Disadvantaged Youth.* New Jersey: Prentice-Hall, 1968.

Gordon, E. W. Perspective on Counseling and Other Approaches to Guided Behavioral Change. *The Counseling Psychologist,* 1970, 2, 105–114. (a)

Gordon, E. W. Guidance in an Urban Setting. *ERIC-IRCD Urban Disadvantaged Series,* 1970, 15, 1–14. (b)

Grantham, R. J. Effects of Counselor Sex, Race, and Language Style on Black Students in Initial Interviews. *Journal of Counseling Psychology,* 1973, 20, 553–559.

Gunnings, T. S.; & Simpkins, G. A Systemic Approach to Counseling Disadvantaged Youth. *Journal of Non-White Concerns,* 1972, 1, 4–8.

Haettenschwiller, D. L. Counseling College Students in Special Programs. *Personnel and Guidance Journal,* 1971, 50, 29–35.

Hardy, R. E.; & Cull, J. G. Verbal Dissimilarity Among Black and White Subjects: A Prime Consideration in Counseling and Communication. *Journal of Negro Education,* 1973, 42, 67–70.

Harper, F. D. What Counselors Must Know About the Social Sciences of Black Americans. *Journal of Negro Education,* 1973, 42, 109–116. (a)

Harper, F. D. Counseling the Poor Child. *Journal of Non-White Concerns,* 1973, 1, 79–84 (b).

Hayes, W. A.; & Banks, W. M. The Nigger Box or a Redefinition of the Counselor's Role. In Reginald L. Jones (ed.), *Black Psychology.* New York: Harper & Row, 1972.

Heffernon, A. R.; & Bruehl, D. Some Effects of Race of Inexperienced Lay Counselors on Black Junior High School Students. *Journal of School Psychology,* 1971, 9, 35–37.

Himes, J. S. Guidance in Negro Secondary Schools in the Southeastern Region. *Journal of Negro Education,* 1948, 17, 106–113.

Hypps, I. C. The Role of the School in Juvenile Delinquency Prevention (With Especial Reference to Pupil Personnel Services). *Journal of Negro Education,* 1959, 28, 318–328.

Irvine, D. J. Needed for Disadvantaged Youth: An Expanded Concept of Counseling. *School Counselor,* 1968, 15, 176–179.

Island, D. Counseling Students with Special Problems. *Review of Educational Research,* 1969, 39, 239–250.

Jackson, G. G. Black Youth as Peer Counselors. *Personnel and Guidance Journal,* 1972, 51, 280–285 (a)

Jackson, G. G. The Use of Roleplaying in Job Interviews With Job Corps Females. *Journal of Employment Counseling,* 1972, 9, 130–139. (b)

Jackson, G. G. & Kirschner, S. A. Racial Self-Designation and Preference for a Counselor. *Journal of Counseling Psychology,* 1973, 20, 560–564.

Job Corps Comes to Bates; Girls Discover Passivity. *Bates College Newspaper,* Lewiston, Maine, January 15, 1969, 7.

Johnson, S. H. Presidential Memo. (Association for Non-White Concerns). In *Personnel and Guidance,* December 18, 1973, 1.

Jones, M. H. & Jones, M. C. The Neglected Client. *Black Scholar,* 1970, 1, 35–42.

Jones, L. Rap's Her Way Fighting Drugs. *New York Amsterdam News,* June 6, 1970, p. L83.

Kadota, P.; & Menacker, J. Community-Based Guidance for the Disadvantaged. *Personnel and Guidance Journal,* 1971, 50, 175–181.

Kendrick, S. A.; & Thomas, C. L. Transition from School to College. *Review of Educational Research,* 1970, 40, 151–174.

Kincaid, M. Identity and Therapy in the Black Community. *Personnel and Guidance Journal,* 1969, 47, 844–890.

Lefkowitz, D.; & Baker, J. Black Youth: A Counseling Experience. *School Counselor*, 1971, 18, 290–293.

Lewis, S. O. Racism Encountered in Counseling. *Counselor Education and Supervision*, 1969, 9, 49–54.

Lewis, M. D.; & Lewis, J. A. Relevant Training for Relevant Roles: A Model for Educating Inner-city Counselor. *Counselor Education and Supervision*, 1970, 10, 31–38.

Lindberg, R.; & Wrenn, C. G. Minority Teachers Become Minority Counselors. *Personnel and Guidance Journal*, 1972, 50, 219–222.

Manley, A. E.; & Himes, J. S. Guidance: A Critical Problem in Negro Secondary Education. *School Review*, 1948, 56, 219–222.

McDaniels, R. Counseling the Disadvantaged Negro. Paper presented at American Personnel and Guidance Association Convention, Monday, April 8, 1968, 1–4.

McGrew, J. M. Counseling the Disadvantaged Child: A Practice in Search of a Rationale. *School Counselor*, 1971, 18, 165–176.

Mickelson, D. & Stevic, R. Preparing Counselors to Meet the Needs of Students. *Counselor Education and Supervision*, 1967, 7, 76–77.

Mitchell, H. The Black Experience in Higher Education. *Counseling Psychologist*, 1970, 2, 30–36.

Patterson, F. D. The Place of Guidance in Education. *Quarterly Review of Higher Education Among Negroes*, 1947, 15, 76–81.

Patterson, L. The Strange Verbal World. *Journal of Non-White Concerns*, 1973, 1, 95–101.

Payne, P. A.; & Mills, R. B. Practicum Placement in a Counseling Employment Agency for Disadvantaged Youth. *Counselor Education and Supervision*, 1970, 9, 189–193.

Phillips, W. Counseling Negro Pupils: An Educational Dilemma. *Journal of Negro Education*, 1960, 29, 504–508.

Phillips, W. Notes From Readers. *Harvard Educational Review*, 1961, 31, 324–326.

Proctor, S. A. Reversing the Spiral Toward Futility. *Personnel and Guidance Journal*, 1970, 48, 707–712.

Record, W. Counseling and Color: Crisis and Conscience. *Integrated Education*, 1966, 4, 34–41.

Rosenthal, R.; & Jacobson, L. F. Teacher Expectations for the Disadvantaged. *Scientific American*, 1968, 19–23.

Rothenberg, L. Relevance is a Many-Splendored Thing. *School Counselor*, 1970, 17, 367–369.

Rousseve, R. J. Counselor Education and the Culturally Isolated: An Alliance for Mutual Benefit. *Journal of Negro Education*, 1965, 4, 395–403.

Rousseve, R. J. Reason and Reality in Counseling the Student-Client Who is Black. *School Counselor*, 1970, 48, 561–567.

Russell, R. D. Guidance Developments in Negro Colleges. *Occupations*, 1949, 27, 25–27.

Russell, R. D. Black Perceptions of Guidance. *Personnel and Guidance Journal*, 1970, 48, 721–728.

Sager, C. J.; Brayboy, T. L.; & Waxenberg, B. R. Black Patient-White Therapist. *American Journal of Orthopsychiatry*, 1972, 42, 415–423.

Sattler, J. M. Racial Experimenter Effects in Experimentation, Testing, Interviewing, and Psychotherapy. *Psychological Bulletin*, 1970, 73, 137–160.

Scheffler, L. M. What 70 SEEK Kids Taught Their Counselor. *New York Times Magazine,* November 16, 1969, 54–55, 109, 110, 112, 114, 116, 119, 120, 122, 126.

Schumacher, L. C.; Banikiotes, P. G.; & Banikiotes, F. G. Language Compatibility and Minority Group Counseling. *Journal of Counseling Psychology,* 1972, 19, 255–256.

Sedlacek, W. E.; & Brooks, G. C. Racism and Research: Using Data to Initiate Change. *Personnel and Guidance Journal,* 1973, 52, 184–188. (a)

Sedlacek, W. E.; Brooks, G. C. Racism in the Public Schools: A Model for Change. *Journal of Non-White Concerns,* 1973, 1, 133–143.

Siegel, B. Counseling the Color-Conscious. *School Counselor,* 1970, 17, 168–170.

Simpkins, G.; Gunnings, T.; & Kearney, A. The Black Six-Hour Retarded Child. *Journal of Non-White Concerns,* 1973, 2, 29–34.

Smith, D. H. The White Counselor in the Negro Slum School. *School Counselor,* 1967, 14, 268–272.

Smith, P. M. Counselors for Ghetto Youth. *Personnel and Guidance Journal,* 1968, 47, 279–281.

Smith, P. M. Alienation or APGA's Black Image. *Personnel and Guidance Journal,* 1970, 18, 312.

Smith, P. M. The Role of the Guidance Counselor in the Desegregation Process. *Journal of Negro Education,* 1971, 11, 347–351. (a)

Smith, P. M. Black Activists for Liberation, Not Guidance. *Personnel and Guidance Journal,* 1971, 49, 721–726. (b)

Smith, P. M. Help: Change the Emphasis. *Journal of Non-White Concerns,* 1973, 2, 42–45.

Stikes, C. S. Culturally Specific Counseling—The Black Client. *Journal of Non-White Concerns,* 1972, 1, 15–23.

Stranges, R. J.; & Riccio, A. C. Counselee Preference for Counselors: Some Implications for Counselor Education. *Counselor Education and Supervision,* 1970, 10, 39–45.

Sue, S. Training of "Third-World" Students to Function as Counselors. *Journal of Counseling Psychology,* 1973, 20, 73–78.

Taylor, P. Research for Liberation: Shaping a New Black Identity in America. *Black World,* 1973, 22, 7, 4–14, 65–72.

Thomas, A. Pseudo-Transference Reactions Due to Cultural Stereotyping. *American Journal of Orthopsychiatry,* 1962, 32, 894–900.

Toldson, I. L. The Human Potential Movement and Black Unity: Counseling Blacks in Groups. *Journal of Non-White Concerns,* 1973, 1, 69–76.

Toldson, I. L.; & Pasteur, A. B. Soul Music: Techniques for Therapeutic Intervention. *Journal of Non-White Concerns,* 1972, 1, 31–39.

Tolson, N. Counseling the 'Disadvantaged.' *Personnel and Guidance Journal,* 1972, 50, 735–738.

Trueblood, D. L. The Role of the Counselor in the Guidance of Negro Students. *Harvard Educational Review,* 1960, 30, 324–326.

Tucker, S. J. Action Counseling: An Accountability Procedure for Counseling the Oppressed. *Journal of Non-White Concerns,* 1973, 2, 35–41.

Vontress, C. E. Counseling Negro Adolescents. *School Counselor,* 1967, 15, 86–91.
Vontress, C. E. Counseling Negro Students for College. *Journal of Negro Education,* 1968, 37, 37–44.
Vontress, C. E. Cultural Differences: Implications for Counseling. *Journal of Negro Education,* 1969, 37, 266–275. (a)
Vontress, C. E. Cultural Barriers in the Counseling Relationship, *Personnel and Guidance Journal,* 1969, 48, 11–17. (b)
Vontress, C. E. Racial Differences: Impediments to Rapport. *Journal of Counseling Psychology,* 1971, 18, 7–13.
Vontress, C. E. The Black Militant as a Counselor. *Personnel and Guidance Journal,* 1972, 50, 574, 576–580.
Vontress, C. E. Counseling the Racial and Ethnic Minorities. *Focus on Guidance,* 1973, 5, 1–12.
Vriend, T. High-Performing Inner-City Adolescents Assist Low-Performing Peers in Counseling Groups. *Personnel and Guidance Journal,* 1969, 47, 897–904.
Ward, E. J. A Gift from the Ghetto. *Personnel and Guidance Journal,* 1970, 48, 753–756.
Washington, B. Perceptions and Possibilities. *Personnel and Guidance Journal,* 1970, 48, 757–761.
Washington, K. S. What Counselors Must Know About Black Power. *Personnel and Guidance Journal,* 1968, 47, 204–208.
Washington, K. S. & Anderson, N. J. Scarcity of Black Counselors: A Crisis in Urban Education. *Journal of Non-White Concerns,* 1974, 2, 99–105.
Waters, E. W. Problems of Rural Negro High School Seniors on the Eastern Shore of Maryland: A Consideration for Guidance. *Journal of Negro Education,* 1953, 22, 115–125.
Williams, C. T. Special Consideration in Counseling. *Journal of Educational Sociology,* 1949, 22, 608–613.
Williams, R. L.; & Kirland, J. The White Counselor and the Black Client. *Counseling Psychologist,* 1971, 4, 114–116.

11 Dimensions of the Relationship between the Black Client and the White Therapist
A Theoretical Overview
Alison Jones
Arthur A. Seagull

ABSTRACT: The psychological issues involved in having white therapists treat black clients are explored. The topics examined are the importance of the white therapist understanding his or her own feelings, countertransference, the detrimental effect of therapist guilt, and the impact of the therapist's need to be powerful. Also explored are the need for awareness of client-therapist interpersonal similarity and the need for an understanding of our social system for effective psychotherapy. Concrete suggestions are offered for helping therapists deal more effectively with black clients. The white-therapist—black-client relationship is proposed as a paradigm of how people with differing values learn to help each other.

The issue of white therapists treating black clients is complicated by the fact that blacks in this country have been systematically oppressed economically, politically, educationally, and socially for hundreds of years by whites (Frazier, 1965; Kardiner & Ovesey, 1951); that is, racism is deeply embedded in our predominantly white culture (Clark, 1965). Against that background, questions about how and in what capacity whites can help blacks in a counseling situation are extremely relevant, especially since white persons far outnumber black persons in the helping professions, and blacks are going to request their fair share of mental health resources. So, white therapists are going to have black clients to counsel. Given this reality, in this article we examine the conditions under which white counselors can be of most assistance to black clients and make concrete suggestions about ways of understanding and handling areas of difficulty.

White Feelings

First, the white therapist working with black clients must examine and understand his or her feelings about blacks. Quite obviously, a white therapist who has blatantly racist attitudes toward blacks should not counsel blacks. (In fact, people with this pathology should be in therapy themselves.) However, for the therapist not in this category, introspection regarding his or her own racial attitudes is still essential. Rosen and Frank (1962), two white psychiatrists, state, "Few of us are entirely free from race prejudice; with some, this is overt; with others it may be below the level of conscious awareness" (p. 456). Further, according to Sager, Brayboy, and Waxenberg (1972), "This latent reserve of racism, this submerged sense that the black man is 'different,' not governed by the white's warm, human emotions or worthy motivations, is part of our American heritage" (p. 417).

The prejudiced, ill-trained, or inexperienced may stereotypically see blacks as nonverbal, concrete, and hence ill-suited for psychotherapy. They may see blacks as a group as untrusting and with character disorders that are unchangeable (Pinderhughes, 1973). But such preconceived notions may elicit these very responses as self-fulfilling prophesies.

Furthermore, white therapists who view all blacks as "culturally deprived," "disadvantaged," "underprivileged," etc., are demonstrating the subtle form of racism inherent in the use of these labels and are simply misinformed. For example, although black culture differs from white culture and has different forms and assumptions, it would be ethnocentric to label it deprived. According to Vontress (1969),

> The problem is not that certain population segments are without culture; rather it seems to be that the powerful dominant cultural group rejects subcultural groups in society. By their rejection, they convey the notion that those unlike themselves are inferior, deprived, or disadvantaged. (p. 12)

If the therapist views blacks stereotypically, she or he neither sees nor treats an individual (Kagan, 1964). As Calia (1966) warns, "Such generalizations lead to categorical prescriptions and the attendant loss of the client's uniqueness and worth" (p. 102). Tolson (1972) adds, "Some of these adjectives, such as 'black,' have become so culturally powerful that they control our perceptions and thereby limit our ability to apply what we know to be good counseling techniques" (p. 735). One must accept that such stereotypical attitudes are held by most whites toward blacks, and it is important that these feelings be understood and "owned" so that one does not unknowingly let them interfere in the therapeutic process.

This is not to say, however, that these stereotyped client behaviors may not sometimes be manifested by fearful blacks (or whites) in therapists' offices. But, we insist, "nonverbal," "mumbling," "unsophisticated," "nonconceptualizing" clients may be responding with a 300-year-old method called "shuckin," which was used by field slaves as a defense against their masters (Foster, 1974). It has been successfully utilized by other groups that feel oppressed and powerless, such as adolescents (Foster, 1974), incarcerated prisoners, who call it "dummying up" (Spewack & Spewack, 1953), and concentration camp inmates (Bettleheim, 1960; Frankl, 1963).

One fights the oppressor with the weapons one has. If weakness is what one has, one uses that. For example, Gandhi forced the British to give up India through nonviolent resistance, the limiting case of powerlessness used as a power maneuver (Ghandi, 1960). Haley (1971) made the same point in his provocative essay "The Power Tactics of Jesus Christ."

The issue in therapy should not be that the client acts as if she or he had no power, but that she or he cannot exhibit other behaviors when she or he wishes, even though the old pattern has proved ineffective, demeaning, and ultimately destructive and leads to a loss of positive self-concept. The task of the therapist is to help the client distinguish when the use of powerlessness is to his or her advantage, and when other forms of interaction seem more efficacious, such as self-disclosure, retreat, confrontation, distraction, or flattery.

As to the alleged "lack of verbal skills" of the black, lower-socioeconomic-level client, the problem may lie in the situation or in the examiner's lack of skill. What are the verbal skills of a black youth who composes the following poetic insult?

> Aw, man, you trying to show you grandma how to milk ducks. Best you can do is to confidence some kitchen-mechanic out of a dime or two. Me, I knocks de pad with them cack-broads up on Sugar Hill and fills 'em full of melody. Man, I'm quick death and easy judgement. Youse just a home-byoy [sic], Jelly, don't try to follow me. (Foster, 1974, p. 220)

Now imagine how this same black person would speak if sent to a white therapist by his parole officer!

It is interesting to note that therapists who would reject a client's complaints that he can "do nothing" about an inability to argue with a friend or maintain an erection, tend to accept without further investigation a client's seeming inability to verbalize feelings. Yet the differences between a black client and a white therapist can be enormous. They may differ in color, sex, socioeconomic level, vocabulary, accent, syntax, mores, religion, and attitude toward time. They meet, perhaps, in the therapist's well-appointed business suite, within a posh office building, in an unfamiliar part of town for an appointment exactly 50 minutes long! And the therapist then wonders why the client doesn't express his deepest feelings.

Clients may also seem "nonverbal" because one does not speak their language (Bernstein, 1958; Foster, 1974), one fears their rage (Grier & Cobbs, 1969), one exhibits countertransference (Vontress, 1971), one lacks knowledge and skill (Foster, 1974), or because of a subtly racist assumption that blacks are inherently less intelligent (Jensen, 1969). So there may be reluctance to challenge the client's use of lack of verbal clarity as a defense (Foster, 1974).

Countertransference

Countertransference occurs when a therapist does not fully understand and acknowledge his or her own feelings and it influences the therapy. Stereotypic reactions toward blacks are also countertransference. According to Vontress (1971), "Countertransference refers to the counselor's reacting to the counselee as he has reacted to someone else in his past. It means that the white counselor unconsciously perceives the black counselee as he always has perceived other blacks" (p. 9). Since many white counselors have middle-class values and mores, they may well bring with them certain feelings about and attitudes toward blacks, which may influence the process of therapy negatively. Because therapy is ambiguous and unstructured, it is possible for the therapist to influence its process by the emotional reactions she or he has toward the client.

Bloch (1968), in "The White Worker and the Negro Client in Psychotherapy," discussed the symbolic value of black persons for whites in America and its influence on the course of therapy. She observed that whites have projected their own unacceptable drives and impulses on to blacks, who are then seen as being supersexual or more aggressive than the white norm. An uninsightful white therapist may feel threatened by his or her own repressions in treating a black client and may thus tend to protect his or her own comfort in the setting at the expense of the client (see Pinderhughes, 1973).

The white therapist must understand his or her own motivation for working with black clients if he or she seeks them out. According to Vontress (1971),

> Productive counseling depends on the ability of the counselor to permit himself to become a part of the total counseling situation. . . . The counselor must know what he is doing and why, and this is not possible unless he understands to some degree his own psychodynamics and his cultural conditioning. (p. 12)

Therapists must understand their own feelings to deal effectively with minority clients or those differing from them on other powerful dimensions such as age, sex, religion, politics, sexual mores or preferences, wealth, or education.

Guilt and the White Conscience

Guilt about their own racism motivates some whites who want to counsel blacks and seek them as clients. Such a therapist is likely to be quite *in*effective. First, according to Heine (1950), a person acting from feelings of guilt is likely to identify with the client and to be too sympathetic to be of much assistance. This type of counselor is likely to fear a realistic confrontation and try to be ingratiating, so that the chance to use the therapy relationship as a springboard for reality testing is lost.

Second, feelings of guilt on the part of the therapist are likely to communicate to the client that the therapist is anxious, which will cause the client to strengthen his or her defenses and cease to explore certain areas either in deference to or from compassion for the therapist, or because the client correctly senses that the therapist will not be helpful for that problem.

Third, guilt feelings on the therapist's part can cause the therapist to become overzealous in helping the black client. "Trying too hard" can defeat therapy. If the therapist is working very hard to help, and the client chooses not to respond to the therapist's efforts to help him or her, the therapist can become angry with the client and, through lack of self-awareness, thwart the client's progress.

Fourth, the guilt-ridden therapist may tend to react defensively or to misperceive the black client's rage (Grier & Cobb, 1969) and hence, rather than encouraging the expression of anger, discourage it. Or the therapist may waste time trying to prove to the client that he or she is different from other whites.

Fifth, the therapist who is motivated by a sense of guilt may easily become unrealistic about the client's real-life problems. He or she will not be respected by the client, and hence will be of little value to the black person.

Any of the above could make therapy ineffective, since the dishonest relationship on which the therapy would be based would make the interaction essentially "duplicitous," in Kaiser's phrase (Fierman, 1965). That is, the therapist would be saying through his or her behavior, "I will appear empathetic, but I am motivated by my own sense of guilt rather than by true concern for the client."

The Need to Be Powerful

Some whites counseling blacks exhibit a need to be powerful and to be in a dominating role. According to Pinderhughes (1973),

> One problem area for many patients lies in the unconscious needs of many psychotherapists to be in helping, knowledgeable, or controlling roles. Unwittingly they wish to be initiators and have patients accommodate to them or to their style or approach. More Black patients than White perceive in this kind of relationship the basic ingredients of a master-slave pattern. (p. 104)

The therapist trying to meet this need is likely to behave in a paternalistic, patronizing fashion toward the client. For example, the therapist might see all of the client's problems as stemming from his or her blackness rather than being able to see him or her as a human being who has racial concerns. Needing to help the black client for one's own power needs constitutes "the great white father syndrome" (Vontress, 1971) and is condescending, paternalistic, and ultimately enraging.

> The counselor must communicate to the black client that he is not only somewhat omnipotent (probably because he is white) but that he literally guarantees the black counselee that he can "deliver," if he will only put himself in his hands. Simultaneously, he communicates, albeit unconsciously, the implication that if the black client does not depend on him, he will be doomed to catastrophe. (Vontress, 1971, p. 9)

The dangers stemming from the "great white father syndrome" are apparent. If the counselor assumes an omnipotent, all-knowing role, the chances of the client feeling helpless and at his or her mercy are increased. This role parallels the client's problem vis-à-vis society and hence is counterproductive.

Those who counsel blacks should be familiar with and understand black culture, life-styles, and heritage. The counselor should have some feel for what the client's environment and experiences are like if he or she is going to be of help. According to Sager et al. (1972),

> It is essential that the therapist know and, more importantly, want to know and to understand the living conditions, cultural patterns, and value systems of the people he seeks to help. Without this appreciation it may be difficult for persons removed from the ghetto to accept the style of life of those who are part of it and to refrain from attempting to impose a Puritan-ethic-tinged morality upon it. (p. 417)

The Role of Client-Therapist Similarity

Real awareness of interpersonal similarity between client and therapist is essential. It increases the ability of the counselor to accept, understand, and emphathize with clients and permits unconditional positive regard, genuineness, and empathy, which are emotional ingredients required for effective, growth-promoting relationships (Rogers, 1962). Accordingly to Calia (1966), the qualities of unconditional positive regard and empathy correlate positively with perceived similarity between counselor and counselee. Although a white person can never become black, certainly his or her familiarity with blacks and black culture will help to decrease the interpersonal differences between them.

The issue is even more complex. Hollingshead and Redlich (1958) found that counselors had better feelings toward clients of their own social class, a finding that supports the importance of perceived similarity for acceptance by a therapist. When therapists have an understanding of themselves and their clients, they will try to be open and honest, which means taking the risk of not being accepted by their clients. If therapists present therapeutic facades or personae, they will most likely be seen as insincere and will have trouble establishing relationships.

The establishment of trust, which is essential for self-disclosure in therapy, also increases as the similarities between the therapist and client increase (Jourard, 1964). According to Vontress (1971), "People disclose themselves when they are fairly sure that the target person (the person to whom they are disclosing) will evaluate their disclosures and react to them as they, themselves, do" (p. 10). (See also, for example, Bienenfeld and Seagull [Note 1], for a case study illustrating the resolution of culturally determined misunderstandings between a middle-class, white therapist and a tough, black, welfare client.) Thus, a therapist with a knowledge of a client's culture and background will be perceived as being more similar to the client and hence will be better able to establish an effective, productive relationship.

There is experimental support for the position that prejudice is a function of perceived differences in belief systems (Rokeach, 1960; Stein, Hardyck, & Smith, 1965). "The prejudiced person does not reject a person of another race, religion, or nationality because of his ethnic membership per se, but rather because he perceives that the other differs from him in important beliefs and values" (Stein et al., 1965, p. 281). Having the white counselor learn about the black perspective can help dispel his or her stereotypes. In doing so, he or she will gain a better understanding of black society and help bridge the gap between himself or herself and the client. She or he will become realistic about the problems presented.

Understanding Our Social System

Understanding our social system and the ways in which blacks in this country have been oppressed, discriminated against, and systematically denied equal opportunity is essential for a white therapist working with black clients. It is no service simply to fit black people back into the society that has trapped them. According to Gladwin (1968), "The clinic does the walking wounded of the Negro community no favor by patching them up and sending them back into battle against a system everyone knows they cannot beat" (p. 479). Psychotherapy can be oppressive rather than constructive, according to Pinderhughes (1973):

> Many psychotherapists have value systems which encourage them to help patients to adjust to oppressive conditions rather than to seek changes in the conditions. . . . This is one reason why psychotherapy has sometimes been labeled as an opiate or instrument of oppression. (p. 99)

Instead of merely helping the black client adjust to a destructive social system, goals for therapy should include helping the client work for change in that system if the client so desires. Further, Kincaid (1969) emphasizes that the counselor who is truly working in the black client's best interests will encourage him or her in making choices that may be alien to the values of mainstream, middle-class America. She says,

If the counselor is committed to his client's freedom, then he must see his task as one of helping black clients understand the discrepancy between their values and those of the larger society and make choices based on their own values, free of the threat of external evaluation and condemnation by the counselor for "wrong choices." (p. 887)

And finally, the white therapist working with black clients should be sensitive to the clients' needs, rather than working within his or her own rigid framework and imposing his or her own goals. The counselor should discover the clients' needs and wants. For example, the therapist does a grave disservice to any client by insisting on approaching the client in a traditional manner when the client comes in with questions about how to live in the slums with rats and roaches, how to make ends meet on a welfare budget, where to take the children when both parents go to work, etc. The therapist owes it to the client to deal with these more immediate real-life problems, either directly or through referral, before dealing with intrapsychic issues. In the statement, "I'll talk about my father if you want me to, but you have to know that there's no food to feed my kids tonight," lies a real dilemma. However, it can also be destructive for a therapist, white or black, to insist that the black client become more politically aware and fight for racial or social betterment if this is not what the *client* perceives as his or her problem. (See Foster, 1974, especially p. 245.) This is not to say that the aims of the therapist may not be moral or valid, but only that the client must set the goal with the therapist. There is a contradiction inherent in having the client blindly follow the dictates, however well-meaning, of the therapist, and that is that the client must be completely dependent in order to learn autonomy! (See Seagull and Johnson [1968] for a discussion of this issue, which we termed "the problem of form and function.")

If the therapist is to help the client meet his or her own needs and grow, it is essential that the therapist understand what the client is saying or asking for before working for change. For example, the counselor who interprets the black client's expression of anger toward whites as displacement, transference, or a defense against dealing with other issues, as does Adams (1950) in his article "The Negro Patient in Psychiatric Treatment," both undermines the client's trust and interferes with his or her reality testing. According to Gochros (1966), "In denying the validity of just complaints or by seeing the mere voicing of anger as an end in itself . . . workers may appear to the client as either insincere or ineffectual" (p. 34). Further, Sager et al. (1972) state,

It can be disastrous for the therapist either to deny the suspicion and hostility of the black patient or to feel guilty that these negative sentiments exist. The therapist works with these powerful negative feelings as distortion and resistance when they are unfounded, and, conversely, accepts them when they are accurate. (p. 417)

It is essential for the therapist to understand the client and to work toward having black clients gain pride in themselves, their culture, and their identity just as he or she would for any other clients. Wilson (1971) sums up the direction in which we feel therapy should move when he says,

Counselors should relate to clients with cultural differences in ways that will enhance the cultural identities of their clients. Counselors should relate to clients in ways which will permit the cultural identities of their clients to become positive sources of pride and major motivators of behavior. To do less is to denigrate a client's identity. To do less is to ask a client to give up his values in order to participate in the dominant culture. To do less is to contribute to the destruction of life; and our mission is not to destroy life but to enhance life. (p. 424)

The White Therapist—Alternatives

So what can be done by white therapists who want to help those who come to them yet who feel that they lack the requisite skills or harbor some racist feelings of which they are not proud but which are real none the less? Clearly the first step is self-knowledge, just as it would be for any therapist who found that she or he harbored irrational or potentially destructive feelings. Talking to colleagues, white and black, about it, playing tapes for colleagues, or organizing discussion groups and arranging speakers on the topic through professional groups would be useful.

Second, the issue of color difference should be brought up early in the relationship, certainly not later than the second session, preferably in the first. "I wonder if the fact that I'm white and you are black is affecting our working together?" "How do you feel about that?" The therapist must be willing to explore the issues in depth, including being willing to verbalize nonverbal cues indicating that the client is telling the therapist what she or he feels the therapist wants to hear. The white therapist should model such openness by examining his or her own feelings if they are relevant to the relationship.

Third, books can be read that give one a view of black culture, aspirations, and mores. And fourth, a willingness to accept one's own fallibility with some humor and wry grace is helpful. Therapists are not perfect, but their openness to change is the one attribute they possess that allows them to try to help others.

Foster (1974, pp. 243–245) writes of the traits necessary for the "natural inner-city teacher" to teach black children successfully. We think the concepts are relevant to the white therapist who genuinely wants to help black clients. The assumptions underlying these traits are honesty, interpersonal/personal integrity, and a respect for others as human beings, which includes the belief that people can learn to change. In a larger sense, these issues of black-white interaction are really the most salient example of the constant, basic issue in therapy—namely, How do we treat with dignity and positive regard those who differ from us on some major dimension such as age, color, wealth, sex, politics, religion, sexual mores, or personal beliefs? This is the task of the "helping professions" and a task, basically, for the whole country.

Reference Note

1. Bienenfeld, S., & Seagull, A. A. *Treating a difficult black client: Some observations by a white therapist in supervision.* Manuscript submitted for publication, 1977.

References

Adams, W. A. The Negro patient in psychiatric treatment. *American Journal of Orthopsychiatry,* 1950, *20,* 305–310.

Bernstein, B. A. Some sociological determinants of perception—An inquiry into subculture differences. *The British Journal of Sociology,* 1958, *9,* 159–174.

Bettelheim, B. *The informed heart; Autonomy in a mass age.* Glencoe, Ill.: Free Press, 1960.

Bloch, J. B. The white worker and the Negro client in psychotherapy. *Social Work,* 1968, *13*(2), 36–42.

Calia, V. F. The culturally deprived client: A re-formulation of the counselor's role. *Journal of Counseling Psychology,* 1966, *13,* 100–105.

Clark, K. *Dark ghetto.* New York: Harper & Row, 1965.

Fierman, L. B. (Ed.). *Effective psychotherapy: The contribution of Hellmuth Kaiser.* New York: Free Press, 1965.

Foster, H. L. *Ribbin', jivin', and playin' the dozens: The unrecognized dilemma of inner city schools.* Cambridge, Mass.: Ballinger, 1974.

Frankl, V. E. *Man's search for meaning; An introduction to logotherapy.* Boston: Beacon Press, 1963.

Frazier, E. F. *Black bourgeoisie.* New York: Free Press, 1965.

Gandhi, M. K. [*An autobiography; The story of my experiments with truth*] (M. Desai, Trans.). Boston: Beacon Press, 1960.

Gladwin, T. The mental health service as conspirator. *Community Mental Health Journal,* 1968, *4,* 475–481.

Gochros, J. S. Recognition and use of anger in Negro clients. *Journal of Social Work,* 1966, *11,* 28–34.

Grier, W. H., & Cobbs, P. M. *Black rage.* New York: Bantam Books, 1969.

Haley, J. *The power tactics of Jesus Christ, and other essays.* New York: Avon, 1971.

Heine, R. W. The Negro patient in psychotherapy. *Journal of Clinical Psychology,* 1950, *6,* 373–376.

Hollingshead, A. B., & Redlich, F. C. *Social class and mental illness.* New York: Wiley, 1958.

Jensen, A. R. How much can we boost IQ and scholastic achievement? *Harvard Educational Review,* 1969, *39,* 1–123.

Jourard, S. M. *The transparent self.* Princeton, N.J.: Van Nostrand, 1964.

Kagan, N. Three dimensions of counselor encapsulation. *Journal of Counseling Psychology,* 1964, *11,* 361–365.

Kardiner, A., & Ovesey, L. *The mark of oppression.* New York: Norton, 1951.

Kincaid, M. Identity and therapy in the black community. *Personnel and Guidance Journal,* 1969, *47,* 884–890.

Pinderhughes, C. A. Racism and psychotherapy. In C. Willie, B. Kramer, & B. Brown (Eds.), *Racism and mental health.* Pittsburgh: University of Pittsburgh Press, 1973.

Rogers, C. R. The interpersonal relationship: The core of guidance. *Harvard Educational Review,* 1962, *32,* 416–429.

Rokeach, M. (Ed.). *The open and closed mind.* New York: Basic Books, 1960.

Rosen, H., & Frank, J. D. Negroes in psychotherapy. *American Journal of Psychiatry,* 1962, *119,* 456–460.

Sager, C. J., Brayboy, T. L., & Waxenberg, B. R. Black patient—white therapist. *American Journal of Orthopsychiatry,* 1972, *42,* 415–423.

Seagull, A. A., & Johnson, J. H. ". . . But do as I preach": Form and function in the affective training of teachers. *Phi Delta Kappan,* 1968, *50,* 166–170.

Spewack, S., & Spewack, B. *My three angels.* New York: Random House, 1953.

Stein, D. D., Hardyck, J. A., & Smith, M. B. Race and belief: An open and shut case. *Journal of Personality and Social Psychology,* 1965, *1,* 281–289.

Tolson, H. Counseling the "disadvantaged." *Personnel and Guidance Journal,* 1972, *50,* 735–738.

Vontress, C. E. Cultural differences: Implications for counseling. *Journal of Negro Education,* 1969, *38,* 266–275.

Vontress, C. E. Racial differences: Impediments to rapport. *Journal of Counseling Psychology,* 1971, *18,* 7–13.

Wilson, M. E. The significance of communication in counseling the culturally disadvantaged. In R. Wilcox (Ed.), *The psychological consequences of being a black American.* New York: Wiley, 1971.

12 Counseling Black Clients Effectively
The Eclectic Approach
Roderick J. McDavis

Drawings/ drawn from varied Sources

Several articles have been written that suggest specific counseling approaches and techniques for counselors to use with Black clients. Gunnings and Simpkins (1972) described an approach in which the counselor works to change the system and helps clients learn strategies to cope with the system. This approach is based on the assumption that most problems that were labeled client problems are in fact system problems. Tucker (1973) discussed an action-counseling approach in which the counselor helps clients establish specific goals and attempts to increase the emotional involvement of clients through the arousal of clients' expectancies and hopes. This approach emphasizes an aggressive commitment on the part of the counselor to mobilize the clients' expectancies for help and some direct action by the counselor to help clients attain stated goals. Harper and Stone (1974) presented a theory of transcendent counseling in which the counselor helps clients to satisfy basic needs, develop new life-styles, and transcend racism. This theory advocates that counselors use supportive, directive, action-oriented, and information-giving approaches and techniques with Black clients. All three approaches are specifically designed for counselors to use with Black clients; however, it is not necessary to develop or learn a completely new approach to counsel Black clients effectively. Existing counseling approaches contain many concepts and techniques that can be used effectively with Black clients.

This article proposes the eclectic approach for counseling Black clients effectively. The eclectic approach combines concepts and techniques from six existing counseling approaches. These six approaches are the behavioral, client centered, existential, Gestalt, rational-emotive, and reality. The first part of the article presents the philosophy of the eclectic approach that incorporates concepts from the existential, client-centered, and reality counseling approaches. The second part of the article describes the techniques of the eclectic approach drawn from the behavioral, Gestalt, and rational-emotive counseling approaches. The article concludes with a discussion of ways in which counselors can use the eclectic approach with Black clients.

Philosophy of the Eclectic Approach

The philosophy of the eclectic approach includes concepts drawn from the existential, client-centered, and reality counseling approaches. The concept from the existential approach is its philosophical orientation. The concepts from the client-centered approach are acceptance, understanding, and congruence. The concepts from the reality approach are involvement in the counseling process, not making value judgments about the client's behavior, and encouraging clients to be committed to a plan of action. Counselors can use these concepts to develop positive attitudes toward Black clients, to establish rapport with Black clients, and to develop more effective counseling relationships with Black clients.

Counselors can develop positive attitudes toward Black clients by integrating the philosophical orientation of the existential counseling approach. Existentialism is a school of thought that is concerned with individuals and their attempts to retain their identities, make their own choices, and provide their own self-directions (Strickland 1966). In a practical sense the existential counselor tries to understand clients as they exist in their own worlds (Shertzer & Stone 1974). For counselors, this approach means viewing Black clients as unique and different. The approach also means learning the culture, life-style, and language of Black clients as well as trying to understand what these clients are experiencing.

How can counselors do this? The most effective way is for counselors to place themselves in situations that enable them to feel what it is like to be different. Attending social affairs sponsored by Black organizations, such as dances, parties, and picnics, is one way to understand how it feels to be a member of a minority group. Also, by eating meals with Blacks at Black community restaurants and having informal conversations with Blacks, counselors can begin to learn the culture, life-style, and language of Blacks. Counselors can also use these existential concepts to eliminate whatever negative attitudes they hold toward Blacks and to develop positive attitudes toward Black clients. The aim is to become a counselor who believes that all people have an inherent right to retain their identities, make their own choices, and be self-directed individuals.

Carl Rogers, originator of the client-centered approach, believes that counselors should bring acceptance, understanding, and congruence to the counseling relationship and communicate these characteristics to the client in order to establish rapport and an effective counseling relationship (Cunningham & Peters 1973). It is important for counselors to communicate acceptance and understanding to Black clients during the first counseling session to demonstrate their sincere and genuine interest in these clients and their personal concerns. It is just as important for counselors to be congruent, meaning that there should be no contradiction between what counselors say and what they do (Cunningham & Peters 1973). Congruent counselors are open, honest, and not afraid to be themselves with Black clients.

How can counselors communicate these concepts to Black clients? By sharing some personal information or making small talk counselors can verbally communicate these concepts to Black clients. This approach shows the client that the counselor is a real person. A warm smile, a firm handshake, and a relaxed manner are nonverbal ways of expressing these concepts to Black clients. Essentially, the idea is to make Black clients feel comfortable and secure when they come for counseling so that they are more willing to discuss their personal concerns. It is important to remember that unless rapport has been established with any client, the chances of developing an effective counseling relationship are slim. Counselors who are able to communicate acceptance, understanding, and congruence during the initial interview are better able to establish rapport with Black clients.

The reality counseling approach developed by William Glasser provides three concepts that counselors can use to develop more effective counseling relationships with Black clients. One concept of the reality approach is that counselors should be involved in counseling relationships (Glasser & Zunin 1973). Basic to reality counseling is the idea that counselors discuss their own experiences with clients. A second concept is that counselors should not make value judgments about clients' behavior (Glasser & Zunin 1973). Reality counseling asks clients to make a value judgment as to whether their behavior is responsible and therefore good for them and those with whom they are involved (Glasser & Zunin 1973). A third concept is that counselors should encourage clients to be committed to carry out a plan of action (Glasser & Zunin 1973).

How can counselors use these concepts with Black clients? First, use of the pronouns I, you, and we by counselors and clients is encouraged because it facilitates involvement by counselors and clients in the counseling process (Glasser & Zunin 1973). It is important that counselors share their own experiences with Black clients because these experiences serve as models for these clients and show them that counselors are willing to disclose themselves. Thus, it becomes less threatening for Black clients to disclose their own experiences. Second, counselors should not make value judgments about Black clients' behavior but rather guide them to an evaluation of their own behavior. Because Black clients may hold values different from those of the counselors, counselors should not judge Black clients' behavior as good or bad but rather seek to help them understand how their values can lead to a happier life. By not making value judgments about Black clients' behavior, counselors are able to facilitate personal growth with them. Third, if counselors have shared some of the behavior changes they have made in their own lives and have accepted and not judged the behavior of Black clients as good or bad, these clients may be more open to commit themselves to a plan of action to change their behavior.

Techniques of the Eclectic Approach

The techniques of the eclectic approach are drawn from the behavioral, Gestalt, and rational-emotive counseling approaches. The techniques include goal setting, role playing, and modeling from the behavioral approach; enhancing awareness and sharing hunches from the Gestalt approach; and the ABC method and homework assignments from the rational-emotive approach.

The behavioral approach contains three techniques that counselors can use to help Black clients find solutions to their personal concerns. Goal setting, role playing, and modeling can help Black clients learn to acquire those behaviors that they believe will help them become better individuals. For example, many Black clients perceive the counseling relationship as a process in which both the counselor and client are actively involved in seeking solutions to their concerns. By assisting Black clients to set realistic goals for the counseling relationship, counselors can demonstrate that they are willing to share their thoughts and feelings with these clients and that the clients' concerns can be resolved. Role playing and modeling are effective ways in which counselors can help Black clients acquire new behaviors because they emphasize demonstrating appropriate behavior. Through both of these techniques counselors and clients are actively involved in the counseling process. Counselors can use these behavioral techniques to counsel Black clients if the techniques are used in a spirit of cooperation.

Frederick Perls's theory of Gestalt counseling offers some techniques that counselors can use to help Black clients understand themselves and their environments. The aim of Gestalt counseling is to assist individuals to discover that they need not depend on others but can be independent (Shertzer & Stone 1974). A major focus of Gestalt counseling is to help the individual make the transition from environmental support to self-support (Shertzer & Stone 1974). In counseling Black clients, counselors must keep in mind that although society may provide obstacles or impasses for Black clients, it is necessary for them to overcome these impediments and become fully functioning, responsible individuals.

Gestalt counseling contains several techniques that can help Black clients to become more aware of themselves and their environments. Enhancing awareness is a Gestalt technique that helps clients focus their attention on immediate behavior (Shertzer & Stone 1974). Counselors can help Black clients become aware of their present behavior by asking how and what questions. Many Black clients' concerns are a part of their immediate past experiences, and these need to be resolved during the first counseling session. By enhancing Black clients' awareness of their concerns, counselors demonstrate that they are ready to offer immediate help.

Sharing hunches is a Gestalt technique that encourages clients to explore inner feelings (Shertzer & Stone 1974). By introducing statements about clients' concerns with phrases such as I see you as being or I imagine that you feel, counselors can help Black clients discuss their feelings and concerns in more depth. Because many Black clients are emotional and want counselors to become actively involved in the counseling relationship, sharing hunches can help Black clients see that counselors are listening to them, are aware of their emotions, and want to hear more about their concerns.

Albert Ellis's theory of rational-emotive counseling provides two techniques that counselors can use to help Black clients become more rational problem-solving individuals. These techniques are the ABC method and the use of homework assignments. The ABC method is the application of principles from rational-emotive counseling that helps clients to change their irrational thinking or beliefs to rational thinking or beliefs (Cunningham & Peters 1973). This method encourages clients to use rational thinking to control their emotions. Counselors' active role in this method can motivate Black clients to think in ways that help them solve their own problems. For Black clients who seek concrete ideas and suggestions for resolving their concerns, the ABC method can be quite effective.

Also, the use of homework assignments with Black clients provides ways for them to work on solutions to their concerns outside counseling relationships. These assignments should be practical; that is, they should be assignments that clients can accomplish (Cunningham & Peters 1973). The assignments should be jointly agreed on by counselor and client to ensure that both parties understand what is to be done by the client. Both the use of the ABC method and homework assignments are techniques that counselors can use to help Black clients reach practical solutions to their concerns and develop rational ways of thinking. There is no specific time during the counseling relationship when the concepts or techniques of the eclectic approach should be used. Rather, the primary aim is for counselors to consider individual differences among Black clients and the nature of the clients' concern and be prepared to respond by using one or more of these concepts and techniques. For example, if Black clients come to counseling for help in establishing better interpersonal relationships, goal setting, role playing, or modeling are effective techniques for counselors to use because these techniques emphasize demonstrating appropriate behavior and involving counselors and clients in the counseling process. On the other hand, if Black clients come to counseling because of a disagreement with a family member, enhancing awareness and sharing hunches are effective techniques for counselors to use because these techniques help clients focus on their concerns and become aware of their feelings.

The eclectic approach is flexible in that it can be adapted to meet the individual needs of Black clients. The approach may be used to help verbal and nonverbal Black clients resolve their personal and nonpersonal concerns. The key point is that the eclectic approach does not advocate that counselors use any single counseling approach with Black clients but that they focus on the clients' concerns and use appropriate concepts and techniques to help clients. Thus, the eclectic approach can be an effective approach for counselors to use with Black clients.

The use of most of these concepts and techniques requires that counselors be active participants in the counseling process. Because of the hesitance of many Black clients to disclose themselves in counseling relationships, counselors must be willing to take risks and become actively involved in the counseling process. Active involvement by counselors demonstrates to Black clients that they are genuinely interested in them as people and in their concerns. Therefore, it is important for counselors to remember that being actively involved in counseling relationships can help them become more effective with Black clients.

Counselors can learn to use the eclectic approach with Black clients by first learning to apply the behavioral, client-centered, existential, Gestalt, rational-emotive, and reality counseling approaches. If counselors can effectively apply each of these six approaches, then they can begin to use a combination of the concepts and techniques with Black clients. The main idea is to be able to counsel Black clients effectively by using a variety of concepts and techniques from these six approaches. For some counselors, this technique means learning or relearning how to use these six approaches effectively. For other counselors who already know how to use these approaches, the technique means being more eclectic when they counsel Black clients.

References

Cunningham, L., & Peters, H. *Counseling theories.* Columbus, Ohio: Charles E. Merrill, 1973.

Glasser, W., & Zunin, L. Reality therapy. In R. Corsini (Ed.), *Current psychotherapies.* Itasca, Ill.: F. E. Peacock, 1973.

Gunnings, T., & Simpkins, G. A systemic approach to counseling disadvantaged youth. *Journal of Non-White Concerns in Personnel and Guidance,* 1972, *1,* 4–8.

Harper, F., & Stone, W. Toward a theory of transcendent counseling with Blacks. *Journal of Non-White Concerns in Personnel and Guidance,* 1974, *3,* 191–196.

Shertzer, B., & Stone, S. *Fundamentals of counseling* (2nd ed.). Boston: Houghton Mifflin, 1974.

Strickland, B. Kierkegaard and counseling for individuality. *Personnel and Guidance Journal,* 1966, *44,* 470–474.

Tucker, S. Action counseling: An accountability procedure for counseling the oppressed. *Journal of Non-White Concerns in Personnel and Guidance,* 1973, *2,* 35–41.

1. Assume you have just been hired by a social service agency that has contracted to provide home-liaison services between the local schools and the parents of students attending these schools. Although a large number of the students are Black (approximately 35%), your agency to date has hired only one Black home-liaison counselor (of a staff of 12 counselors). As a home-liaison counselor, your responsibilities include home visits to acquaint parents with community services available to them and to establish rapport between the parents and the schools.

   a. What expectations would you have for your first home visit with a Black family?

   b. What are some examples of "small talk" you might use to "break the ice" with the parents of a fourteen year old Black student who is consistently truant from school?

   c. Assuming none exists when you are hired, what courses and experiences related to Black culture would you recommend that the school district offer to students?

2. Assume you have just accepted a counseling position in a correctional facility where a large number of Black inmates are incarcerated, most of whom come from nearby urban centers.

   a. What expectations do you have for your own performance as a counselor in this setting?

   b. Do you anticipate Black inmates will avail themselves of your services as a counselor? Why?

   c. What psychological needs can you anticipate Black inmates may have which you as a counselor might attempt to fulfill? How will you attempt to fulfill them?

3. Assume you are a counselor in a small midwestern college that is predominately White but recruits Black athletes. One of the Black athletes (Bill) has been dating a White cheerleader (Mary) you have seen before for counseling. Mary, seeing you alone, has just informed you that Bill has moved in with her and she fears her parents will disown her

when they find out. She has also asked you if she may bring Bill for an appointment the next day.

a. How do you feel about Mary and Bill's cross-racial living arrangement?
b. What are some of the issues you will want to explore with Mary and Bill when they come to see you together?
c. What do you suppose Mary and Bill each want to get out of meeting with a counselor?

The Black Client
Role Playing Exercise

Divide into groups of 4 or 5. Assign each group member to a role and the responsibilities associated with the role as follows:

Role	Responsibilities
1. Counselor	1. Assume role as a counselor or mental health worker who encounters a Black. Attempt to build rapport with the client.
2. Client	2. Assume role of a Black. To play this role effectively, it will be necessary for the student client to (a) identify cultural values of the Black group, (b) identify sociopolitical factors which may interfere with counseling, and (c) portray these aspects in the counseling session. It is best to select a few powerful variables in the role play. You may or may not be initially antagonistic to the client, but it is important for you to be sincere in your role and your reactions to the counselor trainee.
3. Observers	3. Observe interaction and offer comments during feedback session.

This exercise is most effective in a racially and ethnically mixed group. For example, a Black student can be asked to play the Black client role. However, this is probably not possible in most cases. Thus, students who play the client role will need to thoroughly read the articles for the group they are portraying.

Identifying the barriers that could interfere with counseling is an important aspect of this exercise. We recommend that a list be made of the group's cultural values and sociopolitical influences prior to the role playing.

Role playing may go on for a period of 5–15 minutes, but the time limit should be determined prior to the activity. Allow 10–15 minutes for a feedback session in which all participants discuss (within the group) how they felt in their respective roles, how appropriate were the counselor responses, what else they might have done in that situation, etc.

Rotate and role play the same situation with another counselor trainee *or* another Black client with different issues, concerns, and problems. In the former case, the group may feel that a particular issue is of sufficient importance to warrant reenactment. This allows students to see the effects of other counseling responses and approaches. In the latter case, the new exposure will allow students to get a broader view of barriers to counseling.

If videotaping equipment is available, we recommend that the sessions be taped and processed in a replay at the end. We have found this to be a powerful means of providing feedbacks to participants.

Part 5
The Latino Client

Photo by Jean-Claude Lejeune

As with the labels Asian American, Black, and American Indian, there is a danger that by identifying a group of people as Latino (Hispanic), we tend to overlook very real differences that exist within the group. Yet these labels serve an important purpose. Individuals within each group share a common cultural heritage, knowledge of which can enhance the counselor's effectiveness when working with clients from each group. Latinos, primarily consisting of immigrants from Cuba, Mexico, and Puerto Rico, share a similar heritage with regard to language and many values and traditions. Beyond these similarities, very important differences exist among the various Latino populations, and these differences are discussed in some detail in several of the chapters that follow.

Presently the second largest ethnic minority in the United States, it is projected that by the year 2030 or sooner, Latinos will represent the largest minority group. Although the Bureau of Census lists 12 million persons of Spanish origin, it is estimated that there are already 20 million Latinos in this country (Here comes the Latino era, 1977). It has also been estimated that in California, one of our most populated states, Latinos will comprise a majority of the population by the year 2000.

Despite these impressive statistics, there is evidence that Latinos have received less than their fair share of the American dream. Fewer than 42 percent of the Latinos over 25 years of age have completed a high school education as compared to 70 percent for the White population (U.S. Bureau of Census, 1979a). Although educational gains are being made by Latinos, recent data suggest they still lag behind other ethnic groups; 38 percent of the Latinos aged 20 to 24 have less than four years of high school education, a percentage that compares unfavorably with Blacks of the same age (25 percent) and even more unfavorably with Whites of the same age (14 percent, U.S. Bureau of Census, 1979a). The median family income for Latino families in 1978 was $12,566 (despite larger families and more members who work) as compared to a $17,912 median for all other families. Twenty percent of all Latino families exist on incomes below the poverty level as compared to nine percent for all other families (U. S. Bureau of Census, 1979b).

This situation can be accounted for to a large degree by a cycle of poverty set in motion with the earliest migration of Latinos to this country. Ancestral immigrants of many present-day Latinos came to the United States from non-industrial, agrarian-based countries and, for the most part, were unskilled and spoke little or no English. (A major exception was the Cuban population, many of whom were middle class and skilled when they migrated.) Their lifestyle, customs, and language set them apart from the dominant society, making them the objects of stereotyping, prejudice, and discrimination. Thus handicapped, Latinos were forced to join the millions of other American ethnic minorities in competition for scarce jobs and low pay. Hence the pattern was set, and each new generation has been condemned to the perpetual cycle of poverty and group discrimination. Often the result of this process is loss of hope and motivation and an increase in mental health related problems.

In chapter 13, Padilla, Ruiz, and Alvarez suggest that although Latinos are subject to conditions that foster mental health related problems, they tend to underutilize existing mental health service facilities. The authors examine several reasons for this underutilization and conclude that discouraging institutional policies are largely responsible. Three models of mental health services are discussed that are designed to meet the special needs of the Latino community. The chapter concludes with a number of recommendations for the delivery of mental health services to the Latino population.

In the second article to this section, "Counseling Puerto Ricans: Some Cultural Considerations," Christensen provides a brief introduction to the Puerto Rican in America. Important differences between native-born Puerto Ricans and Neo-Ricans are discussed as well as the values and traits linked to the Puerto Rican ethos. Most helpful to the counselor is a section in which Christensen offers a number of specific suggestions that apply directly to counseling Puerto Ricans.

In the final article to this section, "Counseling Latinos," Ruiz and Padilla present a demographic picture of the various sub-groups which constitute the larger Latino population, demonstrating how these sub-cultures differ from the general population. Their examination of Latino ethno-history and culture is highly instructive. Similarities found in each of the various sub-cultures, as well as the distinguishing features which make each unique, are examined in some detail. The need to view both intra-psychic and extra-psychic sources of stress, a theme presented throughout this text, is emphasized by Ruiz and Padilla when counseling Latinos. In the final portion of this article, the authors present several case histories of Latino clients, with the intention of providing guidelines for developing culturally relevant counseling programs for Latinos.

Here comes the Latino era. *Nuestro: The Magazine for Latinos,* 1977, *1* (1), 12, 15, 17–19.

U. S. Bureau of Census. Educational Attainment in the United States: March, 1979 and 1978. In *Current population reports,* (Series P-20, No. 356). Washington, D. C.: U. S. Government Printing Office, 1979. (a)

U. S. Bureau of Census. Persons of Spanish Origin in the United States: March, 1979. In Current population reports, (Series P-20, No. 354). Washington, D. C.: U. S. Government Printing Office, 1979. (b)

13 Community Mental Health Services for the Spanish-Speaking / Surnamed Population

Amado M. Padilla
René A. Ruiz
Rodolfo Alvarez

In the United States, the Spanish-speaking/surnamed (SSS) population receives mental health care of a different kind, of a lower quality, and in lesser proportions than any other ethnically identifiable population. Demographers consistently agree that ethnic minority group members, and particularly minority group members who are poor, receive less health care than the rest of the population. Studies surveyed confirm the demographic findings; in fact, some indicate that the problem may be more serious in mental health care (e.g., see Abad, Ramos, & Boyce, 1974; Cobb, 1972; Hollingshead & Redlich, 1958; Kolb, Bernard, & Dohrenwend, 1969; Padilla & Ruiz, 1973; Srole, Langer, Michael, Opler, & Rennie, 1962; Padilla, Note 1). This article delineates why the SSS receive poorer mental health care than other U.S. citizens and offers some recommendations for remedying this situation.

It should be clear from the onset that by SSS we are referring to the more than nine million residents of the United States who have been identified by the U.S. Bureau of the Census (1971a, 1971b) as people of "Spanish origin." The three largest groups of U.S. residents include more than five million Mexican Americans, approximately one and one-half million Puerto Ricans, and more than 600,000 Cubans. The remaining two million SSS members include Central or South Americans and "other" people of Spanish origin. In all, the SSS represent the second largest minority group in the United States. Further, in spite of geographic and in some cases racial differences between the SSS subgroups, all share cultural and socioeconomic similarities that allow us to speak here with relative ease of the SSS as a homogeneous group.

Use of Available Services

A review of the scant literature available indicates that the SSS population has been seriously underrepresented among the clientele of existing mental health service facilities. For example, Karno and Edgerton (1969), using California census figures, estimated that Mexican Americans made up 9%–10% of the state's population in 1962–1963. They found that during this same period, the percentages of Mexican Americans receiving treatment in California were as follows: 2.2% admissions to the state hospital system, 3.4% to state mental hygiene clinics, .9% to the Neuropsychiatric Institute, and 2.3% to state or local facilities. The resident inpatient population was 3.3%. Thus, underrepresentation ranges from 6.6% to 9.1%. Although these data emanate from one state only, other localities also report high degrees of underrepresentation. For example, Jaco (1960), after surveying the incidence rate of mental disorders during a period from 1951 to 1952 in the state of Texas, also reported a lower frequency of the use of private and public mental hospitals by Mexican Americans. More recently, Abad et al. (1974) have reported that statistics available at the Connecticut Mental Health Center indicate that from July 1, 1971, to March 1, 1972, admissions and readmissions of Puerto Ricans were at least 3.5 times lower than that of blacks, a group comparable in terms of poverty and minority status.

Several investigators have suggested that although the SSS receive comparatively less mental health care than the general population, they actually need more. One reason for this is that the SSS as a group are only partially acculturated and marginally integrated economically and, as a consequence, are subject to a number of "high-stress" indicators. These indicators, known to be correlated with personality disintegration and subsequent need for treatment intervention, include: (a) poor communication skills in English; (b) the poverty cycle—limited education, low income, depressed social status, deteriorated housing, and minimal political influence; (c) the survival of traits from a rural agrarian culture that are relatively ineffectual in an urban technological society; (d) the necessity of seasonal migration (for some); and (e) the stressful problem of acculturation to a society that appears prejudicial, hostile, and rejecting (see also Abad et al., 1974; Karno, 1966; Karno & Edgerton, 1969; Torrey, 1972). These authors all concluded that demographic data *underestimate* the frequency and severity of mental health problems among the SSS, and that the underutilization of mental health services by the SSS is therefore even greater than we know. The latter conclusion is particularly telling because a wide range of mental health modalities does not seem available for the SSS as it does for other U.S. citizens.

Type and Quality of Treatment

If referred or committed to a mental health service facility for treatment, what type of assistance is extended to SSS clients? In an effort to answer this question, Yamamoto, James, and Palley (1968) reported data on the psychiatric care of 594 men and women from four groups: 387 Caucasians, 149 Negroes, 53 Mexican Americans, and 5 Orientals. Each of these persons had applied for treatment at the Los Angeles County General Hospital Outpatient Clinic. Yamamoto et al. reported that compared to Anglo controls, SSS patients were referred for individual or group psychotherapy less often and received less lengthy and intensive treatment (e.g., terminated sooner or were not recommended for continued sessions). Karno (1966) reviewed case records of Nego, Mexican-American, and Caucasian patients of the psychiatric outpatient clinic of the Neuropsychiatric Institute, UCLA, and his findings corroborated the Yamamoto et al. findings. Karno stated:

> The prospective ethnic patients are less likely to be accepted for treatment than are the nonethnic patients. Ethnic patients who are accepted for treatment receive less and shorter psychotherapy than do nonethnic patients of the same social class characteristics. Ethnicity tends to be avoided by clinic personnel. (p. 520)

In an extensive review of the quality of treatment delivered to ethnic minority group and lower-socioeconomic-status patients, Lorion (1973) stated explicitly that "psychiatrists refer to therapy persons most like themselves, that is, whites rather than non-whites and those in the upper rather than in the lower income range" (p. 266). Continuing further, Lorion stated that the proportion of ethnic minority group patients receiving treatment at the Manhattan mental health clinics was, in proportion, "far below the general population rate for that area" (p. 266). He further maintained that in the review of a number of studies, "socioeconomic status correlates significantly and negatively with acceptance for and duration of individual psychotherapy, with experience level of assigned therapists, but not with a patient's diagnostic category or source of referral" (p. 266). These findings take on greater significance because the data were drawn from clinics in which ability to pay was not a condition for treatment.

In a related article, Lorion (1974) discussed the expectations of members of the lower socioeconomic classes toward psychotherapy. Such a person typically hopes for advice rather than reflection and for the resolution of "social" rather than "intrapsychic" problems. Thus, if a psychotherapist naively approaches such a patient with an extensive and historical view of childhood, the patient is confused and the therapist frequently experiences frustration when treatment is terminated "prematurely." On the other hand, if the psychotherapist is sophisticated and sensitive enough to recognize that his patient needs to learn the discrimination between personal and social problems, and better ways of responding to both, then treatment has a much greater potential of achieving the success toward which both patient and therapist are striving. This point is supported by Abad et al. (1974), who stated:

> They [Puerto Ricans] expect to see a doctor who will be active in his relationship with them, giving advice, and prescribing medication or some form of tangible treatment. The more passive psychiatric approach, with reliance on the patient to talk about his problems introspectively and take responsibility for making decisions about them, is not what the Puerto Rican patient expects. This discrepancy between the patient's expectations and his actual experience may well determine whether he continues in treatment. (p. 590)

Thus far we have documented the fact that the SSS underutilize existing mental health services; further, when they do present themselves for service, they tend to receive less frequent care or treatment that is not addressed to their needs or expectations. To understand how these problems have come about and, more importantly, to develop practical means of circumventing them, it is necessary to turn our attention to several explanations that have been used to account for the lower use of mental health facilities by the SSS.

Basically two minor formulations and one major formulation explain why SSS subgroups receive proportionately less mental health care than the general population and why, when delivered, such care tends to be less relevant to patient needs and expectations.

Lower Frequency and Severity of Mental Illness

Some evidence exists for the point of view that certain aspects of SSS subcultures protect members against mental breakdown or provide continued familial support after a breakdown (Jaco, 1959, 1960; Madsen, 1964). Jaco, after finding that Mexican Americans are underrepresented in residential care facilities for the mentally ill, argued that the social structure of Mexican Americans provides protection against stress for its members. Madsen generally concurred with this "stress resistance" formulation but added an elaboration of the protective role of the extended family system. He suggested that Mexican Americans discourage the referral of family members to mental health centers—as they would to any other majority group institutional structure—because the centers are perceived as alien and hostile.

The argument that SSS members are better prepared to tolerate stress or to require less support from social institutions must be interpreted with caution. Both Jaco and Madsen have predicted an increase in emotionally related problems once the SSS undergo a lessening of their traditional social structure (i.e., acculturation). As noted earlier, Karno and Edgerton (1969) and Torrey (1972) identified five sources of massive psychological stress for the SSS that are detrimental to adaptive psychological functioning, including the problems associated with acculturation as one of these. Because the literature on the inadequate mental health treatment delivered to the lower socioeconomic classes essentially corroborates these points, it seems reasonable to conclude that the explanation for the underutilization of mental health resources by the SSS poor must be sought elsewhere.

Use of "Folk" Medicine and/or "Faith" Healers

A small and steadily growing literature exists on the use of folk medicine and the practice of faith healing among the SSS (e.g., Creson, McKinley, & Evans, 1969; Edgerton, Karno, & Fernandez, 1970; Garrison, 1975; Kiev, 1968; Leininger, 1973; Lubchansky, Ergi, & Stokes, 1970; Garrison, Note 2). These investigators either argue or imply that such practices are sometimes selected as alternative solutions for the types of emotional problems for which most majority group members would probably seek more commonplace psychiatric treatment.

One reason why many SSS subgroups may prefer folk healers to more conventional psychiatric treatment may rest in a conceptual difference between lower-class patients and middle-class therapists as to what constitutes mental health or illness. For example, Hinsie and Campbell (1970) defined "mental health" or "psychological well-being" as "adequate adjustment, particularly as community-accepted standards of what human relations should be" (p. 388). This emphasis on adjustment implies a distinction between "mental" and "physical" health, a concept that does not exist among SSS subcultures. The state of well-being is usually conveyed in Spanish as *estar saludable* ("to be healthy"), *ser feliz* ("to be happy"), *sentirse o estar como un cañon* ("to feel or be like a cannon," i.e., the Spanish equivalent of "fit as a fiddle"), or *estar sano y fuerte* ("to be healthy and strong"). All of these Spanish idioms imply that physical and psychological "well-being" are inseparable.

These Spanish phrases reflect the cultural truism that some SSS who "do not feel well" *(que no se sienten sanos)* may consult a physician for help but are quite unlikely to approach a mental health professional for help with an "emotional" (i.e., nonphysical) problem. In support of this, Karno and Edgerton (1969) commented on the active role of the family physician in their study of mental illness among Mexican Americans in Los Angeles. If a problem should be pereived as nonphysical and "spiritual," for example, guilt, shame, a sense of sin, disrespect for elders or family values, then it seems eminently probable that a religious leader would be consulted for solace. It is equally predictable that fellow members of the extended family system, who share the same cultural values, would probably either recommend or support a referral to a physician or a priest or minister. Thus, problems perceived by the Anglo majority as "emotional" in nature and as requiring psychotherapeutic intervention might be perceived differently by the SSS subculture, that is, as subtle problems in physical health or as spiritual malaise.

It should be pointed out that the literature discussing folk psychiatry among Mexican Americans documents the use of such methods among a wide spectrum of the Mexican-American population. Creson et al. (1969) presented data from interviews with 25 Mexican Americans who were receiving treatment in either a pediatric or a psychiatric outpatient clinic. Five subjects admitted having used a faith healer at least once, 7 reported that at least one family member had used one, and 20 demonstrated familiarity with the concepts or language of faith healing. These data imply a substantial degree of recourse to faith healers among Mexican Americans, even among patients receiving conventional medical treatment. A second interpretation is that among this particular SSS group, these beliefs were highly stable. To quote the authors, "the concept of folk illness was deeply entrenched and resistant to the influence of the Anglo culture and its scientific medicine" (Creson et al., 1969, p. 295). Thus, it may be that recourse to faith healing is frequent enough to inhibit self-referrals to mental health centers.

The article by Leininger (1973) illustrated folk illness in depth, using the case-history approach with Spanish, Mexican-American, and lower-class Anglo families. In addition to providing a theoretical model to explain why the families embraced the "witchcraft" model of mental illness, the author outlined a series of therapeutic interventions that were effective in reducing personal and familial stress.

In an attempt to answer why the SSS underutilize mental health services, Torrey (1972) observed that Mexican Americans in California's San Jose and Santa Clara Counties have "their own system of mental health services." He described how this SSS group seeks improved health from self-referral to faith healers. In spite of this community-oriented health system, however, Torrey posited that when and if relevant health services staffed by professionals are available, this will become the preferred mode of health care sought by Mexican Americans.

Similarly, the Karno-Edgerton group recognized the existence of faith healing and described its practice. However, these investigators pointed out that use of the system is minimal and that its existence cannot be used to explain the underutilization of conventional health services (see especially Edgerton, Karno, & Fernandez, 1970).

Similarly, Lubchansky, Ergi, and Stokes (1970) and Garrison (1975; Garrison, Note 2), in studies of Puerto Rican spiritualists in New York City, reported that although spiritualists are consulted, Puerto Ricans also seek professional mental health services. Thus, among Puerto Ricans who believe in folk medical practices, more conventional mental health services are also sought, when available. For this reason, these authors concluded that the efficacy of professional treatment practices is confounded by the existence of this alternative system of mental health.

In sum, the underutilization of traditional mental health services cannot be explained because of the substitution of either folk medicine or faith healing by substantial numbers of the SSS. This conclusion seems warranted despite the seemingly valid conclusion by Leininger (1973) that a limited number of rural and/or migrant peoples still adhere to "witchcraft" beliefs.

Discouraging Institutional Policies

Certain organizational factors and institutional policies are primarily responsible for the use patterns of mental health facilities exhibited by the SSS. A review of the literature by Gordon (1965), concerned with characteristics of patients seeking treatment at child guidance clinics, suggested that the needs of minority group children are not being met (cited by Wolkon, Moriwaki, Mandel, Archuleta, Bunje, & Zimmerman, 1974). Primary factors responsible for this situation are defined as "inflexible intake procedures and long waiting lists." A study of a specific child guidance clinic confirmed the inference based on the literature review (Wolkin et al., 1974). The period between the initial self-referral for service and the intake interview ranged from 1 to 52 weeks, with a median of 28 weeks. The four Mexican-American families seeking treatment had a median wait of 28 weeks, with a range of 24.5–42.5 weeks. In case of "emergency," patients were seen "immediately." At the same clinic, while the median waiting period for Caucasians was only 4.5 weeks, the Mexican Americans had to wait 5.5 weeks. Although these difference failed to achieve statistical significance, it is clear that an "emergency" telephone contact is not generally honored for more than a month in the case of Caucasians but takes almost 6 weeks in the case of Mexican Americans. The inference that delays for ordinary and emergency treatment are discouraging is confirmed by the finding that "77% of the total initial request for services did not receive treatment" (Wolkon et al., 1974, p. 711).

A study even more directly relevant to treatment of the SSS (Torrey, 1972) described mental health facilities located in a catchment area of one million persons, of whom approximately 100,000 were Mexican-American. Torrey evaluated these facilities as "irrelevant" for Mexican Americans because 10% of the local population generated only 4% of the patient referrals. The basis of his judgment was that the bilingual poor should be expected to generate a larger proportion of referrals because they are subject to many stresses known to bring on mental breakdown. His explanation for this discrepancy was based primarily on the following four variables:

1. Geographic isolation is an important casual factor. Mental health services are "inaccessible" to the SSS because they are often located at the farthest distance possible from the neighborhood of the group with the highest need. All too often community mental health services are attached to schools of medicine or universities located outside of the barrio and accessible only by a half-hour, or more, bus ride. Not only does the distance impede the frequency of self-referrals, but both the cost of transportation and the lack of adequate child care during the absence of the mother also serve to decrease the use of mental health facilities by the SSS.

2. Language barriers are a second explanatory factor. Torrey described the "majority" of local Mexican Americans as bilingual. Nevertheless, only 4 members of a professional staff of 120 studied by Torrey spoke any Spanish at all, and none of the directional and/or instructional signs were in Spanish. The interpretation that referrals will decrease if patient and therapist cannot communicate is shared by Edgerton and Karno (1971; Karno & Edgerton, 1969), among others.

3. Class-bound values are a third causal factor. Here the reference is primarily to therapist variables, that is, to personal characteristics of the professional staff that dissuade the patient from continued mental health treatment. Abad et al. (1974), Yamamoto el al. (1968), and Torrey (1972) all indicated that therapists conduct treatment in accord with the value system of the middle class, that is, a system in which the client is seen by the therapist for 50 minutes once or twice a week or in a group therapy in which the client is seen in a group once or twice a week. This approach was proven ineffective with, and discouraging to, lower-class patients. When frustrated because clients fail to respond to this approach, psychologists are more likely not to encourage the SSS client to seek therapy after the first meeting. These points have also been noted by the Karno-Edgerton group as well as by Kline (1960).

4. Culture-bound values are a fourth explanatory factor. Again, Torrey attended to therapist variables. His point was that whenever therapists from one culture diagnose and prescribe treatment for patients from another culture, there is an inherent probability of professional misjudgment. To illustrate, he cited data (p. 156) indicating that 90% of Anglo residents in psychiatry associate the phrase *hears voices* with the word *crazy,* whereas only 16% of Mexican-American high school students make the same association. The concept of intrinsic culture conflict was also advanced by Bloombaum, Yamamoto, and James (1968), the Karno-Edgerton group, Kline (1969), and Phillipus (1971).

Although all four factors operate to minimize self-referral to mental health centers by the SSS, the last three (language, class, and culture) seem to interact in such a way that the SSS are actively discouraged from using mental health services. A review of studies of low-income patients, both white and nonwhite, who apply for mental health services (Lorion, 1973) is particularly relevant here. One major conclusion that emerges from this review is that middle-class therapists are typically members of a different cultural group than their lower-class patients. As a consequence, patient and therapist experience all the difficulties in communication that occur whenever members of two cultures interact. This "culture conflict" was described in much greater detail in a second article by the same author (Lorion, 1974). Therapists, and particularly therapists in training, tend to be "turned off" by low-income patients because they perceive the patients as hostile, suspicious, using crude language, and expecting *merely* "symptomatic relief." Studies reviewed by Lorion reveal that the success of a therapist in working with low-income patients bears a closer relationship to the therapist's personal characteristics than it does to his experience level or treatment approach. Lorion also reported that therapists from low socioeconomic backgrounds are equally successful with patients from all social classes. The reverse does not seem to be true, that is, that upper-class therapists can deal with equal effectiveness across social classes. More interesting is the fact that "low income patients engage in significantly more self-exploration early in treatment if matched with their therapist on race and/or socio-economic background" (Lorion, 1974, p. 346). Cobb (1972), in a review of similar literature, supported an earlier argument made in this article that therapeutic expectations vary to some extent as a function of social class. Low-socioeconomic-status patients seem to expect therapists to assume a more active role, as physicians typically do in dealing with medical problems, as opposed to a passive or "talking" role. As a result, Cobb concluded that such patients will probably respond better to therapists who are more active. Taken together, the reviews of Cobb (1972) and Lorion (1973, 1974) lead to two major conclusions: First, race and social class of the therapist seem to affect the patient's response to treatment; and second, an effective and appropriate "solution" to a problem based upon middle-class values may be totally inappropriate and ineffective for a patient returning to his lower-class environment.

Three Models for Improved Services to the SSS Population

Having reviewed the panorama of complex explanations for the underutilization of mental health services by the SSS population, let us now examine three emerging models for service to this population.

Two points seem relevant here: First, our perusal of the literature suggests that these are the *only* programs designed specifically for the SSS (though there may be others which have not been described in the literature); and second, these programs seem to have been designed primarily for the treatment of adult self-referrals. We return at a later point in this article to the need for child guidance clinics or similar organizations providing treatment programs for younger patients.

Professional Adaptation Model

The major characteristic of the *professional adaptation model* is that the professional and paraprofessional staff of the community mental health center receive some form of specialized nonstandard training or in some way "adapt" themselves to the specific requirements of serving the SSS population. Two examples of the professional adaptation model follow.

First, Karno and Morales (1971) described the effort in east Los Angeles to design a community mental health service that would attract local Mexican Americans. Major innovations were implemented in staffing, service quarters, and treatment programs. At the end of a 2½-year recruitment program, the medical director had attracted 22 full-time professional, paraprofessional, and clerical personnel. Of these 22, 15 were "completely fluent," 4 were "conversant," and 3 had a "rudimentary knowledge" of Spanish. Ten were natives and/or residents of the area. More interesting is the fact that 12 were of Mexican-American and 2 were of other Latin (Cuban and Peruvian) descent. Service quarters selected were "in the heart of the . . . community, convenient for . . . transportation, and comfortable . . . and inviting" (p. 118). The treatment program was based on the philosophy of prevention. Thus, the major thrust was upon mental health consultation to a wide variety of community service agencies. As a backup, the center offers short-term crisis-oriented treatment using individual, family, group, and chemical therapy. The center seems to be fulfilling the objective of providing appropriate treatment for Mexican Americans because the first 200 patients matched local population figures.

A second, but somewhat similar, example of the professional adaptation model has been created for the Hispanic population of Denver (Phillipus, 1971). Three of the eight team members are Spanish speaking, and the center is located in the neighborhood of the target population. It is in a building designed so that the prospective patients enter a reception area furnished to resemble a living room. The initial contact person is usually a secretary-receptionist, who is always Spanish speaking. The patient is referred immediately to a team member to begin whatever action seems necessary. The rationale is that treatment is directed toward crisis resolution that, by definition, is incompatible with rigid adherence to the traditional 50-minute-hour schedule. The staff began to refer to each other and to the patients on a first-name basis when it became apparent that the use of more formal address was estranging some members of the Hispanic group. Unequivocal data bearing on the appropriateness of the program for the SSS are difficult to obtain because of its recency. Nevertheless, new referrals increased to a point that proportional representation of the target population relative to the general population was soon reached. When certain specific elements of the program were eliminated, Hispanic self-referrals began to decline but returned to former levels when reinstituted.

Family Adaptation Model

Under the conception of the "family" (i.e., a strong sense of an extended network of primary social relationships) as an important cultural feature that helps to provide emotional support against stresses experienced by the SSS population, a variant of group psychotherapy appears to be evolving into what we call the *family adaptation model.*

Maldonado-Sierra and Trent (1960) described a "culturally relevant" group psychotherapy program for chronic, regressed, schizophrenic, Puerto Rican males based on assumptions about the Puerto Rican family structure. The father of these families is typically described as a "dominant, authoritarian" figure, and the mother as submissive, nurturant, and loving. The older male sibling is perceived as a figure whom the other siblings respect, admire, and confide in. In this article and in a second (Maldonado-Sierra, Trent, & Fernandex-Marina, 1960), the authors described how these observations were translated into action.

First, three groups of eight patients each spent several weeks together in a variety of activities under the supervision of an individual who represented the older male sibling. A few days before group sessions were initiated, the group was introduced to an older male therapist who represented the father figure. He maintained dignity, remained aloof, and restricted social interaction to brief interchanges. The third therapist was an older female who fulfilled mother-figure expectations by distributing food and chatting informally.

The complexity of the group psychotherapy process of this type is too extensive to describe here. Suffice it to state that this analogy of the Puerto Rican family permitted patients an opportunity to identify their common problems and to resolve them therapeutically.

Although this section is thus far limited to the work of Maldonado-Sierra and his associates with hospitalized schizophrenic patients, the family adaptation model deserves further exploration with less severely disturbed SSS patients. The use of cultural themes such as *machismo, respecto, comadrazco-compadrazco,* the role of women, and *personalismo* in therapy, especially family therapy, could prove extremely valuable in effecting more adequate therapeutic models. Limitations of space preclude a refined definition of these terms, but the basic concepts are that sex roles of SSS men and women are much more rigidly defined: Males value highly the virtues of courage and fearlessness *(machismo);* respect is given elders and there is an adherence to cultural norms and values *(respecto);* extended family relations, especially between godfather-godmother and godchildren, are ritualized and have a religious connotation *(comadrazco-compadrazco);* and interpersonal relations are based on trust for people mingled with a distaste for institutions or organizations that operate on a formal and impersonal basis *(personalismo).*

Barrio Service Center Model

By virtue of the conclusion that the vast majority of the sources of stress experienced by the SSS population are of economic origin, the barrio service center model is emerging and rapidly gaining legitimacy. This model seems to fit particularly well with the "health services catchment area" concept, in which a community center is staffed with personnel who can effectively intervene on behalf of the surrounding population to get jobs, bank loans, and many other basic economic services. Four examples of the barrio service center model exist in the literature:

1. First, Lehmann (1970) described the operation over a two-year period of three storefront neighborhood service centers in New York City as follows:

> [The] typical client [is] a Puerto Rican woman in her mid-30's with two or three children and there is no father present. She is usually an unemployed housewife . . . on welfare . . . with income less than $3,000 a year. She is almost certainly born in Puerto Rico . . . and there is only about one chance in three she speaks English well. (p. 1446)

Lehmann admitted that "their [i.e., the centers'] record for problem solving was less than brilliant" (p. 1454) but attributed whatever successes achieved by the centers to their accessibility, informality, and open-door policy with respect to problems and people, and their use of community residents as staff.

2. A second example of the barrio service center model was described by Abad et al. (1974) in an article identifying demographic and subcultural characteristics of a Puerto Rican sample of residents of New Haven, Connecticut. The "Spanish clinic," or *la clinica hispana* as it is called by the Spanish-speaking community, provides walk-in coverage five days a week and includes psychiatric evaluations and follow-up treatment, medication groups, individual counseling, couple and family therapy, referral services, home visits, and transportation. The staff is bilingual-bicultural and includes a Spanish psychiatrist, a part-time Puerto Rican social worker, and a paraprofessional indigenous staff including community leaders with public visibility. The clinic is prepared to intervene in a variety of problem situations, even if the situations are not of a "clinical" nature. For example, one of the "most frequent roles within the Spanish community is that of intermediary between Spanish speaking clients and other agencies" (p. 592). The article concluded that everyone benefits from such an arrangement: the clientele receive help with problems and this help permits them to function more effectively within their environment, the barrio agency gains the reputation of being a "helpful" institution, and community support of the clinic is enhanced.

3. A third example of the barrio service center model was reported by Burruel (Note 3), who described the creation of *La Frontera,* a mental health outpatient clinic situated in south Tucson, Arizona, designed specifically to provide care for the Chicano community. Burruel described

the ongoing services of the clinic, including "diagnosis and treatment for adults and children with emotional or personality problems and general problems of living" (p. 27). Treatment modalities include "individual therapy, conjoint, family and group therapy" (p. 27). Community representation was originally excluded from planning and administration of the center until "pressure was applied" (p. 29). Currently, the administrative board is a "policy-making board which incorporates representatives from the community" (p. 29). Under the leadership of a Chicano full-time director, deliberate effort was expended "to make the services relevant to the Chicano community . . . by searching for bilingual and bicultural mental health professionals" (p. 29). A deliberate effort to attract patients from the catchment area was implemented by announcing services on the Mexican radio stations and by eliminating the "waiting list" that is typical of traditional mental health clinics. It is stated that patients may be seen "immediately, hours later, or at the latest, the next day" (p. 32). The response to this innovative program is described as follows: "underutilization of mental health services by Mexican Americans has not been the case at *La Frontera;* 61.5% of the total patient population consists of Mexican Americans" (p. 28).

4. The fourth and final example of the barrio service center model was described by Schensul (1974), who brought the insights of an applied anthropologist to the creation of a new mental health center specifically for an SSS subgroup. Schensul described how a group of young Chicanos working in Chicago's west side developed the idea in the summer of 1971 to create a community-controlled youth facility to be called *El Centro de la Causa.* The original operating budget of $1,800 was raised by a community fiesta. According to Schensul, the activist group had, within months, convinced a church organization to provide $40,000 for staff and seed money. Within three years, the operating budget was over $400,000. This funding was used to train community residents as paraprofessionals in mental health and to support mental health training and reading improvement programs, English classes, recreation and youth activities, and programs to prevent drug use. Schensul concluded that whatever success was achieved by *El Centro de la Causa* was primarily because of the youthful Chicano activists and their consistent efforts to maintain community involvement.

The major conclusion is that successful therapeutic models for SSS groups are possible when cultural and social variables are made part of the therapeutic setting. It would be misleading to conclude this discussion without noting that some of the successful programs described here no longer exist (e.g., that described by Phillipus). These programs are only highlighted because they represent the very small number that are described in the literature.

General Conclusions and Recommendations

The preceding review and analysis of the extant literature on the delivery of mental health services to the SSS population clearly reveal a crisis situation. What, then, is to be done? While we are not at this time prepared to generate totally novel institutional mechanisms for the maximum delivery of high-quality mental health services to the SSS population, we are prepared to make a number of recommendations designed to encourage speedier evolution of three promising avenues for improvement of service to this target population. The three models described in the preceding section of this article appear to us to offer considerable promise. Our objective is to focus on their essential distinguishing characteristics and to make compatible recommendations designed to enhance their potential for success.

The recommendations we make here may be viewed as stemming from the intellectual perspective of the community mental health movement. Before proceeding to our recommendations, a word about the community mental health movement is in order. Although there is no exact and technically precise definition of what is still an evolving concept of "community mental health," it can be differentiated from the traditional, exclusively *medical* approach to mental health by four of its major characteristics: First, the community mental health movement seeks an empirical, research-based understanding of the interconnectedness between the family, community, social, economic, and cultural structures, as well as biological and psychic structures, as sources of pressures that directly affect the mental health of individuals. Second, the community mental health movement seeks to promote an improved general state of mental health through intervention techniques in which the recipients of health care have had a measure of knowledge of and participation in the process of development and implementation. Third, the prime objective is positive and preventive, in that it seeks to promote and maintain *health* rather than to dwell on an exclusive concern with the treatment of *illness* that has become too great to be ignored. Fourth, the target of the community mental health movement is the entire population of a defined community in its collective sense, and not simply those individuals whose mental condition has become so acute as to be identified as mentally ill. These, then, are the four intellectual perspectives guiding our recommendations for the improvement of the three models that appear to be making a start toward effective mental health service delivery to the SSS population.

Despite a variety of reasons advanced to explain why the SSS receive proportionately less mental health care, the literature reviewed supports the conclusion that mental health centers across the country are failing to meet the needs of the SSS, with a few notable exceptions. One explanation for this failure is that mental health centers and related agencies are so overly committed to traditional models of health care delivery that they ignore other problems troubling the SSS that are of much greater severity.

Occasionally, centers and agencies offer chemotherapy combined with some variation of individual or group counseling to deal with emotional conflicts of an allegedly intrapsychic nature. These treatment services completely deny, of course, the bona fide problems of a "social" nature that are anxiety provoking, depressing, frustrating, enraging, debilitating, and potentially disruptive to adaptive psychological function. These problems include premature termination of education among the young, elevated rates of arrest and incarceration, widespread abuse of alcohol and illegal drugs, and high rates of unemployment, to cite only the most obvious and destructive.

With regard to treatment programs, a number of investigators have commented that many current modalities, especially those based on majority culture and/or middle-class values, have proven ineffective. Encouraging results have been reported, however, from some centers that emphasize some combination of (a) community consultation as a preventative measure, (b) crisis intervention as a matter of course, and (c) "back-up" treatment with individual, group, family, and drop-in therapies. The literature supports the recommendation that more innovative programs be created and applied on a more widespread basis.

A recommendation for "innovative" treatment programs is self-defeating unless validating research is conducted. Even more critically, demographic and survey research is needed to guide the development of programs with the greatest probability of success. Schensul (1974) spoke of developing "research expertise" among community representatives who lack formal academic, scientific training. Basically, Schensul described an interaction between community activists and researchers that both educates and enhances the quality of the findings that emerge.

In addition, a wide range of innovative programs is necessary to deal with the social problems besetting the SSS (e.g., remedial education, vocational guidance and retraining, drug abuse and crime prevention programs, and possibly even college counseling). The problem of providing appropriate services and attracting clientele can be resolved somewhat by using the agency as a multipurpose center. In addition to providing treatment for a wide range of human problems, the facilities could be used for youth activities (e.g., sports, dances, etc.), for culturally relevant events (e.g., Spanish-language films, fiestas, etc.), or for the satisfaction of any variety of community needs. It makes eminent sense to involve the community in a center in their neighborhood which is situated there to satisfy their needs. The literature supports the contention that the community can be penetrated more effectively, and the quality of services increased, if community representaion is involved in the administration. Even more specifically, Burruel (Note 3) and Schensul (1974) agreed that the use of the community mental health center for a variety of purposes has the beneficial effects of attracting more clientele and delivering services of higher quality.

We also recommend a "business model" approach to attract clientele. There may be some value in using advertising media, in both Spanish and English, to disseminate information to the target population concerning available facilities, therapeutic services, and related activities. Boulette (1973), for example, advocated the use of television to inform clientele of the availability of appropriate services. If one is offended by the "unprofessional" aspects of advertising to provide needed services to an oppressed people, one should reflect upon the extensive publicity suggesting examinations for breast cancer following the illness and surgery of the wives of internationally prominent politicians.

Only slight modifications in existing treatment methods can be created if one is only marginally aware of the nature of the social problems that plague the SSS. Individual psychotherapy, conducted on a once-a-week basis and for the purpose of uncovering alleged unconscious conflicts, is obviously highly ineffective with problems of a social nature. To encourage an SSS youngster to remain in school, it makes much more sense to exploit some modification of family counseling techniques. Peer group psychotherapy has achieved some modest success in reducing delinquency rates among the young. Such an approach will probably be highly unsuccessful, however, if the group is conducted by a non-SSS therapist who attempts to encourage introspection based on psychodynamic formulations. Because many members of SSS subgroups conceptualize "treatment" as something they receive while remaining passive, it makes much more sense to encourage discussion groups among potential drug users, possibly including adults who have "kicked the habit." When a patient has the expectation that he will be helped by "doing something," rather than by just talking, it makes sense to involve potential counseling clients in some form of activity therapy (Cobb, 1972). We turn now to recommendations for improvement of each of the three specific community mental health models.

There is the obvious problem of communication with the professional adaptation model. Potential clients whose predominant language is Spanish will certainly feel unwelcome in settings where they cannot read signs, where they are greeted by clerical personnel to whom they cannot communicate their needs, and where they are subsequently referred to majority-group, monolingual, English-speaking professionals. The use of translators is uneconomical, may not communicate nuances successfully, and seems to possess a vast potential to offend and estrange both patient and professional.

Crash programs in Spanish-language acquisition for monolingual, English-speaking professionals are a partial solution to this problem. But language skill is not enough. As we have indicated at several points, the mental health professional must be knowledgeable about the culture of a particular SSS subgroup he works with in order to be effective. Mental health centers may remedy such educational deficits on the part of their professional staff by presenting lectures, seminars, and films on the particular subgroup being treated. In this context, the use of community representatives as teachers and/or consultants who import insight to a particular subculture can be invaluable.

Federal legislation is currently under consideration (S. 3280, Note 4) which bears directly on the resolution of this problem. Applicants seeking federal funding for programs of health delivery and health revenue sharing to a catchment area in which "a substantial proportion of the residents of which are of limited English-speaking ability" will be *required* to:

> (a) make arrangements for providing services to the extent practical in the language and cultural context most appropriate to such individuals and (b) identify an individual on its staff who is bilingual and whose responsibilities shall include providing for training for members of the applicant's staff, and of the staff of any providers of services with whom arrangements are made, regarding the cultural sensitivities related to health of the population served and providing guidance to appropriate staff members and patients in bridging linguistic and cultural differences. (pp. 151–152)*

Every article describing the delivery of mental health services to SSS subgroups agrees on essentially two major points (Abad et al., 1974; Lehmann, 1970; Schensul, 1974; Burruel, Note 3). First, it is generally agreed that the problem of poor communication between patient and therapist may be partially resolved by the employment of local community representatives who are bilingual and bicultural and their subsequent training at the paraprofessional level in the delivery of mental health services. The consequences of hiring and training community residents appear to benefit everyone. The agency achieves a more positive image in the community when local residents are hired, and the quality of services for the SSS is enhanced when patient and therapist can communicate. The second point on which there is consistent agreement is that community involvement in the administration of the mental health center is critical for success. These articles attest that the SSS refuse to refer themselves for treatment to agencies that are perceived as alien institutions intruding into their community and staffed by non-SSS personnel. It is impressive how closely these recommended practices, based upon empirical evidence, matched the letter and spirit of the suggestions that emerged from the 1974 APA conference held in Vail, Colorado.

The training of paraprofessionals to deliver treatment services and to conduct research leads to an ethical dilemma. Speaking practically, if paraprofessionals are *not* trained, then the SSS will receive essentially no services from anyone who shares their bilingual, bicultural background.

---

*Since the writing of this article, S.3280 was passed by the Senate committee and forwarded to the joint House-Senate conference committee. The bill was passed by the joint conference committee, but pocket vetoed by President Ford at the end of the congressional session in December 1974. Similar legislation has been reintroduced by both the House and the Senate during the present 94th session of Congress.

Whenever paraprofessionals are used for these purposes, however, it is clear that they lack the education, training, and experience of the professionally trained members of the helping professions. But as Ruiz (1971) has indicated, no such cadre of SSS professional mental health specialists exists. Thus, unless professional organizations such as the American Psychological Association and the American Psychiatric Association intervene, a significant number of SSS Americans will receive little or no mental health care. We strongly urge the membership of these two organizations to instruct their elected representatives to assume a posture of moral leadership by working to increase the number of students from SSS subgroups in the mental health professions. Organizations that remain passive and apathetic in the face of problems of this nature and severity can no longer describe themselves as created "to promote human welfare."

A cadre of SSS professionals is needed to provide treatment and to conduct research in the mental health area. Without such SSS professionals, the national problem of underutilization of mental health services by the SSS will probably continue indefinitely. In a survey of selected mental health personnel, Ruiz (1971) identified 58 SSS psychologists from a pool of approximately 28,500, and 20 psychiatrists out of 16,000. Despite the tremendous underrepresentation these data denote, the situation is, in fact, even worse: 30 of the 58 psychologists were Spaniards, a group not ordinarily thought of as a disadvantaged minority group.

Regardless of why the SSS are underrepresented in the mental health professions, it is reasonably certain that this situation will remain essentially unchanged without constructive intervention. Recommendations are for programs to identify those SSS high school students with academic promise, to encourage continued school attendance, to subsidize educational expenses, and to motivate career choices in mental health fields. Implementation of these recommendations will require funding, legislation, and possibly legal pressure on high school counselors and on admission boards at colleges and universities. But a partial solution could be achieved at minimal expense and without new laws if the membership of the American Psychological Association, as well as that of the American Psychiatric Association, would take a more active role in the training of SSS students in the mental health professions as suggested above.

Family Adaptation Model

As we noted earlier, there has been little exploration of SSS family roles as a method of therapeutic entry in working with SSS clients. Such an approach would appear to be successful especially in those situations where several of the family members must be counseled. Therapists knowledgeable about the family dynamics of SSS clients could, for example, use family therapy to better understand the ways in which family members conform to their culturally ascribed roles in times of stress.

Moreover, this technique could be used to analyze how the entire kinship network of an SSS person responds as a support system during periods of extreme mental stress. Weaknesses in the kinship support system could be detected and remedied. Concomitant with this, the knowledgeable therapist could get the SSS client to act out situations demanding elaboration of cultural traits such as *machismo* or *personalismo* in order to better understand points of conflict between the SSS client's cultural values and those of the dominant majority culture. To illustrate this point, Abad et al. (1974) noted that conflict with the *respecto* concept is particularly common in parent-child relationships among Puerto Ricans on the mainland. As Abad et al. stated:

> Influenced by their Anglo peers, children, especially adolescents, strive to be more independent and rebel against restrictions that they might well accept if living on the island. An unknowing therapist in such a situation may too quickly conclude that the adolescent is acting appropriately against rigid expectations, and in so doing, the therapist may alienate himself from the parents, make them defensive, and ruin any chance for further family intervention. (p. 588)

In addition, the family adaptation model would extend to the architectural design of community mental health centers. There is evidence suggestive of the fact that centers with "living room" reception areas appear to be the most attractive to SSS clientele (e.g., Phillipus, 1971). This homelike informality becomes even more attractive, of course, when the SSS patient is greeted by someone who can speak his own language, who can evaluate the problem rapidly, and who can implement immediate disposition. This kind of action based on *personalismo* is similar to the kind of brokerage system employed in Latin America and to which many SSS clients are accustomed.

Barrio Service Center Model
New centers should be situated in the appropriate neighborhoods. Centers established at a distance from the target population must "attract" clientele, perhaps by following a business model. Possibilities include arranging transportation (e.g., a busing service or a patient share-a-ride system), providing child-care facilities for parents (e.g., at the center or home-visit "babysitters"), and encouraging regular attendance at therapy sessions (e.g., through reduced fees or by remaining open "after hours").

Two clinics located in high-density-population urban areas (Abad et al., 1974; Schensul, 1974) report remarkable success by "word-of-mouth" advertising among their Spanish-speaking clientele. While this informal communication network generated self-referrals in a more sprawling geographic area with a smaller population (south Tucson, Arizona), Burruel (Note 3) described a "tremendous" response to an announcement of services on the Mexican radio stations. The inference of significance is clear. If mental health centers for the SSS are to fulfill the purposes for which they are designed, they must exert effort to contact the target population.

The next consideration involves the selection procedure of community representatives to serve as paraprofessionals and the nature of the training program designed for them. Both Abad et al. (1974) and Burruel (Note 3) agree that faith healers and other practitioners of folk medicine are highly qualified as students for paraprofessional training programs. These individuals already enjoy some degree of community acceptance and probably possess skill in responding appropriately to human problems. This statement should not be misconstrued as indicating that ethnic minority group membership is a necessary condition for therapeutic effectiveness. As Sue (1973) has demonstrated, it is possible to develop highly sophisticated and effective training programs to train ethnic minority group students to serve as counselors for clients from their own ethnic minority group. Programs of equivalent validity must be developed for the SSS, and it is assumed that the efficacy of any paraprofessional will be related to the quality of whatever program is created for training purposes.

At this point, we shall expand on some of the recommendations presented above dealing with treatment programs. "Crisis intervention" may be defined and applied in a number of ways helpful, or even crucial, to the continued well-being of patients, but which fall well outside the optimal (or even usual) models of mental health care. Imagine, for example, a widow whose sole source of support is her monthly welfare check. If this check were delayed only a few days, the family might be literally in a "crisis." A center sensitive to the needs of the target population in this hypothetical instance might furnish emergency funding, might contact tradesmen requesting credit, might implore creditors to wait a "few more days," or might ask the welfare agency for immediate reimbursement. Because this type of crisis intervention does not require professional education, the patient could be rendered a tremendous service by a paraprofessional who spoke her language, grasped her plight, was knowledgeable concerning other community agencies, and responded immediately.

This type of "crisis intervention" represents the flexibility that community mental health centers must adopt if they are to respond appropriately to the human problems of the SSS. This point is elaborated in great detail by several writers (see especially Martinez, 1973) who agree that intrapsychic conflict represents only a small portion of the numerous human and social problems that trouble the SSS.

Reference Notes

1. Padilla, A. M. *Special report to the Planning Branch of the National Institute of Mental Health on the mental health needs of the Spanish speaking in the*

United States. Unpublished manuscript, 1971. (Available from author, Department of Psychology, University of California, Los Angeles, California 90024.)

2. Garrison, V. *Social networks and social change in the "culture of poverty."* Paper presented at the meeting of the American Association for the Advancement of Science, Philadelphia, Pennsylvania, December 1971.

3. Burruel, G. *La Frontera,* a mental health clinic in the Chicano community. In *Report on the Southwest States Chicano Consumer Conference* (DHEW Publication No. HSM 73–6208). Washington, D.C.: U.S. Department of Health, Education, and Welfare, 1972.

4. S. 3280. 93rd Congress, second session, September 5, 1974. *A bill to amend the Public Health Service Act to revise and extend programs of health delivery and health revenue sharing.*

References

Abad, V., Ramos, J., & Boyce, E. A model for delivery of mental health services to Spanish-speaking minorities. *American Journal of Orthopsychiatry,* 1974, *44,* 584–595.

Bloombaum, M., Yamamoto, J., & Evans, Q. Cultural stereotyping among psychotherapists. *Journal of Counseling and Clinical Psychology,* 1968, *32,* 99.

Boulette, T. R. *Problemas familiares:* Television programs in Spanish for mental health education. *Hospital and Community Psychiatry,* 1974, *25,* 282.

Cobb, C. W. Community mental health services and the lower socioeconomic class: A summary of research literature on outpatient treatment (1963–1969). *American Journal of Orthopsychiatry,* 1972, *42,* 404–414.

Creson, D. L., McKinley, C., & Evans, R. Folk medicine in Mexican American subculture. *Diseases of the Nervous System,* 1969, *30,* 264–266.

Edgerton, R. B., & Karno, M. Mexican American bilingualism and the perception of mental illness. *Archives of General Psychiatry,* 1971, *24,* 286–290.

Edgerton, R. B., Karno, M., & Fernandez, I. Curanderismo in the metropolis: The diminishing role of folk-psychiatry among Los Angeles Mexican Americans. *American Journal of Psychotherapy,* 1970, *24,* 124–134.

Garrison, V. *Espiritismo:* Implications for provision of mental health services to Puerto Rican populations. In H. Hodges & C. Hudson (Eds.), *Folk-therapy.* Miami, Fla.: University of Miami Press, 1975.

Gordon, S. Are we seeing the right patients? Child guidance intake: The sacred cow. *American Journal of Orthopsychiatry,* 1965, *35,* 131–137.

Hinsie, L. E., & Campbell, R. J. *Psychiatric dictionary.* New York: Oxford University Press, 1970.

Hollingshead, A. B., & Redlich, F. C. Social class and mental illness. New York: Wiley, 1958.

Jaco, E. G. Mental health of the Spanish American in Texas. In M. F. Opler (Ed.), *Culture and mental health: Cross-cultural studies.* New York: Macmillan, 1959.

Jaco, E. G. *The social epidemiology of mental disorders: A psychiatric survey of Texas.* New York: Russell Sage Foundation, 1960.

Karno, M. The enigma of ethnicity in a psychiatric clinic, *Archives of General Psychiatry*, 1966, *14*, 516–520.

Karno, M., & Edgerton, R. B. Perception of mental illness in a Mexican-American community. *Archives of General Psychiatry*, 1969, *20*, 233–238.

Karno, M., & Morales, A. A community mental health service for Mexican Americans in a metropolis. *Comprehensive Psychiatry*, 1971, *12*, 115–121.

Kiev, A. *Curanderismo: Mexican-American folk psychiatry.* New York: Free Press, 1968.

Kline, L. Y. Some factors in the psychiatric treatment of Spanish Americans. *American Journal of Psychiatry*, 1969, *125*, 1674–1681.

Kolb, L. C., Bernard, V. W., & Dohrenwend, B. P. *Urban challenges to psychiatry.* Boston: Little, Brown, 1969.

Lehmann, S. Selected self-help: A study of clients of a community social psychiatry service. *American Journal of Psychiatry*, 1970, *126*, 1444–1454.

Leininger, M. Witchcraft practices and psychocultural therapy with urban U.S. families. *Human Organization*, 1973, *32*, 73–83.

Lorion, R. P. Socioeconomic status and traditional treatment approaches reconsidered. *Psychological Bulletin*, 1973, *79*, 263–270.

Lorion, R. P. Patient and therapist variables in the treatment of low-income patients. *Psychological Bulletin*, 1974, *81*, 344–354.

Lubchansky, I., Ergi, G., & Stokes, J. Puerto Rican spiritualists view mental illness: The faith healer as a paraprofessional. *American Journal of Psychiatry*, 1970, *127*, 312–321.

Madsen, W. Value conflicts and folk psychiatry in South Texas. In A. Kiev (Ed.), *Magic, faith and healing.* New York: Free Press, 1964.

Maldonado-Sierra, E. D., & Trent, R. D. The sibling relationship in group psychotherapy with Puerto Rican schizophrenics. *American Journal of Psychiatry*, 1960, *117*, 239–244.

Maldonado-Sierra, E. D., Trent, R. D., & Fernandez-Marian, R. F. Cultural factors in the group-psychotherapeutic process for Puerto Rican schizophrenics. *International Journal of Group Psychotherapy*, 1960, *10*, 373–382.

Martinez, C. Community mental health and the Chicano movement. *American Journal of Orthopsychiatry*, 1973, *43*, 595–601.

Padilla, A. M., & Ruiz, R. A. *Latino mental health: A review of literature.* Washington, D.C.: U.S. Government Printing Office, 1973.

Phillipus, M. J. Successful and unsuccessful approaches to mental health services for an urban Hispano-American population. *Journal of Public Health*, 1971, *61*, 820–830.

Ruiz, R. A. Relative frequency of Americans with Spanish surnames in associations of psychology, psychiatry, and sociology. *American Psychologist*, 1971, *26*, 1022–1024.

Schensul, S. L. Commentary: Skills needed in action anthropology: Lessons from El Centro de la Causa. *Human Organization*, 1974, *33*, 203–209.

Srole, L., Langer, T. S., Michael, S. T., Opler, M. K., & Rennie, T. A. C. *Mental health in the metropolis: The Midtown Manhattan study.* New York: McGraw-Hill, 1962.

Sue, S. Training of "Third World" students to function as counselors. *Journal of Counseling Psychology*, 1973, *20*, 73–78.

Torrey, E. F. *The mind game: Witchdoctors and psychiatrists.* New York: Emerson Hall, 1972.

U.S. Bureau of the Census. Persons of Spanish origin in the United States: November 1969. In *Current population reports* (Series P-20, No. 213). Washington, D.C.: U.S. Government Printing Office, 1971. (a)

U.S. Bureau of the Census. Selected characteristics of persons and families of Mexican, Puerto Rican, and other Spanish origin: March 1971. In *Current population reports* (Series P-20, No. 224). Washington, D.C.: U.S. Government Printing Office, 1971. (b)

Wolkon, G. H., Moriwaki, S., Mandel, D. M., Archuleta, Jr., Bunje, P., & Zimmermann, S. Ethnicity and social class in the delivery of services: Analysis of a child guidance clinic. *American Journal of Public Health,* 1974, *64,* 709–712.

Yamamoto, J., James, Q. C., & Palley, N. Cultural problems in psychiatric therapy. *Archives of General Psychiatry,* 1968, *19,* 45–49.

14 Counseling Puerto Ricans
Some Cultural Considerations
Christensen, Edward W.

Puerto Ricans comprise a significant percentage of potential clients for many counselors. The migration of Puerto Ricans to the mainland over the years has created cultural differences between Puerto Ricans raised in Puerto Rico and those raised in the U.S., but both groups are at a disadvantage in the dominant American culture. Migration back to the island in recent years is creating some problems for Puerto Rico, so Puerto Ricans often find prejudice both here and there. In this article the author, who married into a Puerto Rican family, discusses some values and traits that characterize Puerto Ricans and the behaviors that emerge from these traits. He offers practical suggestions for those counselors who have Puerto Rican clients.

In recent years the educational world has become increasingly concerned with students whose cultural backgrounds are different from those of the dominant culture in the U.S. This concern, though belated and still insufficient, has prompted other helping professions to follow the lead. Thus there has recently been increased publication on counseling members of minority groups, writers advocating giving more attention to the needs of clients who are culturally and ethnically different.

One of the outcomes of the increased attention given minority groups has been a tendency on the part of many to lump all minority individuals together. Thus, although early legislation and educational endeavors were designed to help blacks, American Indians, Mexican-Americans, and Puerto Ricans, they often served only to identify them all as having the same needs and disadvantages. Each group has protested this treatment, and all have insisted that their uniqueness be recognized and preserved. This need to understand the uniqueness of clients from specific cultural and ethnic backgrounds motivated the preparation of this article about counseling Puerto Ricans.

Some Facts about Puerto Rico

There is a great deal of ignorance among mainland Americans with regard to Puerto Rico. A few years ago, when I was in the U.S. on sabbatical leave from the University of Puerto Rico, I brought my automobile, which had Puerto Rican license plates. A number of people asked if the car had been driven from Puerto Rico! Other typical questions reveal a lack of knowledge concerning this significant group in our society. Mainland Americans have asked: "Aren't all Puerto Ricans dark-skinned?" "Does one need a passport to go there?" "You won't serve me that hot and spicy food, will you?"

Puerto Rico is an island in the Caribbean, about 1,050 miles from Miami and 1,650 miles from New York. The island is about 35 miles by 100 miles and has a population of over 2.8 million. Its population density is greater than that of China, Japan, or India. Puerto Ricans are all American citizens, proclaimed so by the Jones Act of 1917. The population is a mixture of Taino Indians, Africans, and Spaniards, although the Indian influence is much more cultural than biological, as conflicts with the Spaniards practically decimated that group. Skin colors range from as white as any Scandinavian to as black as the darkest African, with all shades and mixtures in between.

It is impossible in this article to clear up all the myths and misunderstandings about Puerto Rico and Puerto Ricans. Indeed, there is currently much study, debate, and conflict regarding many issues of Puerto Rico's culture, identity, and political future. (Readers will find relevant material cited in the list of suggested readings at the end of this article.) These larger issues will not be easily resolved, but the present reality concerning Puerto Ricans is crucial for today's educators and counselors. In order to perform in a helpful and ethical way in assisting clients to grow and make viable decisions, a counselor must recognize personal prejudices and erroneous assumptions.

The problem of understanding Puerto Ricans is confounded by the fact that today there are really two groups of Puerto Ricans. From a crowded island not overly endowed with natural resources beyond its people and its climate, thousands of Puerto Ricans have come to the mainland, especially in the period since World War II. Many have stayed. Scarcely a state is without any Puerto Ricans, and some places, such as New York City, Boston, Hartford (Connecticut), and several areas in New Jersey, have large numbers of Puerto Ricans. Many have raised families on the mainland, and these second- and third-generation Puerto Ricans are different in many significant ways from those who were raised on the island.

The mainland-raised Puerto Rican, sometimes called Neo-Rican, is generally English-dominant with respect to language. This Puerto Rican has adapted, as one might expect, to the unique environment of the urban setting but has retained a strong influence from and linkage to a primarily Latin American setting. Thus, having been brought up in another climate, with another language, with different fears and aspirations, and perhaps often with a different reference group, the mainland Puerto Rican is understandably different from the island Puerto Rican. Yet the culturally dominant group in the U.S. defines all Puerto Ricans in the same way, and the Neo-Rican often suffers from the same prejudices inflicted on the recent arrival from San Juan, Ponce, or Ciales.

In many ways, however, Puerto Ricans from the mainland and those from the island do share common cultural characteristics. As dangerous as generalizations can be, it is important for counselors to consider some of the qualities a Puerto Rican client might possess.

Cultural Characteristics

There are certain values and traits that are generally agreed on as being linked to the Puerto Rican ethos. Chief among these are *fatalismo, respeto, dignidad, machismo,* and *humanismo* (Hidalgo undated; Wagenheim 1970). Wells (1972) has added *afecto* to this list. (See the glossary at the end of this article for definitions of Spanish words used.) These cultural attributes are important to any group, and a wise counselor should have some understanding of them. The reader who has difficulty conceptualizing these terms may find it helpful to empathize with what the Puerto Rican experiences on entering an alien culture. The following explanations may help.

There is a certain amount of overlap in the words used above. *Dignidad* and *respeto,* which have to do with the dignity of an individual and respect for those deserving of it, are interrelated concepts. *Machismo,* generally connoting male superiority, is also part and parcel of the other cultural traits. Because these concepts are so central to the Puerto Rican as an individual and as a representative of a culture that is—at least politically—bound to this country, it is very important that the counselor understand how some of these attributes are translated into behaviors. The behaviors discussed apply in some degree to most Puerto Ricans, but in some instances they may be less typical of second-generation Puerto Ricans on the mainland.

Typically the Puerto Rican is highly individualistic, a person who is not used to working in concert with others, following in single file, and, in general, organizing in ways that Anglos would call "efficient." Whether in a traffic jam or a line of patrons in a bank, a Puerto Rican may break line and take a position ahead of others. But the Puerto Rican will also offer another person the same privilege, being much more tolerant than Anglos of this demonstration of individuality.

Another characteristic of Puerto Ricans is their demonstration of love and tolerance for children. It is rare that a baby or tot, taken down any street in Puerto Rico, is not exclaimed over, chucked under the chin, and generally complimented. This love for children is stronger than its stateside equivalent; generally speaking, in fact, the family unit is stronger among Puerto Ricans. Perhaps because of the love for children, illegitimacy is not frowned on or punished among Puerto Ricans. It is not unusual for families to add to their broods with nephews, nieces, godchildren, and even the children of husbands' alliances with mistresses. It is therefore difficult for the Puerto Rican arriving at a mainland school to understand all the fuss about different last names and shades of skin color and all the confusion about birth certificates among siblings.

The characteristic of gregariousness, a trait common to nearly all Puerto Ricans, often dismays many Americans, who view it as excessive when compared with their own culture. The existence of large families and extended families, the *compadrazgo* (godparent) relationship, and life on a crowded island are probably causes as well as effects of this gregariousness. Puerto Ricans love to talk, discuss, gossip, speculate, and relate. No one needs an excuse to have a fiesta. Music, food, and drink appear instantly if someone comes to visit. Group meetings, even those of the most serious nature, often take on some aspect of a social activity. I remember more than one dull and pedantic committee meeting at the University of Puerto Rico that was saved from being a total loss because refreshments and chatting were an inseparable part of the meetings. A colleague used to reinforce attendance at meetings in her office by furnishing lemon pie and coffee.

"Puerto Ricans are seldom found in professional or managerial jobs; they are usually working in low-paying, menial occupations, to an even greater degree than blacks."

Puerto Ricans' hospitality is related to their gregariousness. In the poorest home in a San Juan slum or in a remote mountain shack, a visitor will be offered what there is or what can be sent out for on the spot. And it is not good manners to refuse this hospitality; it is offered from the heart, and refusal is rejection. The visitor in this situation will give more by partaking of the hospitality than by bringing a gift.

As might be deduced from the preceding comments, Puerto Ricans are sensitive. Social intercourse has significant meaning, and Puerto Ricans typically are quite alert to responses they evoke in others and to others' behavior, even behavior of a casual nature. Often Puerto Ricans avoid a direct confrontation, and they do not like to give a straight-out no to anyone. Marqués (1967) is among those who have described Puerto Ricans as passively docile, and indeed docility is a noticeable Puerto Rican characteristic. Silén (1971), however, has interpreted this characteristic as actually having aggressive overtones, pointing out that historically this docility was simply a refusal to engage in battles that were impractical. Silén has also reminded us of some of the past and present revolutionary stirrings of the "docile" Puerto Rican. Whichever interpretation is accepted, there is evidence that there has been some change in this behavior, especially among younger Puerto Ricans on the island and those Puerto Ricans who have been raised on the mainland.

Puerto Ricans on the Mainland

For most readers of this article, the Puerto Rican living on the mainland is likely to be of greatest interest and relevance. There are approximately two million Puerto Ricans living in the U.S. They come to the mainland primarily for jobs. They generally do not intend to remain here and, as economic conditions for the family improve, increasingly return to the island. In recent years Puerto Rico has made some economic progress and some advances in creating jobs, and thus Puerto Ricans, who typically aspire to live in Puerto Rico, find it increasingly attractive to go back.

This return migration has created some economic, social, and educational problems for Puerto Rico. For example, when younger Puerto Ricans who have been raised in New York City or other areas return to the island, they face certain cultural assimilation problems not at all unlike those their parents faced when they came to the mainland. English-dominant young people must master Spanish for school, work, social life, and participation in family and civic affairs. These youngsters' modes of behavior are often in conflict with the attitudes and values of grandparents, uncles, and the general society. Some efforts are being made to deal with these conflicts, including the establishment of special classes given in English and even the employment of a bilingual counselor or two, but the island's resources are too limited to permit extensive help in this regard. It is fair to say, however, that the Puerto Rican returning to Puerto Rico is treated considerably better than the islander who comes to the U.S. mainland.

Puerto Ricans coming to the mainland often encounter prejudice. Part of this seems to be due to the fact that they are "foreign"; most Americans—even those whose parents were born in another country—are inclined to be cool, to say the least, toward people different from themselves.

"A person's name *is* that person, and a counselor's mispronouncing it—whether through carelessness or laziness—can easily be construed as the counselor's lack of interest in the client."

Certainly racism is another significant element in the prejudice against Puerto Ricans. Senior (1965) has reported:

> Census figures show that fewer non-white Puerto Ricans come to the States than whites, in comparison with their proportion of the population, and a special study indicates that a larger percentage of the non-whites return to their original homes after a sojourn on the mainland. (p. 46)

But problems for the Puerto Rican are not limited to prejudice. For those young people newly arrived in the States or born here of Puerto Rican parentage, the generation gap becomes compounded by what Senior has called "second-generationitis." These youngsters must contend not only with the expectancies and pressures of a different and dominant culture but also with conflicts of values representing two different cultures. Mainland Puerto Ricans may not be able to identify completely with the Puerto Rican culture, but neither are they a part of the dominant mainland culture. Social scientists often refer to this situation as the "identity crisis" of the Puerto Rican in the States.

As has been shown in the tragic treatment of blacks in the U.S., social and personal prejudice against a group is generally accompanied by a lack of economic opportunities for that group. Puerto Ricans are seldom found in professional or managerial jobs; they are usually working in low-paying, menial occupations, to an even greater degree than blacks. There are many causes for this. The low educational levels of Puerto Ricans on the mainland is undoubtedly a significant factor. Prejudice, suspicion, language difficulties, and the familiar self-fulfilling prophecy of low aspirations leading to lowly positions also play heavy roles in maintaining the Puerto Rican on the bottom rung of the economic and vocational ladder.

Practical Considerations for the Counselor

The following suggestions offered for counseling Puerto Ricans are based on my eleven years of experience as a counselor in Puerto Rico and on those human relations tenets to which all counselors presumably subscribe. The suggestions may seem simple and obvious to the reader; they are purposely so. They are intended as exhortations for those who are thoughtless, as reminders for those who forget, and as reinforcements for those who truly attempt to accept and understand their clients.

Examine your own prejudices. Counselors should consider their attitudes toward poor, rural, Spanish-speaking, racially mixed, culturally different clients. Knowledge alone cannot overcome prejudice, and an intellectual understanding expressed with emotional distaste will only serve to exacerbate the situation. If a counselor has negative stereotyped feelings about Puerto Ricans, it is not likely that his or her counseling relationships with them will be open and warm.

Call students by their right names. In Spanish, people are given two last names. The first last name is from the father's side of the family, the second from the mother's. The American custom is to look for the last word, and this becomes the last name. If this logic is followed with Latins, a student named Angel Rodríguez López gets called Angel López, thus dropping his father's family name. Not only might the father and son be understandably insulted by such cavalier treatment, but the boy's identity—in a real as well as a cultural sense—is in question. For those who fervently desire to maintain their cultural and personal identities without being antagonistic to the larger society, acknowledgment of the correct name can be critical.

Another element in this linguistic area is simply pronouncing names in reasonably accurate ways. Even though other students and staff may pronounce names inaccurately, it would seem that a counselor who espouses the establishment of good relationships might make a special effort in this area. A person's name *is* that person, and a counselor's mispronouncing it—whether through carelessness or laziness—can easily be construed as the counselor's lack of interest in the client. Counselors can check with a client about pronunciation. (Spanish, incidentally, is much more consistent in pronunciation than English, because each vowel is pronounced the same way in all words.)

Work with the family. For the Puerto Rican, the family is much more important than it is for the typical American. If possible, the counselor should deal not only with the young person but also with the family, getting to know them as well as the youngster. If this is not possible, the counselor can at least talk with the client about his or her family. Among Puerto Ricans, the family and extended family are often sought out for help more readily than is a counselor; research, in fact, indicates that the family is the source of greatest help (Christensen 1973). The counselor should realize that others are helping and should work with them, understanding that each person has something to offer. Ignoring this fact is equivalent to refusing to recognize that a client is also receiving help from another professional.

Refrain from using the child as an interpreter. In cases where a parent knows little English and the child is reasonably bilingual, it is a temptation to rely on the son or daughter to carry a message to the parent. This should be avoided whenever possible. Even though it might be a source of pride for the child, it might place the parent in a dependent position, preventing the parent from entering into the counseling relationship as a full partner. There is an additional concern: the possibility that the child might twist others' statements. Puerto Rican families are close, but a situation in which a parent continually communicates only through the child can alter relationships and create family strains.

Understand that to the Puerto Rican you are the foreigner. One cannot jump into instant relationships. The counselor must give the client time to know and trust him or her. To facilitate this, the counselor may need to meet the client outside of the school or the counselor's office. The counselor should share and be somewhat self-disclosing, revealing some things about his or her family, ideas, home, and so on, in order to give the client a chance to know the counselor as a person. Counselor self-disclosure can be a sign of trust for any client, but it is even more crucial where some feeling of "foreignness" is present in both counselor and client.

Understand the concept of "hijo de crianza." This term refers to someone other than the child's parents raising the child—either family members (such as an aunt or a grandmother), extended family members (such as a godparent), or even a friend or neighbor. It also may refer to a family's raising the father's children from another marriage or even from outside a legal union. Counselors must not apply their moral values in such situations. The child is the parents' child through love and acceptance, and exact relationships are not that important.

Be patient. This should be a given for all counselors with all clients, but it is especially true when counselors desire to establish any kind of relationship with clients from a different culture. Puerto Ricans have many obstacles to overcome, some of which are not of their own making. In the counseling relationship, counselors have to overcome some of these same hurdles. Counselors must demonstrate their credibility, honesty, and reliability, just as their Puerto Rican clients must do almost daily in an alien society. The difference is that the counselor is in a more advantageous position, and therefore the counselor's initiative is crucial. The Puerto Rican client may expect the counselor to be prejudiced, arrogant, and lacking in knowledge about Puerto Ricans. The burden is on the counselor to demonstrate that these expectations will not be fulfilled.

The Fruits of Labor

The counselor who works with Puerto Ricans of any age and in any setting may find some difficulty in doing so. But counselors who are willing to learn will find the effort rewarding. Puerto Rican clients need counselors as much as—or more than—other clients do. Moreover, in the final analysis, we Americans need them also. For they, along with all people of differing ethnic and cultural backgrounds, offer all of us a richness that even a wealthy country cannot afford to be without.

Glossary of Spanish Terms

afecto   literally means "affect." Refers to the affective side of life—warmth and demonstrativeness.

compadrazgo   refers to the relationship entered into when a person becomes a godfather (*padrino*) or godmother (*madrina*). This person then becomes a *compadre* or *comadre* with the parents of the child and traditionally not only takes on certain responsibilities for the child but also is closely related to the entire family of the other person. In some cases this may also involve even other *compadres,* and then the total relationships derived from this system of *compadrazgo* are complex and far-reaching and form the basis for what sociologists term the extended family, which is so characteristic of many societies.

dignidad   dignity, but of special importance in Puerto Rico and closely related to *respeto.* One can oppose another person, but taking away a person's respect or dignity in front of others is about the worst thing one can do.

fatalismo   fatalism.

humanismo   humanism, especially as contrasted with the more pragmatic set of the typical Anglo.

machismo   related to male superiority and, in its original form, implying the innate and biological inferiority of women. Characterized as an overcompensatory reaction to the dependence-aggression conflict, *machismo* is acted out through fighting and sexual conquest.

respeto   signifies respect, especially respect for authority, family, and tradition.

References

Christensen, E.W. (Ed.) Report of the task force for the study of the guidance program of the Puerto Rican Department of Education, vocational and technical education area. San Juan, Puerto Rico: College Entrance Examination Board, 1973.

Hidalgo, H.A. The Puerto Rican. In National Rehabilitation Association (Ed.), *Ethnic differences influencing the delivery of rehabilitation services: The American Indian; the black American; the Mexican American; and the Puerto Rican.* Washington, D.C.: National Rehabilitation Association, undated.

Marqués, R. *Ensayos (1953-1966).* San Juan, Puerto Rico: Editorial Antillana, 1967.

Senior, C. *The Puerto Rican: Strangers—Then neighbors.* Chicago: Quadrangle Books, 1965.

Silén, J.A. *We, the Puerto Rican people: A story of oppression and resistance.* New York: Monthly Review Press, 1971.

Wagenheim, K. *Puerto Rico: A profile.* New York: Praeger, 1970.

Wells, H. *La modernización de Puerto Rico: Un analisis politico de valores e instituciones en proceso de cambio.* San Juan, Puerto Rico: Editorial Universitaria, 1972.

Suggested Readings

Adams, J.F. Population: A Puerto Rican catastrophe. Address delivered to the Puerto Rican League of Women Voters, Hato Rey, Puerto Rico, February 1972.

Cordasco, F., & Bucchions, E. *Puerto Rican children in mainland schools.* Metuchen, N.J.: The Scarecrow Press, 1968.

Espin, O.M., & Renner, R.R. Counseling: A new priority in Latin America. *Personnel and Guidance Journal,* 1974, *52*(5), 297-301.

Fernández Méndez, E. (Ed.) *Portrait of a society: Readings on Puerto Rican sociology.* San Juan, Puerto Rico: University of Puerto Rico Press, 1972.

Fitzpatrick, J.P. *Puerto Rican Americans: The meaning of migration to the mainland.* Englewood Cliffs, N.J.: Prentice-Hall, 1971.

15 Counseling Latinos

Ruiz, René A.

Padilla, Amado M.

Our purpose here is to provide background information and techniques that will enable counselors to communicate more effectively and to counsel more successfully with Latino clients. To achieve this, we have summarized information that communicates the many ways in which Latino clients are similar and dissimilar to other non-Latino clients. Deliberate effort is made to identify resource documentation to provide interested counselors an opportunity to explore contact areas in greater depth, if desired. This summary material, which is designed to facilitate understanding of typical and unique problems faced by Latinos, is organized around the following topical outlines: (a) Demographic characteristics of the target population, (b) Ethnohistory and culture, (c) Sources of psychological stress, (d) Utilization of services, and (e) Factors reducing self-referral.

Following presentation of this introductory material, case histories of two Latino clients appear. These were deliberately selected to illustrate points made in preceding sections; but, in addition, they serve to facilitate the presentation of specific recommendations for the counseling of Latino clients. The case histories are followed by a concluding section presenting general recommendations for counselors and the settings in which they function.

Demographic Characteristics of the Target Population

The term ''Latino'' is used in this article as a generic label including all people of Spanish origin and descent. United States Bureau of the Census reports (1971a, 1971b) indicate the existence of at least 9,000,000 Latino residents in the United States. While this figure almost certainly underestimates the current size of the Latino group, it appears adequate for our purposes. Analyzing the Latino group by geographic area of origin, and rounding by millions, population estimates as of 1972 are as follows: Central and South America (0.5), Cuba (0.6), Mexico (5.0), Puerto Rico (1.5), and other (1.5).

The census data further indicate that an absolute and relative majority of Latinos are urban-dwellers; 82.5 percent compared with 67.8 percent for the total population and 76 percent for Blacks. Furthermore, locus of residence and Latino subgroup membership are related. More specifically, Chicanos are heavily represented in the Southwest United States; 87 percent reside in Arizona, California, Colorado, New Mexico, and Texas. Most Puerto Ricans reside in either Connecticut, New Jersey, or New York (76%); while most immigrants from Cuba are situated in Florida.

In addition to being urban dwellers, disproportionately large numbers of Latinos are members of the lower income groups. The 1971 census reports that 2.4 million Latinos or 26.7 percent were classified as living ''in poverty.'' Closer examination of census data on personal and family income support the inference that the standard of living among Latinos is relatively lower than the general population. In 1970, for example, the median income for Latino males was $6,220 compared with $8,220 for non-Latino males. Examination of family income confirms the general trend; overrepresentation for Latinos in the lower income groups and underrepresentation in the higher income groups. More specifically, 23 percent of the families reported income of less than $5,000 a year compared with 14.7 percent of the general population; while only 18.4 percent had incomes greater than $15,000 compared with 35.5 percent of the general population. There is no reason to believe that this situation has improved from 1970 to 1976.

Difference in patterns of employment and unemployment between Latinos and the non-Latino population exist, and these are interpreted as representing additional stress for Latinos. With regard to status of employment, Latinos are overrepresented in occupations that are menial and low paying; for example, 76 percent are blue-collar workers. With regard to unemployment, a 1975 Bureau of Labor Statistics report indicates that during the third quarter of 1974 the unemployment rate among Latinos was 8 percent, which is intermediate between the national level (5%) and that among Blacks (10.5%). These data are somewhat deceptive, however, unless one considers the increase in unemployment during the preceding year was 29 percent among Latinos, compared with 22 percent among the general population and 8 percent among Blacks.

With respect to education the US census reports the following for Anglos, Black, and Latino males aged 25 years and older; median years of education: 12.2, 9.6, and 9.3 years; fewer than five years of schooling: 5.0, 13.5, and 19.5 percent; and, graduation from high school: 56.4, 34.7, and 32.6 percent. Thus, regardless of which of three educational criteria is examined, the inference remains unchanged. Latinos are provided the least education, compared with either the general population or to American blacks.

In conclusion, Latinos are, on the *average,* urban dwellers, poor and low paid, menially employed and fearful of layoffs, and undereducated relative to age peers who are not Latino. Factors such as these are unquestionably significant sources of stress in US society. It also follows that we would expect, because of increased stress, a relatively higher frequency of self-referrals for counseling and psychotherapy among Latinos. Keep this syllogism in mind while examining subsequent sections of this article.

Ethnohistory and Culture

Above, we presented demographic data that demonstrates how Latinos differ from the general population. Here we describe the Latino experience from a historical perspective as a means of documenting three major points. First, we maintain that Latinos may be thought of as members of a single cultural group in the sense they share historically similarities in language, values, and tradition. Second, we simultaneously maintain that this Latino culture group is highly heterogeneous, and that for some purposes, *should* be conceptualized as an aggregate of distinct subcultures, each possessing a recognizable pattern of unique traits. Third, we believe that information on ethnohistory and culture is important for non-Latino counselors who need to be able to differentiate between members of different Latino subcultures.

In terms of a commonsense example of relevance to our topic, we are arguing that a particular counseling program designed to deal with a specific type of problem might be highly successful with Chicanos, moderately successful with Cubans, and of only limited success with Puerto Ricans because of subcultural differences across groups.

The preceding argument is complex and subtle. What is involved is the identification of patterns of similarity among *individual* members of different subcultural groups, who are by definition unique in many aspects. The next step, of course, is to create "culturally relevant" programs of counseling and psychotherapy based on intragroup subculture similarities that achieve maximum success rates in constructive behavior change and personal growth. The interested reader is referred to Padilla and Ruiz (1973) and Padilla, Ruiz, and Alvarez (1975) for an analysis of culturally relevant counseling programs for Latinos.

Our ethnohistorical account begins with the Spanish explorers who arrived in the New World in the early 16th century, bringing with them a relatively homogeneous culture similar in language, values, tradition, and costume. In Mexico, they overthrew the Aztec empire, intermarried with the natives, and soon thereafter began to migrate north. The Rio Grande, or "Big River," current border between the United States and Mexico, was crossed in 1528. By the mid-16th century, settlements had been created in what today is Northern New Mexico. These original immigrants included Spaniards from Europe, native Americans from Mexico, and the *mestizo* or "mixed blood" progeny of these two groups.

These events contribute to our thesis in three ways. First, genetic merger resulted in the gradual creation of a new Indo-Hispanic culture. Second, Spaniards as well as the *mestizo* offspring sought new lands to explore and colonize. Third, the settlers who reached Northern New Mexico remained relatively isolated from Mexico and Spain, because of geographic distance and dilatory transportation. Later, they were outgrouped by the immigrants who came to call themselves the ''Americans'' of the United States. These Latinos came to refer to themselves as ''Spanish-Americans,'' or Hispanos, and coincidentally were the first people of European or European-Indian stock to settle in what is present day United States.

This process of Spanish-Indian intermarriage and cultural fusion was occurring simultaneously in other parts of the New World. In some areas, native inhabitants were slain or driven off their land, and their cultures destroyed. Slaves from Africa were sometimes imported (Puerto Rico is a prime example) and the process of intermarriage and culture fusion continued for several hundred years. The net result, of course, was that a number of subculture groups were formed. The subgroups are commonly referred to as Latinos, or ''the Latino culture,'' which blurs significant differences across groups. As our ethnohistorical analysis reveals, Latinos differ in genetic heritage as indicated by observable physical characteristics, and in cultural tradition (the relative extent to which a given subculture is based on influences from Europe, and the New World, or Africa.) Let's examine some of these differences more closely to learn how they can determine need for, and response to, counseling intervention.

Skin color is one obvious physical characteristic with a genetic link that differentiates Latino subgroups. The range in skin coloration is from ''white,'' through *mestizo* and mulatto ''brown,'' to African ''black.'' Considering the long-standing prejudice in this country to people of color, it seems certain that darker Latinos experienced greater discrimination than lighter ones.

The types of subcultures formed were also influenced by original motivations for leaving their country of birth and migrating to a new country. Some Spaniards migrated for immediate personal gain with no thought of creating a new home. These people came to explore, colonize, exploit, and return. Others built new homes: they sought economic opportunity and personal liberty. Still others came because of interactions between complex social, political, economic, and personal factors. Today, Latinos have migrated to the United States in waves, to seek employment or to escape periods of civil strife in their country of origin.

Thus we can see that a large group of Latinos can be identified on the basis of shared characteristics: primarily, language, values, and tradition. Further, this large group includes a number of distinct subcultures that share these characteristics, but to varying degrees. This variation is attributable to the degree of acculturation among Latinos to the majority culture of the United States that is basically WASP and monolingual English. Here we will turn to an examination of acculturation because it bears directly upon the kinds of social stresses experienced by Latinos in the United States, which in turn is one factor that determines need for counseling.

One characteristic that determines rate of acculturation is fluency in English, yet the commitment to Spanish among Latinos is so strong that 50 percent report it as their "native tongue," and as their preferred "home language." What this means in effect is that unlike many other ethnic groups, Latinos overall have tenaciously held on to their Spanish language, despite the fact that English is the language of the school, work, and play.

Latinos also differ from mainstream Americans with regard to values (e.g., religious preference). The vast majority of Latinos profess Roman Catholicism, with only a relatively small percentage professing Protestant faiths. In contrast, the dominant religious preference of the majority culture is reversed; that is, more professed Protestants than Roman Catholics.

The characteristic of Latino tradition is extremely complex, and therefore more difficult to describe succinctly in terms of variation from the majority culture. The most prominent features, and those of greater significance for the counselor formulating programs based on cultural and subcultural differences, appear in the areas of family structure and attendant sex roles. The extended family structure is most common by far, but characteristically includes: (a) respect for the authority of a dominant father who rules the household; (b) unwavering love for the mother who serves a unifying function within the family; (c) formalized kinship relations such as the *compadrazgo* "godfather" system; and (d) loyalty to the family that takes precedence over other social institutions. In addition, sex roles are traditionally more rigid and demarcated more clearly, males are granted greater independence and at an earlier age than females, and there are greater expectations for achievement outside the home for males. Again, the reader is reminded these are summary statements; a more detailed analysis of family structure and sex-role behavior appears in Ruiz and Padilla (unpublished manuscript).

There exists an additional pattern of behavior, which seems to stem from family structure and sex role, which differentiates Latinos from non-Latinos. Latinos typically manifest *personalismo,* a term denoting a preference for personal contact and individualized attention in dealing with power structures, such as social institutions. Anglos, in contrast, seem to favor an organizational approach that follows impersonal regulations (the "chain of command"). Consistent with a preference for more personalized interaction is the observation of relatively more frequent physical contact among Latinos. For example, handshakes between acquaintances and *abrazos* (embraces) among friends are the norm upon meeting and leaving. The influence of *personalismo* appears early and is reflected in play. Mexican children are the most cooperative, Anglo the most competitive, and Mexican-American children are intermediate (Madsen & Shapira 1970). Of more immediate relevance to our thesis is the finding that Latino clients prefer to use first names rather than formal titles in centers dispensing counseling and psychotherapy services (Kline 1969).

Counselors interested in increasing their counseling skills by learning more about Latino culture will probably explore the social science literature.

This may prove to be hazardous, however, because this literature contains a certain degree of misinformation concerning the "true nature" of the Latino character. Unsupported "findings" based on single-study research, or subjective opinions presented in the context of unsubstantiated essays, seem to have been accepted by a segment of the scientific community. What may have occurred is that a certain degree of spurious "validity" has been created through constant repetition rather than through the gradual accumulation of validating research. Without casting aspersions on the motivation of persons creating or perpetuating such myths, it does seem as if the most widely disseminated and firmly held are pejorative in nature.

It has been alleged often, for example, that Latinos are fatalists (Heller 1967). The belief that Latinos adhere to predestination has been supported by a few studies showing, to use more technical language, higher "external reinforcement" scores on tests of "locus of control" (Lefcourt 1966; Rotter 1954, 1966). This finding disappears, however, when socioeconomic status is controlled (Stone & Ruiz 1974). Related to the myth of fatalism and belief in predestination is the idea that Latinos possess distorted attitudes toward time. Specifically, Latinos are presumably present time oriented, unduly emphasizing immediate gratification, and displaying underdeveloped skills in future planning. This tendency to enjoy the moment and to defer unpleasant responsibilities to some vague, indeterminate point in the future, seems widely accepted despite a dearth of supportive evidence. What may be occurring is that some non-Latinos translate common Latino responses such as mañana ("Tomorrow"), or *Lo que Dios desea* ("Whatever God wills"), into literal English equivalents. Any translation that ignores cultural and subcultural *values* runs the risk, of course, of communicating *meaning* inaccurately. It is at least conceivable that a Latino youngster who expends minimal effort in the pursuit of scholastic or academic goals is responding realistically to societal constraints based on discrimination and prejudice, rather than displaying any deficiency in "achievement motivation."

The last concept we explore to better acquaint counselors with the unique aspects of Latino clients is acculturation. Each Latino client, in addition to being a member of the greater Latino culture and some smaller Latino subculture, is simultaneously a member of the majority, Anglo culture to some degree. Degree of acculturation can be inferred from degree of commitment of cultural variables; that is, language values, tradition, diet, and costume. Thus, a Latino client who is monolingual Spanish or bilingual Spanish-English, with Spanish dominant: Roman Catholic; a member of an extended family; and who prefers ethnic food and dress is probably much less acculturated to the majority, Anglo culture of the United States than some other Latino client who is monolingual English, non-Catholic, from or in a nuclear family, and without preferences for the diet or clothing characteristic of his ethnic group. As we hope to show later, these variables of cultural preference and acculturation interact with the variable of *source of stress* to determine what type of counseling approach will be maximally successful with a given Latino client. It now seems appropriate to examine sources of stress for Latino clients.

Sources of Stress

In this section, we differentiate between *intrapsychic* and *extrapsychic* sources of stress. We use the former term (intrapsychic) to identify problems of a personal or individual nature that arise independent of ethnic minority group membership. We propose—although empirical evidence corroborating this supposition has not yet been collected—that Latino clients experiencing intrapsychic stress will respond similarly, if not exactly, as will non-Latino clients experiencing the same stress. For example, if a young person is graduating from high school, uncertain as to whether to attend college or which major to pursue, it probably makes relatively little difference whether this student is Latino or not. Regardless of ethnicity, a young person in such a dilemma would probably complain about feelings of uncertainty, indecision, insecurity, personal inadequacy, and general apprehension concerning his or her own, and familial expectations. Finally, ethnicity would probably have relatively little influence upon the type of counseling approach designed to help such a client formulate and achieve more compatible life goals with less personal discomfort.

We have reserved the term *extra psychic* to refer to sources of stress that stem from outside the person and that are basically societal or environmental rather than personal. Our interest, of course, lies with extrapsychic stress associated with ethnic minority group membership. Thus, we focus upon prejudices against Latinos and the effect of discriminatory practices upon character formation, personality function, and coping. We have already documented earlier, for example, that Latinos are victims of the "poverty cycle": depressed personal and family incomes, fewer years of education, overrepresentation in menial occupations, and elevated rates of unemployment. This cycle is self-perpetuating because the victims are less able to subsidize their own education, those of their children, or to qualify for better, higher paying employment. Furthermore, in comparison with other ethnic groups, Latino students possess fewer "role models" to imitate who have achieved success through continued education or training. Other stressful consequences of poverty include decreased social status, inadequate health care and nutrition, and a generally reduced quality of life.

This discussion suggests that the counselor may anticipate three "types" of Latino clients with regard to the sources of stress that motivate self-referral for counseling. Some will complain of intrapsychic stress and present problems similar to those of non-Latino clients. Others will be experiencing extrapsychic stress and will appear similar to other clients who are victims of prejudice and discrimination. But most Latino clients will probably seek counseling for problems stemming from both sources of stress. In any event, this analysis suggests that rates of self-referral for counseling and psychotherapy are expected to be elevated relative to the general population. Now let's examine relevant data to determine the accuracy of this prediction.

Utilization of Services

Available utilization data of public mental health service facilities indicates that Latinos, contrary to expectations, and despite *greater* stress, refer themselves *less* often for counseling and psychotherapy, relative to the general population (for review see Padilla & Ruiz 1973; Padilla et al. 1975; Ruiz, Padilla & Alvarez, in press). The most recent survey of utilization of state and county mental hospitals across the nation (Bachrach 1975) reveals the following: (a) the age-adjusted rate of admission for Latinos is 155 per 100,000 population, compared with 181 for other white and 334 for non-whites, (b) age-adjusted rate of admission rates are approximately double for Latino males compared with Latino females (212 to 103 per 100,000 population), and (c) adjusting for relative differences in the sizes of ethnic groups, Latino admissions are highest among the youngest (ages 14-25 years), and oldest (age 65 years and older).

Moving from the national scene and turning to geographic areas impacted with Mexican Americans, underutilization of counseling and psychotherapy continues. It has been estimated by Karno and Edgerton (1969) that Mexican Americans made up between 9 to 10 percent of California's population from 1962 to 1968. During this period, the percentages of Mexican Americans admitted for treatment in California facilities were as follows: 2.2 percent to the state hospital system, 3.4 percent to state mental hygiene clinics, 10.9 percent to the neuropsychiatric institute, and 2.3 percent to state and local facilities. The resident in-patient population was 3.8 percent. A similar pattern of underutilization of private and public mental hospitals by Mexican Americans has been found in Texas (Jaco 1960). Of even greater direct relevance are findings reported in an unpublished manuscript by Perez (1975) of significant underutilization of university counseling services by Chicano students.

Factors Reducing Self-Referral

Discouraging institutional policies may be largely responsible for the underutilization of counseling and psychotherapeutic services by Latinos. A sufficiently large body of literature describe counseling services as "inappropriate" or "irrelevant" in meeting the needs of the Latino community. All too frequently, services are provided in agencies or centers situated at unrealistic geographic distances from the residences of the target population. Further, it is obvious that monolingual Spanish, or bilingual Spanish-English clients, cannot be served adequately by monolingual English speaking professionals. Yet, this is precisely the situation at a number of treatment centers as described by Torrey (1972), Edgerton and Karno (1971), and Karno and Edgerton (1969). Other authors (Abad et al. 1974: Kline 1969; Torrey 1972; Yamamoto et al. 1968) have theorized that the process of counseling will be retarded when clients and counselors are members of different socioeconomic class groups or possess different sets of cultural values.

Elsewhere, (Padilla & Ruiz 1973; Padilla et al. 1975; Ruiz et al., in press), we have summarized arguments by others suggesting that Latinos refer themselves less often because of factors such as "pride" or some hypothetical characteristic of Latino culture that somehow functions to reduce the destructive effects of stress. Typical "stress resistant" factors have included the extended family, religious belief, and recourse to *curanderos* or "faith healers." In general, we have rejected these unsupported speculations, and have argued instead that Latinos have rejected traditional counseling services because of discouraging institutional practices, linguistic problems, and culture-class differences that retard communication. It now seems appropriate to review case histories—and to share our recommendations—as a means of showing how the sensitive counselor can create culturally relevant counseling programs that are specific to his Latino clients and that are more valid.

Case Histories

Here, we present case histories from Latino clients seeking counseling. We exercise our ethical responsibility to preserve confidentiality by minimizing identifying information. Nevertheless, these are "real," albeit disguised cases. Furthermore, we have fictionalized certain elements, as you shall see, to communicate theoretical points more lucidly. Even though both clients are "alike" because they are Latinos, we strongly advise the counselor to remain alert to individual differences based upon subculture group membership (such as Chicano versus Cuban), sources of stress (intrapsychic versus extrapsychic), and degree of acculturation (that is, relative degree of commitment to the majority group versus the subculture group). We propose that these are the variables of major significance in designing valid counseling programs for culturally different clients.

Case 1: Maria. This client identifies herself as "Spanish-American." Her ancestors have resided in Northern New Mexico under conditions of relative sociocultural isolation for generations. She is fluent in both Spanish and English, but her Spanish retains regional archaicisms unfamiliar to other Latinos and her English is slightly accented. Her politics are conservative, she was educated in a Roman Catholic school system, is committed to the dicta of her faith, and was reared in the large extended family structure that is traditional in that region.

Maria's life adjustment was uneventful until she left home for the first time and enrolled in a California college. There she was shocked by her encounters with Chicanos and Chicanas who were personally assertive, less inhibited in personal decorum, and more liberal politically. She could not deal with the rejection and disdain she experienced when she identified herself as "Spanish," rather than Chicana. This is her opening statement when she sought counseling.

> Moving away from home had a great psychological impact on me and my ideals. I had some difficulty adjusting myself to a completely new and independent form of life. Being Spanish-American, I was always closely bound to the family. When I tried to deviate from the norm, I was reprimanded and reminded of the obligation I had to the family. Living away from home taught me to appreciate them (family) and their conservative values more than I had before...but we sure are different from the people in California!

The brief history and presenting complaint identify Maria as a Latina whose subcultural identification is Hispano. Our comments on Latino ethnohistory, as well as the clients own opening comments, confirm the contention of differences across Latino subculture groups. Maria voices awareness that she is "different from the people (Chicanos) in California!" and we agree. Furthermore, we argue that Maria would become aware of other subculture group differences if her encounter had been with Puerto Ricans (or Cubans, or other Latinos), rather than California Chicanos.

With regard to degree of acculturation, Maria seems basically bicultural. Available history indicates she is a bilingual who is equally familiar with the values and traditions of both the majority culture and the Latino culture. Examining her personal value system stemming from identification with her Hispano subculture, she seems less assimilated into the Chicano subculture attending California colleges, than to the majority culture in some ways! This is an important point, expanded further in our discussion of sources of stress and recommendations for counseling.

Examining intrapsychic sources of stress first, Maria's major problem seems to be she is a college freshman away from home for the first time. Like other young people in a similar situation (regardless of ethnicity), Maria is almost certainly homesick and lonely. She probably misses friends, relatives, and familiar places. Her opening statement refers to problems in "adjusting." Her ability to tolerate and lessen distress is lowered because of her absence from familiar support systems (home, family, and church), while in a new, taxing, demanding, different, and frightening environment. At a less obvious level of analysis, there are hints that Maria is experiencing an identity crisis. She is clearly uncertain of subculture group identification as reflected by questions such as, "Am I Spanish as we call ourselves within the family, or Chicana as my new friends insist?" Maria has noted that fellow students are more assertive, striving, and goal-oriented; now she is beginning to wonder if perhaps she would get more of what she wanted out of life if she were less passive. For example, feminism and the Chicano movement intrigue Maria, but the people involved seem "pushy" to her in many ways. And at a more personal and intimate level, Maria is beginning to question her traditional conservatism and her decorous sexual mores.

With regard to extrapsychic sources of stress, Maria denies any major hassles with the dominant culture. While she is subjected to the same general level of prejudice and discrimination that other Latinos are, it seems neither personal or excessive at this time. Note, however, the anomalous situation with regard to her treatment by Chicanos and Chicanas. The Chicano student community rejects Maria because her self-designated "Spanishness" is misperceived as an attempt to deny her "Mexicanness."

How does the counselor respond to this complex of problems, and in what priority? We shall outline a culturally relevant treatment program but encourage the reader to anticipate our recommendations and to amplify upon them as he or she goes along. First, it seems to us the problem of priority is Maria's sense of personal isolation. We would recommend a supportive approach to minimize this intrapsychic source of stress. Although unstated, Maria is almost certainly experiencing dysphoric affect, probably depression ranging somewhere between mild to moderate degrees of severity. An initial approach that works well with problems of this sort is to minimize any tendencies toward apathy and social withdrawal by encouraging interpersonal interaction. Specifically, Maria, like any young person with depressive tendencies, should be encouraged to date, to go to parties, to mix with people her own age and so on. Simultaneously, Maria's major assets should be identified and reflected back to her, repeatedly, if necessary to enhance self-esteem. For example, if she is doing well academically she should be reminded of her intellectual assets: her bright mind, her good study habits, her perseverance, and so on. This supportive approach of confronting Maria with positive aspects of her life adjustment will tend to retard movement in the direction of increased depression.

A problem of second-order priority for Maria is her estrangement from the local Chicano student community. This is particularly lamentable for Maria because this group represents a "natural" but underutilized resource to combat what has been termed Maria's "first problem": her combined sense of low self-esteem, loneliness, mild depression, and isolation. Maria is a Chicana in more ways than she is not; and mutual realization of this aspect of her identity will facilitate Maria's admission into the Chicano group; in turn, it can provide her with much needed emotional support.

One reason Maria and the Chicano group have failed to achieve harmonious rapprochement may be a mutual misjudgment of how each perceives the other. It is conceivable that Maria is unaware that Chicanos perceive Mexican Americans who call themselves "Spanish" as denying their heritage; and some of the Chicanos may not know that Mexican Americans from Northern New Mexico refer to themselves in that manner with no connotation of deliberate efforts to "pass" from one ethnic group to another. Reconciliation may be achieved if both parties become more familiar with their own ethnohistory. While this goal could be attained by the counselor bringing this issue to the attention of the ethnic studies department, if one exists, and having them plan a course or lecture on ethnohistory, we propose an alternative course. We recommend Maria be informed of the possible source of the mutual misunderstanding discussed here, and that she be encouraged to confront those Chicanos who have been scornful. This approach has several advantages: Maria will be required to become more assertive; her approach behavior toward others will counteract her withdrawal tendencies; and everyone involved examines the problem from a fresh perspective.

The third problem for Maria is her blurred, changing, and developing sense of personal identity. She seems to be going through a psychological growth phase that involves questioning life values, but this process is evaluated by us as "normal" or "healthy" (Wrenn & Ruiz 1970). She is not exactly certain "who she is" as yet, but continued self-exploration should be encouraged by her counselor because enhanced self-awareness will minimize subjective discomfort and expediate self-actualization. The counselor maintains the responsibility, of course, for determining whether this third general recommendation is appropriate for Maria; and if so, of selecting the techniques and methods thought to be maximally growth-inducing for this client.

Case 2: Antonio. Like Maria, Antonio is bicultural and bilingual. Unlike Maria, however, he is a native Californian Chicano, he only attends college parttime, and he is a committed activist politically. In fact, Antonio attends so many Chicano meetings that his grades are suffering and his employers have chided him for his absenteeism and tardiness. Let's examine part of his opening statement during an initial interview to get a stronger sense of what he is like as a person.

> Because of Mexican American descent my parents wish to see their son attend a college or university and further the Chicano cause. We speak Spanish frequently at home and maintain the Mexican heritage. We are a proud family—of our home, community, and heritage . . .I wish to become something proud, an example to my thousands of little brothers and sisters in the barrios across the nation.

In a subsequent session, Antonio complained of oppression by local police due to their alleged prejudice against La Raza. When pressed for details, Antonio reported this pattern: he would visit one of the elementary school playgrounds in the neighborhood, introduce himself to small groups of children at play, and begin to instruct his "little brothers and sisters" in Chicano culture. Parents or school officials would contact the police, who would come to investigate "loitering" by a grown man in his late twenties. Antonio also complained of snide remarks made by various officers to the effect that he should shorten his hair length and stop wearing a decorated leather headband ("He looks like a damned Indian in a John Wayne movie.").

Here we present the same type of analysis as with Maria, but we can be more succinct because our theoretical approach is familiar by now. In terms of cultural group membership, Antonio is self-identified as "Chicano," and we concur with his opinion. He fails to recognize, however, the degree to which he is acculturated into the majority culture. Despite his Chicanismo, for example, his unaccented English is fluent and he is already far beyond the average Chicano in terms of number of years of education and potential employment and earning power.

The discrimination between intrapsychic and extrapsychic sources of stress becomes especially difficult when the two are conmingled, as with Antonio. Regardless of source of stress we can be fairly certain he is uncomfortable since he referred himself for counseling. His complaint that "people just don't understand" (elicited in a later part of the first meeting), can be interpreted in at least two ways. He may feel he may try harder to communicate more effectively. That is, he may believe major change must come from within. This is a classic example, of course, of motivation for personal change based on intrapsychic stress. On the other hand, Antonio may believe "he's O.K.," but that society is "not O.K." (Harris 1973). In such a case, he would experience stress as extrapsychic: that is, he would identify the source of his discomfort as environmental, rather than personal.

The first step in formulating a counseling program for Antonio is to render an opinion concerning the accuracy of his reporting and the quality of his judgment. To state the proposition as bluntly as possible, we are recommending that the counselor deal immediately with the question of whether or not Antonio is distorting reality. One needs to know, to use Antonio's polemic rhetoric, whether he is a hapless victim of "police oppression" as he claims, or, which is equally possible given the sparse information provided here, whether his relations with figures of authority are essentially "paranoid."

The answer to this question is important, because it tells us whether stress is mainly internal or external. This information can be used to create treatment programs of maximum relevance and efficacy. If it turns out that Antonio is psychotic and is imagining or exaggerating police intervention, then the counselor may respond with immediate support, seek psychiatric consultation concerning the need for ataractic medication or institutionalization, and begin preparing for whatever intervention model has the greatest probability for change in the direction of less inappropriate behavior. With regard to this latter point, we are referring to preferred modes of therapeutic theory and technique, such as, nondirective counseling versus psychoanalytic psychotherapy, reflection versus free association, and so on. If on the other hand, Antonio is not psychotic and is reporting accurately, then a much different approach is called for. Before describing a counseling program for Antonio based upon the opinion he is neither psychotic nor paranoid, but is reporting discrimination accurately, we discuss how such an opinion might be reached.

At the risk of appearing melodramatic, we ask the reader to examine his or her own biases concerning relations between ethnic minority group people and organized power structures such as civic agencies, government bureaucracies, or the police. This exercise in introspection bears upon points that follow and may be illuminating, particularly if the reader has given relatively little thought to the issue.

Our first point concerning this issue is that preconceptions and prejudices are dangerous since they obscure critical judgment. The skilled and responsible counselor responds to the needs of the client, not to idiosyncratic prejudgments. Regardless of whether your exercise in introspection revealed a "conservative" or "liberal" perception of relations between police and ethnics, it is a fact that some police, in some locales, at some times, do harass ethnics. It is equally true that some ethnics develop paranoid reactions of psychotic proportions and that imaginary police harassment is sometimes incorporated into a delusional system. Thus when ethnic clients report harassment, it is especially crucial that counselors avoid prejudgment and evaluate each report on its own merits.

In cases such as Antonio's, the accuracy of reporting of interaction with the police can be evaluated in several ways. If Antonio presents additional material for discussion that is unbelievable; for example, religious delusions, then it is more likely (but not absolutely certain) that his description of interactions with the police are equally distorted. His veracity can also be evaluated through the use of informants; for example, contacts with family members, friends, fellow employees, and so on. It goes without saying, of course, that evidence of previous delusional periods—whether reported by informants or documented by official records—tends to discredit current reporting. Psychological assessment devices, including tests and interviews, can help determine current personality functioning, but they may be of questionable validity when used by professionals with only superficial understanding of the client's culture (Padilla & Ruiz 1975).

The issue of Antonio's questionable judgment permeates the area of interpersonal relations. He appears relatively insensitive to the impact of certain aspects of his behavior and appearance upon others. Specifically, almost any stranger approaching unknown children on a playground will arouse suspicion. This seems especially true if the stranger is dressed in a manner that a more conservative school administrator or police would perceive as unusual or exotic. We are not recommending that counselors assume the function of sartorial consultants; but from what we know of Antonio, it appears he would benefit from some dispassionate and disinterested feedback concerning how he affects other people.

Little is known of Antonio's social life outside of his involvement with the Chicano movement. Regardless of ethnicity of client, many counselors would explore with a client his age-related peer interactions, his marital status, marriage plans, dating behavior, and heterosexual interest. Because Antonio is a member of a cultural group with a tradition of close family ties, and because he verbalizes the importance of family life, he would also recommend exploration of relevant experiences. Where does Antonio reside? Who does he live with? What is the extent of his interactions with related family members. Answers to questions about social and family life will help counselors determine whether or not Antonio experiences problems in these areas.

One final comment about Antonio. He states he wants a college degree, and even works part-time to subsidize his education, but his performance at school and on the job is marginal. We are *not* arguing that everyone must adhere to the so-called "Protestant ethic" by formulating life goals and by striving arduously to achieve them. Antonio has formulated life goals all right; he wants a college degree to further the cause of the Chicano movement. His goal-oriented behavior is so inefficient, however, that both goals are in jeopardy. Most people, Antonio included, would experience anxiety and frustration in such a life situation. Our recommendation for Antonio is that these aspects of his life be explored more closely with him. He may elect to reorder the priorities of his life, he may choose to modify his life schedule, or he may do both. But he must change something in order to reduce frustration, to achieve a more satisfying life adjustment, and to become more efficient in getting what he wants out of life.

Conclusion

Here we present general principles that can be applied in formulating more culturally relevant counseling programs for Latinos. For instance, the counselor knowledgeable of the importance of *personalismo* among Latinos may wish to greet Latino clients as soon as they arrive at the agency, even if it requires brief interruption of an ongoing session. A counselor sensitive to the Latino culture will immediately extend his hand and introduce himself, including first name rather than formal title. So-called small talk at this initial meeting, and at the beginning of subsequent sessions, is believed to be very important with Latino clients to establish and maintain rapport. Because of possible differences in the perception of time, we urge counselors to make an appointment to meet with the prospective client immediately, and to schedule that meeting as soon as possible, preferably that same morning, afternoon, or evening. As we have indicated earlier, cultural differences in temporal perspective are not perceived by us as pathological procrastination. We have argued elsewhere (Padilla et al. 1975) that Latinos *tend* to perceive psychological problems as more similar to physical problems than do non-Latinos. Thus nondirective approaches, requests for reviews of childhood history, or instructions to introspect should be used judiciously. In general, many Latino clients may have preconceptions of counseling interviews and sessions based on an analogue of a medical examination. Thus, they may anticipate a more active approach from the counselor; for example, inquiry that is goal-oriented and leading to concrete solutions for identified problems.

The higher frequency of extended family structure and the greater importance of family interaction in the daily lives of most Latinos indicate that family and other group approaches should be used more often.

Family-oriented therapies would probably yield higher success rates among Latinos than among non-Latinos regardless of whether the problem is intrapsychic or extrapsychic. It is important to keep in mind, however, that sex roles are more rigidly defined, sons have more and earlier independence, fathers have more prestige and authority, and the aged receive more respect. Such knowledge can be exploited to shape more valid counseling intervention. Thus the culturally sensitive counselor will not impute unconscious incestuous desire to a Latino father who expresses sharp interest in his daughter's suitors; nor would such a counselor misperceive the Latino daughter who tolerated such supervision as immature, unduly submissive, or pathologically compliant. Therapeutic responses based on an understanding, rather than a misinterpretation, of the meaning of certain behaviors within a given cultural context will obviously be more effective. Furthermore, familial interdependence, for example, married sons visiting their parents frequently, does not carry the connotation of pathological dependency such behavior might imply in other cultures.

These recommendations for culturally relevant counseling programs are meaningless unless Latinos can be motivated to refer themselves with greater frequency. To achieve this end, the centers and agencies that offer counseling services will have to be modified. Again, we summarize here recommendations presented in greater detail elsewhere (Padilla & Ruiz 1973; Padilla et al. 1975; Ruiz et al., in press).

First, we advocate that counseling centers emphasize a "business model" approach, and aggressively pursue clientele for their services. For example, one might begin with a local needs assessment program, simultaneously contacting and involving community people in planning, training, administration, and delivery of services. Once community needs have been identified and the relevant service programs established, it is time to advertise the availability of services. A multimedia approach in both English and Spanish would probably reach the largest number of Latinos. Second, new services are needed to deal with the Latino pattern of extrapsychic problems that make Latino clients different from non-Latino clients. Counseling centers could and should offer innovative services for Latinos such as these: written and oral translation contact with government agencies, building skill in obtaining employment and securing promotions, remedial education, and some type of course work teaching rights, responsibilities and privileges of a politico-legal nature. One example of the course work indicated in the final recommendation would be an educational experience teaching the structure of government, the effectiveness of political coalition, voting, and the impact of legislation on equal opportunity and affirmative action.

The third general recommendation for agency change concerns staffing. Our interpretation of the literature is that Latino clients will obtain maximum benefit from counselors knowledgeable with Latino ethnohistory and culture. To be effective, the counselors must "speak the language" of the client, both literally and figuratively. The number of Latino professionals already available is infinitesimally small (Ruiz 1970), and the disproportionately small number of Latinos enrolled in baccalaureate or doctoral programs (El-Khawas & Kinzer 1974) indicates underrepresentation of Latinos in the professions is going to continue in the foreseeable future. The short-range solution to this problem is two-fold; teach Spanish and Latino culture to non-Latino counselors, and teach counseling skills to Latinos at the paraprofessional level.

The fourth recommendation has been implied but is now made explicit. To become successful in delivering counseling services to the Latino community, agencies offering services must first gain the confidence and support of prospective clients. To accomplish this end, members of the community must infiltrate the agency at all levels of administration, be active in policy change and decision making, and be involved as teachers or students in the educational programs described earlier. To convince community people the agency is truly theirs, and therefore for their benefit, it would probably be wise to encourage the use of agency facilities for community events. In this context, the agency might celebrate Latino holidays in some appropriate way in addition to occasionally offering programs in the arts and humanities that would interest and attract potential users of available services. Consistent with our statements on the "business model," programs attracting participants represent excellent opportunities to inform people of agency activities. Latinos come to participate in a cultural program sponsored by the centers but simultaneously receive information via a brochure or brief announcement of the services offered by the agency.

(The preparation of this article was supported in part by Research Grant MH 24854 from the National Institute of Mental Health to the Spanish Speaking Mental Health Research Center at the University of California, Los Angeles.)

References

Abad, V.; Ramos, J.; and Boyce, E. A model for delivery of mental health services to Spanish-speaking minorities. *American Journal of Orthopsychiatry,* 1974, *44,* 584-595.

Bachrach, L.L. *Utilization of state and county mental hospitals by Spanish Americans in 1972.* Statistical Note 116. DHEW Publication No. (ADM), 1975, 75-158.

Edgerton, R.B., and Karno, M. Mexican American bilingualism and the perception of mental illness. *Archives of General Psychiatry,* 1971, *24,* 286-290.

El-Khawas, E.H. and Kinzer, J.L. Enrollment of minority graduate students at PhD granting institutions. *Higher Education Panel Reports.* Number 19, August, 1974.

Harris, T.A. *I'm OK—You're OK.* New York: Avon, 1973.

Heller, C. *Mexican-American Youth.* New York: Random House, 1967.

Jaco, E.G. *The social epidemiology of mental disorders: A psychiatric survey of Texas.* New York: Russell Sage Foundation, 1960.

Karno, M., and Edgerton, R.B. Perception of mental illness in a Mexican American community. *Archives of General Psychiatry*, 1969, *20*, 233-238.

Kline, L.Y. Some factors in the psychiatric treatment of Spanish Americans. *American Journal of Psychiatry*, 1969, *125*, 1674-1681.

Lefcourt, H.M. Internal versus external control of reinforcement. *Psychological Bulletin*, 1966, *65*, 206-220.

Madsen, M.C. and Shapira, A. Cooperative and competitive behavior of urban Afro-American, Anglo-American, Mexican-American, and Mexican village children. *Developmental Psychology*, 1970, *3*, 16-20.

Padilla, A.M. and Ruiz, R.A. *Latino Mental Health*. Washington, D.C.: U.S. Superintendent of Documents, 1973.

Padilla, A.M. and Ruiz, R.A. Personality assessment and test interpretation of Mexican Americans: A critique. *Journal of Personality Assessment*, 1975, *39*, 103-109.

Padilla, A.M.; Ruiz, R.A.; and Alvarez, R. Community mental health services for the Spanish-speaking/surnamed population. *American Psychologist*, 1975, *30*, 892-905.

Perez, M.S. Counseling services at UCSC: Attitudes and perspectives of Chicano students. Unpublished manuscript, 1975.

Rotter, J.B. *Social Learning and Clinical Psychology*. Englewood Cliffs, N.J.: Prentice-Hall, 1954.

Rotter, J.B. Generalized expectancies for internal versus external control of reinforcement. *Psychological Monographs*, 1966, *80*, 1-28.

Ruiz, R.A. Relative frequency of Americans with Spanish surnames in associations of psychology, psychiatry, and sociology. *American Psychologist*, 1971, *26*, 1022-1024.

Ruiz, R.A. and Padilla, A.M. Chicano psychology: The family and the *macho*. Unpublished manuscript, 1973.

Ruiz, R.A.; Padilla, A.M.; and Alvarez, R. Issues in the counseling of Spanish-speaking/surnamed clients: Recommendations for therapeutic services. In L. Benjamin (Ed.). *Counseling Minority Students*, in press.

Stone, P.C. and Ruiz, R.A. Race and class as differential determinants of underachievement and underaspiration among Mexican Americans. *Journal of Educational Research*, 1974, *68*, 99-101.

Torrey, E.F. *The mind game: Witchdoctors and psychiatrists*. New York: Emerson Hall, 1972.

U.S. Bureau of the Census. Persons of Spanish origin in the United States: November 1969. In *Current population reports* (Series P-20. No. 213). Washington, D.C.: U.S. Government Printing Office, 1971 (a).

U.S. Bureau of the Census. Selected characteristics of persons and families of Mexican, Puerto Rican, and other Spanish origin: March 1971. In *Current population reports* (Series P-20, No. 224). Washington, D.C.: U.S. Government Printing, 1971 (b).

Wrenn, R.L. and Ruiz, R.A. *The normal personality: Issues to insight*. Monterey, Calif.: Brooks/Cole, 1970.

Yamamoto, J.; James, Q.C.; and Palley, N. Cultural problems in psychiatric therapy. *Archives of General Psychiatry*, 1968, *19*, 45-49.

Selected Readings

Acosta, F.X. & Sheehan, J.G. Preferences toward Mexican American and Anglo American Psychotherapists. *Journal of Consulting and Clinical Psychology,* 1976, *44,* 272-279.

Christensen, E.W. When counseling Puerto Ricans...*Personnel and Guidance Journal,* 1977, *55,* 412-415.

Cross, W.C. & Maldonado, B. The counselor, the Mexican American, and the stereotype. *Elementary School Guidance and Counseling,* 1971, *6,* 27-31.

Edgerton, R.B. & Karno, M. Mexican-American bilingualism and the perception of mental illness. *Arch. Gen. Psychiat.,* 1971, *24,* 286-290.

Karno, M. & Edgerton, R. Perception of mental illness in a Mexican American community. *Archives of General Psychiatry,* 1969, *20,* 233-238.

Maes, W.R. & Rinaldi, J.R. Counseling the Chicano child. *Elementary School Guidance and Counseling,* 1974, *8,* 279-284.

Medina, C. & Reyes, M.R. Dilemmas of Chicano counselors. *Social Work,* 1976, *21,* 515-517.

Oragon, J.A. & Wibarri, S.R. Learn Amigo learn. *Personnel and Guidance Journal,* 1971, *50,* 87-89.

Padilla, A.M.; Ruiz, R.A.; & Alveraz, R. Community mental health services for the Spanish-speaking/surnamed population. *American Psychologist,* Sept., 1975, 892-905.

Palomares, U.H. Nuestros sentimientos son iguales, la diferencia es en la experiencia. *Personnel and Guidance Journal,* 1971, *50* (2), 137-144.

Ruiz, A.S. Chicano group catalysts. *Personnel and Guidance Journal,* 1975 *53,* 462-466.

The Latino Client
Cases and Questions

1. Assume you are a counselor at a large state university that has publicly stated support for all its federally mandated affirmative action programs. Recently, however, the Sociology Department's graduate admission procedure has been under fire by the campus newspaper for its practice of reserving twenty percent of its new admissions for Chicano students (the state in which the school is located is composed of 20% Chicanos).

   a. How do you feel about the selection procedure described?
   b. What action would you take in view of your feelings?
   c. What impact would you expect this to have on your ability to relate to Chicano students?

2. Assume you are a counselor in a state run rehabilitation agency. A Puerto Rican paraplegic enters your office looking very sullen and begins to question your ability to help her. She points out that you can not possibly understand her problems since you are not encumbered, as she is, by the forces of multiple oppression.

   a. How will you respond to her charges?
   b. What doubts do you have about your ability to work with this client?
   c. What are some of the cultural factors to which you need to be sensitive in working with this client?

3. Assume you are a counselor in an urban elementary school with a student enrollment that is 60% Anglo, 40% Chicano. Several physical confrontations have occurred in the school cafeteria recently, apparently the result of insult trading between Anglos and Chicanos over "Mex" and "Gringo" food. The school principal has asked you to work with some of the students involved.

   a. How do you plan to work (what is your role) with these students?
   b. Do you anticipate any difficulty in establishing a relationship with either the Anglo or Chicano students? How will you deal with the difficulty?
   c. What community resources might you want to tap in dealing with this problem?

The Latino Client
Role Playing Exercise

Divide into groups of 4 or 5. Assign each group member to a role and the responsibilities associated with the role as follows:

Role	Responsibilities
1. Counselor	1. Assume role as a counselor or mental health worker who encounters an Hispanic. Attempt to build rapport with the client.
2. Client	2. Assume role of an Hispanic. To play this role effectively, it will be necessary for the student client to (a) identify cultural values of the Hispanic group, (b) identify sociopolitical factors which may interfere with counseling, and (c) portray these aspects in the counseling session. It is best to select a few powerful variables in the role play. You may or may not be initially antagonistic to the client, but it is important for you to be sincere in your role and your reactions to the counselor trainee.
3. Observers	3. Observe interaction and offer comments during feedback session.

This exercise is most effective in a racially and ethnically mixed group. For example, an Hispanic student can be asked to play the Hispanic client role. However, this is probably not possible in most cases. Thus, students who play the client role will need to thoroughly read the articles for the group they are portraying.

Identifying the barriers that could interfere with counseling is an important aspect of this exercise. We recommend that a list be made of the group's cultural values and sociopolitical influences prior to the role playing.

Role playing may go on for a period of 5–15 minutes, but the time limit should be determined prior to the activity. Allow 10–15 minutes for a feedback session in which all participants discuss (within the group) how they felt in their respective roles, how appropriate were the counselor responses, what else they might have done in that situation, etc.

Rotate and role play the same situation with another counselor trainee *or* another Hispanic client with different issues, concerns, and problems. In the former case, the group may feel that a particular issue is of sufficient importance to warrant reenactment. This allows students to see the effects of other counseling responses and approaches. In the latter case, the new exposure will allow students to get a broader view of barriers to counseling.

If videotaping equipment is available, we recommend that the sessions be taped and processed in a replay at the end. We have found this to be a powerful means of providing feedbacks to participants.

Part 6
Implications for Minority Group Cross-Cultural Counseling

16 Future Directions in Minority Group/Cross-Cultural Counseling

Counseling Practice

In chapter 2 it was noted that a great deal of criticism by minority individuals has been directed at the traditional counseling role. Timebound, space-bound, cathartic counseling is rejected by these critics as largely irrelevant to minority life experiences and needs. The counselor, they argue, needs to get out of the office and meet the client on the client's ground. Rather than demanding the the client adapt to the counselor's culture, the counselor should adjust to and work within the client's culture. Furthermore, minority individuals are by definition oppressed, and it is highly unlikely that any minority client problem is ever totally free of this oppression. Providing an empathic ear so that the client can reassess past experiences, or even changing the client's behavior so that he or she can cope better with the environment, does not eliminate the oppression.

Several roles that overcome at least some of the criticisms leveled by minority critics, have been proposed as alternatives to the traditional counseling role. For the most part, these roles are not really new, since they have been proposed and to some degree implemented in the past (Pine, in his 1972 article, refers to them as "old wine in new bottles"). They are "new," however, in that they have not gained widespread acceptance by the counseling profession, and the traditional counseling role remains solidly entrenched as the counselor's primary modus operandi.

In general it can be said these alternative roles involve the counselor more actively in the client's life experiences than does the traditional role, and the former often require the counselor to move out of his/her office into the client's environment. They also share a preventative thrust rather than the more traditional remedial focus. Because of this there is considerable overlapping of the role functions, but each includes some aspects which are unique to the role. The alternative roles to be discussed are: (1) outreach role, (2) consultant role, (3) ombudsmun role, (4) change agent role, and (5) role as facilitator of indigenous support systems.

Outreach Role

The outreach role requires that counselors move out of their offices and into their clients' communities (Weinrach, 1973; Mitchell, 1971a). Minority clients in educational settings are often hesitant to contact counselors

(Calia, 1966); and Haettenschwiller (1971) urges counselors to make the initial contact with minority students on the students' home ground, thus establishing the counselor as a person, ". . . to whom the student can turn when confronted by the uncertainty and ambiguity of institutional demands" (p. 31). Meeting clients in this manner allows the counselor to divest him/herself of the Establishment association that an office visit can generate. Woods (1977) describes a counseling services program that relies heavily on group counseling and group activities rather than on traditional one-to-one counseling and, in keeping with an outreach philosophy, the group sessions are often, ". . . conducted at students' apartments for potluck dinners, and at local beaches and parks for picnics and games" (p. 417).

By making him/herself available in the client's environment, the counselor is in a better position to respond to client needs at the time they are experienced. Exposure to the client's world may also help the counselor understand the cultural experience of the client and may enhance the counselor-client relationship. Furthermore, the counselor as an outreach worker may be in a position to directly observe the environmental factors that are contributing to the client's problems, and the counselor is thus less likely to attribute deviations from majority norms to pathology. In addition to direct exposure to the environment of minority clients, counselors should become actively involved in community and social programs and activities in their minority clients' communities (Wilson & Calhoun, 1974).

Consultant Role

The goal of consultation is the development of a nurturing ecological system designed to optimize each client's self-growth (Blocker & Rapoza, 1972). In this role the counselor works with teachers, parents, peers, and others who have an impact on the minority client (Maes & Rinaldi, 1974).

Perhaps the most effective way a counselor can function as a consultant vis a vis minorities is by designing and implementing a peer counseling program. Minority client populations frequently find it easier to trust a peer than a professional, regardless of the professional's membership-group status. Gravitz and Woods (1976) describe a peer counseling program in which Third World students function as liaison between the University and minority students. Peer counselors focus their efforts on the ". . . clinically asymptomatic student who has problems of living in a complex university community" (p. 231). The primary philosophy of this peer counseling program is to serve a preventative function; to anticipate minority student difficulties and to alleviate them before they become aggravated. In order to do this, peer counselors often spend much of their time outside the counseling center, meeting minority students in residence halls, student centers, and minority centers. In addition to providing direct services to minority students, one result of the peer counseling program reported by Gravitz and Woods is that an increased number of minority students make contact with the counseling center's professional staff.

The training of minority peers is an important aspect of any minority peer or paraprofessional program. D. W. Sue (1973) has described a training program for Third World student counselors; this includes a course on peer counseling of minority students offered for credit. The course stresses six content areas: (1) the cultural backgrounds of the minorities to be served, (2) techniques of counseling, (3) crisis intervention, (4) ethical issues, (5) behavior pathology, and (6) referral sources. In addition, trainees spend 1½ hours a week role-playing counselor-counselee interactions in small groups supervised by a professional counselor. In general, the role-playing sessions are aimed at helping trainees develop skills associated with facilitative and action conditions (Carkhuff, 1971) of the helping relationship. Sue reports that an important aspect of the training procedure is the feedback provided by fellow trainees.

Lewis and Lewis (1977) have pointed out that counselors can also serve as consultants with groups of minority people who want to organize in order to improve the conditions under which they live. They describe four ways the counselor can serve in this capacity: the counselor can assess community needs, coordinate activities and resources, provide training in skill building, and advocate change.

Ombudsmun and Change Agent Roles

In both the ombudsmun role and the change agent role the counselor discards entirely the intrapsychic counseling model, and clearly views the problem as existing outside the minority client. Economic, political, social, emotional, and other forms of oppression are identified as the underlying causes of minority client problems, and the counselor's role is to combat oppression. The two roles differ slightly, however, in terms of focus.

Ombudsmun. The ombudsmun role (spelled with a *u* to avoid a sexist connotation) originated in Europe where it functions as a protector of citizens against bureaucratic mazes and procedures (Bexelius, 1968). A number of colleges and universities in this country have instituted the ombudsmun role, and recently school counselors have been urged to serve as student advocates (Ciavarella & Doolittle, 1970). In this role the counselor represents a client or group of clients who have brought a particular form of oppression to the counselor's attention. Being an empathic counselor who suggests alternative ways of coping with a particular problem is not enough; the counselor must be willing to pursue actively alternative courses with or for the client, including making "a personal contact for the student who is overwhelmed by the bureaucracy" (Mitchell, 1971, p. 36). Not infrequently the injustice involves the institution employing the counselor, either directly or indirectly, making the counselor somewhat unpopular at times with institutional administrators. If the client's goals are in conflict with those of the institution, "the counselor must decide to represent the student and not the institution or the system" (Williams & Kirkland, 1971, p. 114), presumably within ethical restrictions imposed by the profession. When a minority client is involved, the ombudsmun has the added responsibility for making certain that the minority person can benefit fully from the social and economic resources of the majority culture without losing what is unique and valued in his/her own culture (Maes & Rinaldi, 1974).

Change Agent role. In the change agent role the counselor assumes an alloplastic counseling position, devoting considerable time and energy to changing the social environment of his/her minority clientele (Banks, 1972). By necessity, this often means changing the social environment of majority peers and superiors in the offending environment. Like the ombudsmun role, counselors in this role must often identify the problem as residing with the very institution that employs them and must be willing to confront their employers (Williams & Kirkland, 1971).

As a change agent the counselor need not represent a particular client or group of clients known to the outsider. Rather, the entire minority culture experiencing an injustice functions as the client. Furthermore, the counselor serving as a change agent frequently assumes a low visibility stature, often finding it useful to mobilize other influential persons in the offending institution so as to bring about change (Waltz & Benjamin, 1977).

Anderson & Love (1973) exhort counselors to, ". . . assume responsibility for making efforts to increase positive human relations and fostering development of a multicultural view of the world" (p. 667), and suggest psychological education as a vehicle to aid this process. The Division 17 Professional Affairs Committee of the American Psychological Association agrees that special measures are needed to combat institutional oppression of minority people in this country.

> Problems of institutional racism are paramount on a university campus. Counseling alone on discrimination issues will be ineffective. Counseling psychologists must involve themselves in affirmative action programs, sponsor symposia and workshops on racism in society, and actively involve themselves in programs of cultural awareness. (Ivey, 1976, p. 10–11).

As a change agent, however, the counselor need not necessarily spend his/her time confronting institutional bureaucracy. The counselor can work directly with majority clients in an attempt to move them toward the goal of reducing racism, sexism, and other discriminatory attitudes toward minorities. Katz and Ivey (1977) describe a racism awareness training program that could easily be adapted to majority attitudes toward non-racial minorities. The program involves a re-education process designed, ". . . to raise consciousness of White people, help them identify racism in their life experience from which their racist attitudes and behaviors have developed, and move them to take action against institutional and individual racism" (p. 487). The six phases of the program are designed to help participants to:

1. Increase their understanding of racism in society and themselves.
2. Confront discrepancies existing between the myths and reality of American ideology and behavior.
3. Sort through some of their feelings and reactions that were triggered by phases 1 and 2.
4. Confront the racism in the white culture that their own actions support.
5. Understand and accept their whiteness.
6. Develop specific action strategies to combat personal and institutional racism (p. 487).

The authors' suggestion that racism is a White problem and White counselors should assume a major role in dealing with it, is plausible. Majority counselors are, in some respects, in the best position to confront the majority population with their own stereotypic attitudes and behaviors.

Role as Facilitator of Indigenous Support Systems

Pedersen (1976) has discussed the need for counselors who are engaged in international cross-cutural counseling to be aware of the culture's indigenous mental health care systems. Focusing specifically on the Native American population, Torrey (1970) has suggested that mental health workers should structure their activities to supplement, not supplant, the existing system of mental health services among American Indians and Eskimos. Within most other United States minority groups, culturally-relevant procedures have evolved to assist the individual who is experiencing a psychological problem. Frequently counselors are unaware of or are disdainful of these procedures, preferring to engage the client in the very counseling process so heavily criticized by minority representatives. The inevitable result is a mismatch of treatment and need, loss of credibility in the counselor, and the client's disengagement from counseling. We would like to suggest that counselors may be able best to serve their minority clientele by attempting to facilitate rather than discourage use of indigenous support systems.

The counselor working with a minority client might begin the facilitative process by exploring with the client how he/she has dealt with similar problems in the past. Familiarity with the client's culture will help the counselor understand culturally relevant support systems that may assist the client. For instance, among some Mexicano groups *curanderos* perform many of the functions of a counselor. In numerous minority cultures the extended family plays an important supportive role. In others (e.g. women, gays), the family may provide little support, but peers provide the reinforcement needed to survive and overcome crisis. The counselor can facilitate problem resolution by encouraging the client to use these support systems where appropriate.

In many cases minority client problems can be linked directly to oppression. Depression, for instance, may result from years and years of futile attempts to achieve some measure of social equality. A facilitative counselor might encourage a client experiencing depression of this nature to participate in an organization within the client's culture that fosters minority community pride.

Not all cultural adaptations to psychological problems engender growth, and in some instances the client may be too acculturated to benefit from procedures developed by the minority culture. In these instances the facilitative process begins with an exploration of processes with which the client feels comfortable. A key distinction in these cases, however, is that the exploration serves to discover a process for resolving the client's difficulty, not as a process for resolving a problem in and of itself.

Counselor Education

In response to the negative view minorities have of counseling, some authors have suggested that indigenous and paraprofessional counselors should be trained for minority group counseling, since it is doubtful whether majority counselors can become truly sensitive to minority needs (Ward, 1970). Yet, in view of the multicultural makeup of American society, it seems highly unlikely that counselors being trained today (especially those being trained for educational settings) will escape contact with culturally different clients. It seems imperative, therefore, that counselors of all cultural backgrounds be at least minimally prepared to work with clients who differ culturally from themselves. In our opinion, programs that train counselors need to do a better job both of increasing the number of minority counselors and of preparing all counselors for cross-cultural counseling experiences.

Recruiting, Admitting, and Supporting
Minority Counselor Trainees

It is probably safe to say that very few counselor education programs in the 1980s intentionally discriminate against minority applicants in their admission's policies and procedures. Yet surveys of psychology departments and American Psychological Association (APA) members consistently reveal that ethnic minorities are still underrepresented in psychology (Kennedy & Wagner, 1979; Padilla, Boxley, & Wagner, 1973; Russo, Olmedo, Stapp, & Fulcher, 1981; Strong & Peele, 1977). According to Russo et al. (1981), ethnic minorities make up 3.1 percent of all APA members, 5 percent of all graduate faculty in psychology, approximately 8 percent of those awarded Ph.D.'s in psychology in 1980, and approximately 10 percent of those enrolled in graduate psychology programs in 1981. These data suggest a slight increase in the production of minority psychologists, but an increase so gradual that it will take decades to achieve a parity with nonminorities in the field of psychology. Although there are no comparable data for ethnic minority representation in counseling and counselor education programs, this underrepresentation is presumably generalizable to the field of counseling. Korchin (1980) has identified five reasons, paraphrased below, why the underrepresentation of ethnic minorities in the mental health professions must be eliminated:

1. It is morally right to do so.
2. Minority mental health workers are better able than are their nonminority colleagues to understand minority clients.
3. Minority mental health workers are more motivated than are their nonminority colleagues to work with minority clients.
4. Minority mental health workers are needed as identification figures for minority clients.
5. Minority mental health workers can enrich the knowledge of their nonminority colleagues by sharing their knowledge of human diversity.

One reason that psychology departments and counselor education programs have not enrolled significant numbers of ethnic minority students in the past is that they fail to recognize counselor-trainee selection as a three-phase process involving recruitment, admission, and support (Atkinson, 1981). Even an admission policy designed to increase minority enrollment can have only a limited impact if the applicant pool includes only a few minority applicants. Further, as victims of oppression, ethnic minorities often need economic, social, and emotional support that nonminorities may not need in order to complete a degree in counseling.

In a survey of a representative sample of counselor education programs, Atkinson and Wampold (1981) found that 57 percent of the respondents stated an interest in enrolling ethnic minorities in the literature describing their program. Slightly less than half (49 percent) indicated that someone from their campus had been identified as an affirmative action recruiter for their program, and only 31 percent said their affirmative action recruiter travels to other colleges or universities to recruit ethnic minorities. Fewer than 3 out of 10 programs (29 percent) responding to the survey said that they send applications to eligible ethnic minorities without request.

A successful affirmative action recruitment effort is designed to identify and solicit applications not only from those minority individuals who already have definite plans to enroll in a counselor education program, but also from those individuals who have ruled out graduate education in counseling for less than valid reasons (e.g., lack of knowledge about financial support available to them) although they have the prerequisite educational and experiential background. Such a recruitment effort is affirmative in the true sense of the word. It reaches out to those who might settle for a less appealing vocation because their oppressive experience has conditioned them to settle for less than what they actually desire. It includes recruitment literature that identifies: (1) the counselor education faculty's commitment to enroll a diversified student population, (2) aspects of the training program (e.g., course content, field-work settings, research focus) that provide a multicultural experience, and (3) support services (e.g., tutorial, financial, social) that are available to minorities. It includes active recruitment by students and faculty at college career days, professional conventions, and in day-to-day encounters. It also includes personal contacts with interested minority persons by department heads and individual faculty to communicate a real interest in enrolling ethnic minorities.

With regard to admission activities, the Atkinson and Wampold (1981) survey found that fewer than half (42 percent) of the responding programs give credit for ethnicity as part of the selection process. Approximately 4 out of 10 (39 percent) of the respondents indicated that credit is given to applicants who have prior experience working with members of an ethnic minority. Only 34 percent of the respondents employed ethnic minority persons to review application materials and only 31 percent used ethnic minority interviewers when they interviewed applicants.

Counselor education programs need to develop admission policies and procedures that will admit as many qualified minority applicants as is legally, morally, and ethically possible in order to eliminate the current underrepresentation of minorities in the field of counseling. Traditional admission criteria of undergraduate GPA and graduate aptitude test scores have been found to discriminate against ethnic minorities (Bernal, 1980) and to be unreliable predictors of counseling performance (Rowe, Murphy, & DeCsipkas, 1975). New and/or additional criteria need to be identified by counselor education programs that will insure minorities are adequately represented in their student populations. As most counselor educators are aware, the famous U.S. Supreme Court decision in *Bakke vs. Regents of the University of California* ruled out the use of quotas as a means of insuring minority admissions. What tends to be overlooked, however, was the court's approval of some admission's procedures designed to insure minority representation. Citing the Harvard undergraduate admission policy as an example, the Court held that a "representational" admission policy designed to insure representation from diverse groups was acceptable as long as it did not involve quotas.

An alternative to the "representational" admission policy has been described by Atkinson, Staso, and Hosford (1978) which seeks to identify counseling-related strengths held by minorities and include them as admission criteria. Briefly, the selection process involves three equally weighted criteria: academic index, experiential background, and personal interview. The traditional criteria of undergraduate GPA and graduate aptitude test are included in the academic index but their negative impact on minority applicants is lessened by using only the higher of the two scores (GPA or test score) relative to other applicants and restricting the weight to one third of the total criteria. Experiential background is measured by a background questionnaire and points are awarded to applicants with multicultural experiences and goals that include working with ethnic minorities. For the personal interview criterion, applicants are asked to respond to videotaped counseling scenerios that involve minority clients and are offered an opportunity to conduct their interview in a second language. The combined effect of this process is to admit increased numbers of minority applicants by structuring the admission criteria around multicultural strengths that anyone may have, but which minorities are more likely to possess than are non-minorities.

In the area of support, the Atkinson and Wampold (1981) survey found that over half of the respondents (57 percent) offered support groups for ethnic minorities. However, only 39 percent reserved special fellowship, teaching assistantships, or other intramural sources of financial assistance exclusively for ethnic minorities and only 28 percent provided special tutorial services for these groups. Less than 4 out of 10 respondents (37 percent) provided special advising services for ethnic minorities.

A variety of support services are needed to insure that ethnic and other minorities, once admitted, are able to complete their graduate education in counseling. Special fellowship funds need to be developed and administered for underrepresented groups that could not otherwise attend graduate school (Bernal, 1980). Whenever feasible, minorities should be employed as research and teaching assistants, since these positions involve not only a financial renumeration but serve as apprenticeships for skills needed as a professional counselor and/or researcher. In addition to financial support, counselor education programs should provide tutorial support to those individuals who may have experienced an inferior education due to their minority status. Since role models for minorities are often missing from counselor education faculties, non-minority faculty need to expand their advising role for minority students to include the functions of mentor (Walton, 1979). As a minority student mentor, the faculty member attempts to minimize the trauma of graduate education and maximize the supportive services for each minority advisee. For emotional/psychological support, many counselor education programs have arranged to have support groups offered for their minority students.

In summary, counselor trainee selection involves recruitment, admission, and support. If counselor education programs are to reduce the underrepresentation of ethnic minorities in the counseling profession, expanded effort in all three areas will be needed in the future.

Need for Cross-Cultural Counseling Emphasis

Very few counselor training programs to date have developed and offered systematic training in multicultural counseling (Bryson & Bardo, 1975).

Even in the much discussed area of cross-racial counseling, very few training centers have ". . . given necessary attention to assisting developing professionals in recognizing, understanding, and resolving the more subtle forms that undesirable attitudes concerning race may take in therapeutic relationships where skin color becomes an important variable" (Gardner, 1971, p. 86).

Where courses in minority counseling have been developed, they have often been instituted at the insistence of a single, vocal, minority group and have tended to focus on a limited clientele. The rationale for such courses is that majority counselors must receive intensive training from a minority perspective (Cross & Maldonado, 1971; Williams & Kirkland, 1971). Since each minority group within the United States is deserving of this sort of professional attention, this approach to course development presumably could result in the proliferation of a large number of courses. Each program would be designed to sensitize majority counselors to the life experiences and special needs of a single minority group. While each of these groups is deserving of such attention, it seems unlikely that counselor education programs will offer more than one or two minority counseling courses (often some version of "counseling Blacks" and "counseling women"). The predictable outcome is that little attention will be focused on the numerous other minority groups with whom counselors may come in contact.

Several additional problems present themselves when classes are developed that focus on counseling one or two minority groups to the exclusion of others. Students and instructors often mistakenly assume that a dynamic applicable to one minority group can be generalized to others. Also, since the professional literature pays little attention to minority counselor-majority client and minority counselor-minority client interaction (Gardner, 1971; Sattler, 1970), these courses seldom focus on the minority counselor condition. This occurs in spite of the fact that minority counseling courses are frequently instituted at the insistence of and are primarily patronized by minority counselors-in-training.

We are not suggesting that specialized courses in counseling particular minority groups should not be developed. Nor are we suggesting that minority group students should not be involved in the design and implementation of training programs. We agree with Bell (1971) who provides a convincing argument in favor of their involvement. The point we are making is that courses are needed in cross-cultural counseling, courses which sensitize counselors to a variety of minority cultures, and examine the common experiences of various minority groups as well as their differences. Such courses should give attention to the minority counselor as well as to the majority counselor role in cross-cultural counseling.

One of the major objectives of a cross-cultural counseling class should be to acquaint the student with etic and emic qualities of favored counseling approaches. For instance, it seems clear that rapport is a culturally generalizable element basic to all counseling interaction

(Vontress, 1971, 1973, 1974, 1979). Techniques to establish rapport, however, may be culturally specific and not capable of generalization. Nondirective techniques presently taught in many training programs as rapport building responses may actually antagonize some minorities or seem meaningless to others (Sue & Sue, 1972a). As Bryson and Bardo (1975) point out, ". . . it can no longer be assumed that techniques and strategies that are successful with one group of clients will work effectively with another group" (p. 14). Yet it would be a serious error to assume that all concepts associated with counseling theory developed to date must be discarded when working with a minority client. For instance, the learning theory principles upon which behavioral counseling is predicated presumably hold true in any culture. It seems axiomatic that operant conditioning, classical conditioning, and vicarious learning concepts apply to one culture as well as another. The ways in which these principles may manifest themselves in a variety of cultures may differ, however, and what may be a reinforcing stimulus in one culture may prove to be aversive in another.

In addition to courses specifically designated as cross-cultural counseling or multicultural counseling courses, all counselor education offerings should be revised to include minority-relevant topics. Mitchell (1917) offers a model of such a program.

Literature Related to Training Counselors of Minority Group Clients

Vontress (1974) has suggested that, "although a course in counseling racial and ethnic minorities may be another exciting and rewarding cognitive exposure, needed most are affective experiences designed to humanize counselors" (p. 164). The experiences which he and other authors suggest are needed are those designed to increase counselor understanding in two areas: first, to understand themselves and their previously unrecognized biases; second, to gain appreciation for the experiences of someone who is culturally different and to become open to divergent life styles (Calia, 1966). In order to achieve these goals, "sensitive training", in which the counselor lives and works in the minority community to experience it first hand, is recommended (Vontress, 1971).

One method for increasing counselors' understanding of themselves and their previously unrecognized biases is the Awareness Group Experience (AGE) described by Parker and McDavis (1979). AGE is a one-day structured workshop for minority and non-minority counselors (the authors recommend 15 members from each group) consisting of five sessions. Session one, *Becoming Aware,* provides for dyadic and large group sharing of individual cross-cultural experiences. Session two, *Eliminating Stereotypes,* involves a role-played social gathering with each participant wearing an ethnic stereotypic label on his/her back followed by a group processing of the experience. In session three, *Ethnic Lunch,* participants eat together at an ethnic restaurant followed by a tour of an ethnic community. Session four, *Minority Student Perceptions of Counselors,* is designed to make counselors aware of how they are viewed by ethnic minority students. Seven to ten students are interviewed by the group leaders in a "fishbowl" procedure with the participants seated around them. In session five, *Action Plan,* the participants are divided into groups of five to develop plans for changing their negative attitudes toward ethnic minorities.

McDavis and Parker (1977) have described a course designed to help counselor education students become aware of their attitudes toward ethnic minorities that includes AGE as one component. Other topics/experiences covered are *Facilitating Interracial Groups, Minority Student Panels, Counseling Ethnic Minorities Individually, Class Projects,* and *Ethnic Dinner.* In addition to increasing self-awareness of ethnic biases, the course is designed to help students learn how to build rapport and counsel ethnic minorities individually and in groups.

Several authors have proposed that prior to direct experience in a cross-cultural setting, counselors in training should be exposed to simulated cross-cultural encounters. Bryson, Renzaglia, & Danish (1974) describe a simulation training procedure designed ". . . to assist counselors in training and other human service workers to function successfully with Black citizens" (p. 219), which might be adapted to other cross-cultural situations. A counselor trainee group is shown a number of videotaped or filmed vignettes in which actors portray the emotions associated with rejection, fear of rejection, intimacy given, and fear of intimacy (p. 219). The trainees are asked to think of the role player as a client, and to respond affectively and empathically. The trainees as a group then discuss their reactions to the simulated situation. During the discussion, trainees are asked to (a) identify the role-played emotion, (b) identify their own emotional reaction, and (c) suggest alternative responses to the role-played emotion.

An intriguing simulation procedure referred to as the *Triad Model* has been described by Pedersen (1977), who views counseling as a power struggle between client and counselor and the problem. Counselor trainees are divided into teams of three in which one trainee portrays the counselor, one the client, and one the "anticounselor." The client and "anticounselor" are matched with respect to cultural factors as closely as possible and the "anticounselor's" role is to use ". . . cultural similarity with the client in order to disrupt the counselor-client cross-cultural coalition" (Pedersen, 1977, p. 95). The "anticounselor" may attempt to build a coalition with the client by privately supplying negative feedback to the client about the counselor, or may attempt to destroy a client-counselor coalition by joining the counseling interaction and attacking the counselor openly. Pedersen (1978) has also identified four skill areas (articulate the problems, anticipate resistance, diminish defensiveness, and recovery skills) covered by the *Triad Model*. He reports that this procedure has been successfully employed with both prepracticum training and in-service workshops (Pedersen, 1977, 1978). Pedersen and his associates (Pedersen, Holwill, & Shapiro, 1978) have provided research evidence that counselors who participate in triad training increase thier ability to interact empathically, genuinely, and with understanding of affective communication. A one-hour videotape consisting of four triad interviews and a training manual have been developed for use in any counselor training program.

Lewis and Lewis (1970) propose a training model in which beginning counselors-in-training are paired with experienced counselors and placed as teams in inner-city schools to work as full-time counselors. While on-the-job experience working with disadvantaged youth would serve as the basic core of this program, didactic course work taught in participating public schools would bridge theory and practice requirements. A major objective of this training model would be to develop counselors ". . . skilled in the processes of consultation and change and group and individual counseling" (Lewis & Lewis, 1970, p. 37).

Mitchell (1971) describes a counselor training model which is similar to the Lewis-Lewis (1970) model but has the advantage of having already been implemented. The program is designed to provide for a Black perspective, but includes several features that could be generalized to cross-cultural situations. For instance, in implementing the new program, internships were developed in predominately minority-attended schools. Also, in addition to developing new courses aimed at understanding the Black experience, core guidance and counseling courses were designed to include minority-relevant materials. This could conceivably be done in any counselor education program. Most programs, for instance, include the equivalent of such courses as Introduction to Guidance/Counseling, Test and Measurements, and Vocational and Educational Information. The Introduction course could include a discussion of how the promise of guidance has fallen short for minority students (Russell, 1970). The testing class could devote considerable attention to cultural test biases as well as to problems of validity and reliability (Barnes, 1972). And the Vocational class could focus on the special problems of minorities in obtaining and retaining jobs (Miller & Oetting, 1977).

A recent approach to defining the training for cross-cultural counseling has been to specify competencies that counselors should have. Arredondo-Dowd and Gonsalves (1980) have proposed that counselor training programs should specialize in bilingual-multicultural education and "assist students in developing basic attitudes, skills, and competencies to be culturally effective counselors" (p. 659). With respect to competencies, the authors specify counseling, cultural, linguistic, and pedagogical competencies needed by counselors who work with a diverse client population.

Perhaps the most extensive discussion of cross-cultural counseling competencies to date has been offered by the Education and Training Committee of Division 17, American Psychological Association. In a position paper, the Committee describes eleven minimal competencies in the areas of beliefs/attitudes, knowledges, and skills that all counselors should possess. The *Position Paper on Cross-Cultural Counseling Competencies* is reprinted in its entirety in appendix A.

Training for Activist Roles Needed

The major challenge in the future to counselor education vis a vis minority group/cross-cultural counseling is the establishment within the profession of activist alternatives to the traditional counseling role. Until such time as counselor education programs define outreach, consultation, ombudsmun, change agent, and facilitator of indigenous support systems roles as viable alternatives to time-bound, space-bound, personal-social counseling, it seems unlikely these roles will be accepted and implemented by the profession in general (Atkinson, Froman, Romo, & Mayton, 1977). Counselor education's long-standing love affair with the intrapsychic model of client problems must cool, and the effects of an oppressive society be acknowledged, before counseling as a profession will achieve credibility with a large portion of the minority populations.

Counseling Research

Sattler (1970) reviewed the research concerned with the effect of *experimenter* race on experimentation, testing, interviewing, and psychology, and found only three studies related to counselor-client interaction. While a number of studies have been carried out since Sattler completed his review, empirical research in this area is still generally lacking. Several reasons for the relative paucity of research concerned with minority group/cross-cultural counseling present themselves. One possibility is that a majority-controlled counseling research establishment has simply not viewed minority status as an important factor in counseling. Counselor educators and researchers who espouse an etic counseling approach may feel cultural factors in counseling play a subordinate role to counseling techniques in affecting counseling outcome.

Another reason may be that majority researchers believe that the topic is a highly controversial issue and prefer to conduct research on less controversial subjects. As Gardner (1971) points out, ". . . many blacks have called for a moratorium on all further efforts by white investigators to study and explain the psychological and social characteristics of blacks" (p. 78). Similar requests have been made by other minority professionals who believe that forays by majority researchers into minority cultures have resulted in reinforced stereotypes rather than enlightened understanding. While aimed primarily at researchers in sociology and psychology who have attempted to explain minority behavior in terms of deviance from majority norms, the attitude that the majority researcher-minority subject combination is destined to produce distorted, biased results has obviously become generalized to counseling psychology.

Furthermore, individual members of various minority groups have grown increasingly resistant to research and refuse to serve as subjects (Sue & Sue, 1972b). Black males are understandably reluctant to participate in any activity that smacks of experimentation. Perhaps the most tragic abuse of research with human subjects in this country occurred when 400 Black men identified during the 1930's as having syphilis were allowed to suffer its effects without treatment (infamously known as the Tuskegee experiment). At least 48 of these men died and numerous others were permanently maimed as a direct result of the disease. A number of other studies with potentially harmful effects have been conducted on inmates (a majority of whom are members of racial/ethnic minorities) in federal and state prisons either without the subjects' knowledge or with direct or indirect coercion.

Proposed Research Model for Minority Group/Cross-Cultural Research

The suggestion has been made that the impacts of the preconceptions or prejudices of the experimenter on cross-cultural counseling research can be minimized when the researcher feels "comfortably polycultural" (Vontress, 1976, p. 2). We feel that the danger of cultural bias on the part of a single researcher, no matter what his/her race, socioeconomic background, sex, sexual orientation, etc., is unavoidable. It seems unlikely that any researcher has totally escaped the impact of cultural stereotyping that may be present as unrecognized bias in the design, implementation, and/or data analysis of a research project.

The possibility of unrecognized bias can be reduced, however, when research teams are composed of at least one representative from each cultural group included in the study. We are proposing, in effect, whenever two or more cultural groups are represented in a research design, that each group have an advocate on the research team, who is likely to be sensitive to cultural bias. Objectivity might also be enhanced if the research team included a person whose cultural background was not directly related to the variables under study. Thus, a research team examining the effectiveness of Black or White counselors with Black or White clients might include an Asian American researcher as well as Black and White investigators.

The American Psychological Association hosted a conference on professional training at Vail, Colorado, in 1973; on that occasion one recommendation developed was that ". . . counseling of persons of culturally diverse backgrounds by persons who are not trained or competent to work with such groups should be regarded as unethical" (Pedersen, 1976, p. 35). We would like to recommend that a similar ethical restriction be placed on minority group/cross-cultural researchers.

Areas Where Research Is Needed

Some barriers and benefits resulting from cross-cultural counseling were presented in the first chapter. For the most part, these variables have been identified through clinical observation, with little solid research evidence to support their effect on the counseling relationship. Research is needed to establish this effect, then to determine how benefits can be maximized and obstacles minimized. Also, since much of the writing in this area has been done by Black theorists, research is needed to determine if these factors can be generalized and applied to other cultures.

Research is also needed to determine the etic quality of current counseling approaches. What are the underlying assumptions of behavioral counseling, transactional analysis, gestalt therapy, rational emotive therapy, reality therapy, existential approaches to counseling, which apply to all cultures? Which techniques based on these assumptions are equally applicable to all cultures? What assumptions are obviously not applicable to all cultures, and what implications does this have for associated techniques? What are the emic solutions to psychological problems that have been developed within the various cultures in American society? How can counseling be used to increase the effectiveness of these procedures? Draguns (1976) argues that both etic and emic counseling approaches are needed and that both ". . . are equally valid and complimentary. . . . The crucial thing is to recognize these orientations for what they are; practical and conceptual pitfalls appear only when the etic orientation is mistaken for the emic or vise versa" (p. 3). Research is sorely needed that identifies etic and emic qualities of current counseling procedures.

In chapter 3 we proposed a Minority Identity Development model that we hope will stimulate research in minority group/cross-cultural counseling. The Minority Identity Development model itself needs empirical verification. Hall, Cross, & Freedle (1972) found experimental support for a Black Identity Development model, and their study could serve as a prototype for research on Minority Identity Development.

Research that examines the effect of membership group and attitude similarity on counseling process and outcome also appears promising. The relationship of racial, sexual, socioeconomic, religious, and sexual orientation similarities to counseling effectiveness is yet to be determined. The relationship of membership group and attitudinal similarities to the nature of the client's problems in a variety of dimensions (related or unrelated to client minority status, personal-social-educational-vocational, internal-external locus of problem) needs to be assessed. Given membership group dissimilarity, how can attitudinal similarity be communicated by the counselor? One interesting hypothesis which needs testing is that when the counselor responds with empathy, he/she is perceived by the client as holding similar values. If so, are there more effective ways of communicating attitudinal similarity?

Finally, research is needed to assess the effectiveness of activist counseling roles when dealing with minority clientele. Are counselors who serve as ombudsmuns, change agents, etc., actually perceived by minority clients as more helpful than counselors who function in a more traditional role? More important, what is the actual impact of counselors functioning in these roles?

If this book helps to stimulate research activity in these and other areas related to minority group/cross-cultural counseling, it will have served an important purpose. We are optimistic that the barriers to cross-cultural counseling can be bridged.

References

Anderson, N. J., & Love, B. Psychological education for racial awareness. *Personnel and Guidance Journal*, 1973, *51*, 666–670.

Arredondo-Dowd, P. M., & Gonsalves, J. Preparing culturally effective counselors. *Personnel and Guidance Journal*, 1980, *58*, 657–661.

Atkinson, D. R. Selection and training for human rights counseling. *Counselor Education and Supervision*, 1981, *21*, 101–108.

Atkinson, D. R., Froman, T., Romo, J., & Mayton, D. M. II. The role of the counselor as a social activist: Who supports it? *The School Counselor*, 1977, *25*, 85–91.

Atkinson, D. R., Staso, D., & Hosford, R. Selecting counselor trainees with multicultural strengths: A solution to the Bakke decision crisis. *Personnel and Guidance Journal*, 1978, *56*, 546–549.

Atkinson, D. R., & Wampold, B. Affirmative action efforts of counselor education programs. *Counselor Education and Supervision*, 1981, *20*, 262–272.

Banks, W. The Black client and the helping professionals. In R. I. Jones (Ed.) *Black Psychology*. New York: Harper & Row, 1972.

Barnes, E. J. Cultural retardation or shortcomings of assessment techniques? In R. L. Jones (Ed.) *Black Psychology*. New York: Harper & Row, 1972.

Bell, Robert L., Jr. The culturally deprived psychologist, *The Counseling Psychologist*, 1971, *2*, 104–106.

Bernal, M. E. Hispanic issues in psychology: Curricula and training. *Hispanic Journal of Behavioral Sciences*, 1980, *2*, 129–146.

Bexelius, A. The ombudsman for civil affairs. In D. C. Rowat (Ed.), *The ombudsman: Citizen's defender*. Toronto: University of Toronto Press, 1968.

Blocker, D. H., & Rapoza, R. A systematic eclectic model in counseling-consulting. *Elementary School Guidance and Counseling*, 1972, *7*, 106–112.

Bryson, S.; & Bardo, H. Race and the counseling process: An overview. *Journal of Non-White Concerns in Personnel and Guidance*, 1975, *4*, 5–15.

Bryson, S.; Renzaglia, G. A., & Danish, S. Training counselors through simulated racial encounters. *Journal of Non-White Concerns in Personnel and Guidance*, 1974, *3*, 218–223.

Calia, V. F. The culturally deprived client: A re-formulation of the counselor's role. *Journal of Counseling Psychology*, 1966, *13*, 100–105.

Carkhuff, R. R. *The development of human resources*. San Francisco: Holt, Rinehart, & Winston, 1971.

Ciavarella, M. A. & Doolittle, L. W. The Ombudsman: Relevant role model for the counselor. *The School Counselor,* 1970, *17,* 331–336.

Cross, W. C., & Maldonado, B. The counselor, the Mexican American, and the stereotype. *Elementary School Guidance and Counseling,* 1971, *6,* 27–31.

Draguns, J. G. Counseling across cultures: Common themes and distinct approaches. In P. B. Pedersen, W. J. Lonner, & J. G. Draguns (Eds.), *Counseling across cultures.* Honolulu: The University of Hawaii Press, 1976.

Gardner, L. H. The therapeutic relationship under varying conditions of race. *Psychotherapy: Theory, Research and Practice,* 1971, *8* (1), 78–87.

Gravitz, H. L., & Woods, E. A multiethnic approach to peer counseling. *Professional Psychology,* 1976, *8,* 229–235.

Haettenschwiller, D. L. Counseling black college students in special programs. *Personnel & Guidance Journal,* 1971, *50,* 29–35.

Hall, W. S.; Cross, W. E., & Freedle, R. Stages in the development of Black awareness: An exploratory investigation. In Reginald L. Jones' (Ed.) *Black Psychology,* New York: Harper & Row, 1972, 156–165.

Ivey, A. E. *Counseling psychology, the psychoeducator model and the future.* Paper prepared for APA Division 17 Professional Affairs Committee, 1976.

Katz, J. H., & Ivey, A. White awareness: The frontier of racism awareness training. *Personnel and Guidance Journal,* 1977, *55,* 485–489.

Kennedy, C. D., & Wagner, N. N. Psychology and affirmative action: 1977. *Professional Psychology,* 1979, *10,* 234–243.

Korchin, S. J. Clinical psychology and minority problems. *American Psychologist,* 1981, *35,* 262–269.

Lewis, M. D. & Lewis, J. A. Relevant training for relevant roles: A model for educating inner-city counselors. *Counselor Education and Supervision,* 1970, *10,* 31–38.

Lewis, M. D., & Lewis, J. A. The counselor's impact on community environments. *Personnel and Guidance Journal,* 1977, *55,* 356–358.

Maes, W. R., & Rinaldi, J. R. Counseling the Chicano child. *Elementary School Guidance and Counseling,* 1974, *9,* 279–284.

McDavis, R. J., & Parker, W. M. A course on counseling ethnic minorities: A model. *Counselor Education and Supervision,* 1977, *17,* 146–148.

Miller, C. D., & Oetting, G. Barriers to employment and the disadvantaged. *Personnel and Guidance Journal,* 1977, *56,* 89–93.

Mitchell, H. Counseling black students: A model in response to the need for relevant counselor training programs. *The Counseling Psychologist,* 1971, *2* (4), 117–122. (a)

Mitchell, H. The black experience in higher education. *The Counseling Psychologist,* 1971, *2* (1), 30–36. (b)

Padilla, E. R., Boxley, R., & Wagner, N. The desegregation of clinical psychology training. *Professional Psychology,* 1973, *4,* 259–265.

Parker, W. M., & McDavis, R. J. An awareness experience: Toward counseling minorities. *Counselor Education and Supervision,* 1979, *18,* 312–317.

Pedersen, P. B. The field of intercultural counseling. In P. Pedersen, W. J. Lonner, & J. G. Draguns (Eds.) *Counseling across cultures.*

Pedersen, P. B. The triad model of cross-cultural counselor training. *Personnel and Guidance Journal,* 1977, *56,* 94–100.

Pedersen, P. B. Four dimensions of cross-cultural skill in counselor training. *Personnel and Guidance Journal,* 1978, *56,* 480–484.

Pedersen, P. B., Holwill, C. F., & Shapiro, J. A cross-cultural training procedure for classes in counselor education. *Counselor Education and Supervision,* 1978, *17,* 233–237.

Pine, G. J. Counseling minority groups: A revew of the literature. *Counseling and Values,* 1972, *17,* 35–44.

Rowe, W., Murphy, H. B., & DeCsipkes, R. A. The relationship of counselor characteristics and counseling effectiveness. *Review of Educational* Research, 1975, *45,* 231–246.

Russell, R. D. Black perception of guidance. *Personnel and Guidance Journal,* 1970, *48,* 721–728.

Russo, N. F., Olmedo, E. L., Stapp, J., & Fulcher, R. Women and minorities in psychology. *American Psychologist,* 1981, *36,* 1315–1363.

Sattler, J. M. Racial experimenter effects in experimentation, testing, interviewing and psychotherapy. *Psychological Bulletin,* 1970, *73,* 137–160.

Strong, D. J., & Peele, D. The status of minorities in psychology. In E. L. Olmedo & S. Lopez (Eds.), *Hispanic mental health professionals.* Los Angeles: Spanish Speaking Mental Health Research Center, 1977.

Sue, D. W. Ethnic identity: The impact of two cultures on the psychological development of Asians in America. In D. W. Sue & Wagner (Eds.) *Asian Americans: Psychological perspectives.* Ben Lomand, California: Science and Behavior Books, Inc., 1973, 140–149.

Sue, D. W., & Sue, S. Counseling Chinese-Americans. *Personnel and Guidance Journal,* 1972, *50,* 637–644. (a)

Sue, D. W., & Sue, S. Ethnic minorities: Resistance to being researched. *Professional Psychology,* 1972, *3,* 11–17. (b)

Torrey, E. F. Mental health services for American Indians and Eskimos. *Community Mental Health Journal,* 1970, *6,* 455–463.

Vontress, C. E. Racial differences: Impediments to rapport. *Journal of Counseling Psychology,* 1971, *18* (1), 7–13.

Vontress, C. E. Counseling: Racial and ethnic factors. *Focus on Guidance,* 1973, *5,* 1–10.

Vontress, C. E. Barriers in cross-cultural counseling. *Counseling and Value,* 1974, *18* (3), 160–165.

Vontress, C. E. Racial and ethnic barriers in counseling. In P. B. Pedersen, W. J. Lonner, & J. G. Draguns (Eds.) *Counseling across cultures.* Honolulu: The University of Hawaii Press, 1976.

Vontress, C. E. Cross-cultural counseling: An existential approach. *Personnel and Guidance Journal,* 1979, 58, 117–122.

Walton, J. M. Retention, role modeling, and academic readiness: A perspective on the ethnic minority student in higher education. *Personnel and Guidance Journal,* 1979, *58,* 125–127.

Waltz, G. R. & Benjamin, L. *On becoming a change agent.* Ann Arbor: Eric Counseling and Personnel Services Information Center, 1977.

Ward, E. J. A gift from the ghetto. *Personnel and Guidance Journal,* 1970, *48,* 753–756.

Weinrach, S. Integration is more than just busing. *The School Counselor,* 1973, *20,* 276–279.

Williams, R. L., & Kirkland, J. The white counselor and the black client. *The Counseling Psychologist,* 1971, *2,* 114–116.

Wilson, W., & Calhoun, J. F. Behavior therapy and the minority client. *Psychotherapy: Theory, Research and Practice,* 1974, *11* (4), 317–325.

Woods, E. Counseling minority students: A program model. *Personnel and Guidance Journal,* 1977, *55,* 416–418.

Appendix A Position Paper
Cross-cultural Counseling Competencies
Education and Training Committee
Division 17, American Psychological Association
January 1981

Derald Wing Sue, Chairperson
California State University-Hayward

Joseph E. Bernier, College of St. Rose
Anna Durran, Columbia University
Lawrence Feinberg, University of California, Berkeley
Paul Pedersen, University of Hawaii
Elsie J. Smith, State University of New York, Buffalo
Ena Vasquez-Nuttall, University of Massachusetts, Amherst

Ever since the 1960s, counseling and psychotherapy have been challenged as to the appropriateness of the services they offer to minority clients. A barrage of criticisms have been leveled against traditional counseling practices as being demanding, irrelevant, and oppressive toward the culturally different. Admonitions to develop new methods, concepts, and services more appropriate to the life experiences of minority clients have been plentiful. Yet, many mental health educators continue to argue the merits of including curriculum on ethnic minority groups, and/or incorporating ethnic content into existing courses.

The purpose of this position paper is threefold. First, we would like to outline and challenge some prevalent myths and misunderstandings which have made it difficult to develop appropriate curricula, and relevant counseling/therapy competencies for the culturally different in the United States. Second, we would like to begin the much needed task of defining the term "cross-cultural counseling/therapy" which has been increasingly used in the literature. Last, we would like to recommend the adoption of specific cross-cultural counseling and therapy competencies by the American Psychological Association to be used as a guideline for accreditation criteria.

The Need for a Cross-Cultural Perspective:

Myths and Misunderstandings

One of the main arguments proposed against the need for a cross-cultural perspective in the mental health profession has been *the belief that current research strategies and approaches as well as mental health practices are*

Reprinted with permission from *The Counseling Psychologist*, 1982, *10* (2), 45–52.

adequate and appropriate in application to various minority groups.)This assumption can be seriously challenged when a thorough review of the counseling and mental health literature is undertaken. Below are listed documentation that support this point.

1. Many writers have noted that the mental health literature and specifically research have failed to create a realistic understanding of various ethnic groups in America (Bryde, 1971; Sue & Sue, 1972; Thomas & Sillen, 1972; Williams, 1970; Smith, 1973; Padilla & Ruiz, 1974; Sumada, 1975). The social sciences have generally ignored the study of certain ethnic groups in the United States (D. W. Sue, 1975), and/or tended to reinforce a negative view by concentrating on the pathological aspects of minorities (Billingsley, 1970; E. R. Padilla, 1971; Trimble, 1976, D. W. Sue, 1981). When reading the literature, one gets the impression that the difficulties encountered by minorities are due to intrinsic factors such as racial inferiority, incompatible value systems, and/or inherent pathological forces. Thus, the portrayal of the culturally different in literature has generally taken the form of stereotyping them as "deficient" in certain "desirable" attributes. Minorities have generally been perceived as deficient genetically (the genetic deficient model) and/or culturally (the culturally deficient model). That the genetic deficient model still exists can be seen in the writings of Shuey (1966), Jensen (1969), Hernstein (1971), and Shockley (1972). The position of these writers have been used to support the view that Blacks are genetically inferior and that the accumulation of weak or low intelligence genes in the Black population should be seriously curtailed by not allowing Blacks to bear children.

Even more disturbing has been recent allegations that Cyril Burt, imminent British psychologist, fabricated data to support his contention that intelligence is inherited and that Blacks have inherited inferior brains (Dorfman, 1978; Kamin, 1974; Gillie, 1978). To many minorities, the Cyril Burt fiasco may represent another instance of so-called "scientific racism." The question as to whether or not there are differences between races and intelligence is both a complex and emotional one. Besides the difficulty in defining "race," there exists questionable assumptions regarding whether research on the intelligence of whites can be generalized to other groups, whether middle class and lower class minorities grow up in similar environments to middle and lower class whites, and whether instruments are valid for both minority and white subjects. More importantly, we should recognize that the "average values" of different populations tell us nothing about any one individual. Yet, much of the social science literature continues to portray ethnic minorities as being genetically deficient in one sense or another.

It is important to note that even well-meaning social scientists who challenged the genetic deficient model, and who place heavy reliance on environmental factors were victims to their own cultural biases. Instead of an emphasis on genetics, terms such as culturally "disadvantaged," "deficient" or "deprived" were used. What occurred in the social science literature was that the biological differences that were originally proposed to cause the differences were now shifted to the lifestyles or values of various ethnic groups (Baratz & Baratz, 1970; Sumada, 1975; Smith, 1977). The term "culturally deprived" was inadequate because it meant to lack a cultural background which is contradictory, because everyone inherits a culture. Such terms tend to cause conceptual and theoretical confusions that may adversely affect social planning, educational policy and research. Even more disturbing is the assumption that cultural deprivation is synonymously equated with deviation from and superiority of white middle class values.

2. Western-based social sciences have generally prided themselves on the objectivity of research and its findings. Yet, it has become increasingly clear that what a researcher proposes to study and how he/she interprets such findings are intimately linked to a personal, professional, and societal value system. As we saw in the previous discussion, these societal values may affect the interpretation of data as it relates to minorities. A similar analogy can be drawn with respect to the counseling profession. For example, the professions preoccupation with pathology tends to encourage study of deficits and weaknesses rather than strengths or assets. Racist attitudes, biases and prejudices may intensify this narrow view as minorities may be portrayed in professional journals as neurotic, psychotic, psychopathic and/or parolees instead of a well-rounded person.

Additionally, the Western approach in research has stressed the experimental design as the epitomy of the "scientific method." Associated with this emphasis are characteristics of control, manipulation, and a linear analytic approach. D. W. Sue (1981) has indicated how these characteristics may oftentimes clash with the world views and cultural perspectives of different ethnic groups.

3. Many mental health professions have noted that racial and ethnic factors may act as impediments to counseling and psychotherapy (Carkhuff & Pierce, 1967; Vontress, 1971; D. W. Sue, 1975; Ruiz & Padilla, 1977). Misunderstandings can oftentimes arise from cultural variations in communications that may lead to alienation and/or inability to develop trust and rapport. This may result in an early termination of therapy (Yamamoto, James & Palley, 1968). In a comprehensive study conducted in the state of Washington, S. Sue and Associates (Sue, McKinney, Allen & Hall, 1974; Sue & McKinney, 1975; Sue, Allen & Conaway, 1978) have found supporting evidence that Asian Americans, Blacks, Hispanics and American Indians terminate therapeutic services after only one contact at a rate greater than 50%. This is in sharp contrast to a 30% termination rate for Anglo clients. These investigators along with others have concluded that is may be inappropriateness of interpersonal transactions that might

account for the premature termination. D. W. Sue (1981) points out that language barriers which often exist between the counselor and client, class-bound values which indicate that counselors conduct treatment within the value system of the middle class, and culture-bound values which are used to judge normality and abnormality seriously hinder and distort the counseling therapy process. That counseling and psychotherapy are handmaidens of the status quo and transmitters of society's values lead many minorities to believe that the mental health profession is engaged in a form of cultural oppression. In reviewing the minority group literature on counseling, Pine (1972) found the following views to be representative of those held by many minority individuals:

> that it is a waste of time; that counselors are deliberately shunting minority students into deadend nonacademic programs regardless of student potential, preferences, or ambitions; that counselors discourage students from applying to college; that counselors are insensitive to the needs of students in the community; that counselors do not give the same amount of energy and time in working with minorities as they do with white middle class students; that counselors do not accept, respect, and understand cultural differences; that counselors are arrogant and contemptuous; and that counselors don't know how to deal with their own hangups. (p. 35)

These three points are at odds with the myth that current research and mental health practices are adequate for all ethnic groups and that a cross-cultural perspective is not needed. We need a perspective that allows us to present a balanced realistic picture of minorities in the U.S. For example, much can be learned from the current help-giving networks that exist in minority communities, from the manner in which racial/ethnic minorities have dealt with racism, and from the positive aspects of being bicultural. Indeed, since most minorities are bicultural/bilingual, they are in an advantaged position where cross-cultural counseling is needed. It is ironic that in our society, the social psychological forces continue to reward a mondingual/monocultural orientation which would prove limiting to effective cross-cultural interactions.

Another myth that tends to be prevalent in the counseling and mental health profession is that *ethnic cultural issues are only the province of a select few individuals who are considered experts in the field because it applies to a small segment of the population.* Traditionally, counseling and clinical psychology has emphasized the importance of self understanding as an important component in the development of therapists. Espin (1979) points out how little attention has been given to the importance of the trainee's own ethnicity, cultural biases and prejudices. When these issues are addressed, people believe that they are more appropriate for "minorities" than "Mainstream" counselors/therapists. This position is a fallacy and deprives practitioners and their clients of an understanding of psychological and developmental processes that influence ethnicity.

Ethnicity and culture is a function of every person's development and not limited only to "minorities." Espin (1979) states

> If counselors can acquire a greater understanding of their own ethnicity and its overt and covert influences on their personalities and interpersonal styles, they will be better able to recognize the ways in which ethnic background influence different individual behavior, peer interaction, values and life goals of counselors. (p. 1)

It is also important for us to realize that we live in a multicultural, multilingual and pluralistic society. It is infrequent that we have no contact with people whose cultural backgrounds or lifestyles differs from our own. In one way or another we are bound to interact with individuals who can be classified as "culturally different" and it is our responsibility as practicing psychologists to become more culturally aware and sensitive to our work with different populations. For example, it is estimated that by 1990 over half the population of the state of California will be members of minority groups.

Another reason for a cross-cultural perspective in counseling is the possible scientific contributions it would make to our field (S. Sue, 1980). *The practice of counseling and psychotherapy assumes a universality of psychological theories and concepts.* In many ways, the study of culturally different groups tests the limits and generalities of psychological theories in mental health practices. If traditional assumptions and theories of mental health are valid across cultures and situations, then they constitute "universals." Likewise, means of conducting treatment and or delivering services that are effective with the diverse range of client types would indicate its universal applicability. In the absence of a culturally diverse population of study, it is difficult to know when universals have been found, or when techniques and assumptions are culturally specific. Triandis (1972) indicated the importance of the problems in differentiating etic (universal) and emic (culture specific) phenomena in cross-cultural research. To the extent that the Western theories, assessment procedures, treatment approaches, and research methods are inappropriate for different cultural groups, they must be modified (Brislin, Lonner & Thorndike, 1973).

While we have moved a long way from the "individual centered" approaches of counseling and psychotherapy, the prevalent orientation is still upon the individual. *The belief in "rugged individualism" and that the person is totally responsible for his or her own lot in life* hinders a more realistic understanding of the influence of culture and the sociopolitical influences. As pointed out by D. W. Sue (1981), an overemphasis on the "individual" oftentimes leads to a person-blame orientation while minimizing the contributions of the sociopolitical system. A cross-cultural perspective in mental health work will begin to increase our awareness of the cultural-environmental-contextual perspective on mental health as proposed by Ivey & Authier (1978). It is not enough to study solely different cultural groups in the United States without understanding the sociopolitical history that minorities have undergone. The history and experiences of the culturally different have been the history of oppression, discrimination, and racism (D. W. Sue, 1981). Institutional racism has created psychological barriers among minorities that are likely to interfere with the counseling/therapy process. Feelings of powerlessness, inferiority, subordination, deprivation, anger and rage, and over/covert resistance to factors in interracial relationships are likely to occur and must be dealt with in the counseling/therapy context. It is inappropriate and a fallacy to consider that these issues can be simply dealt with through study of the individual or just cultural differences. It is precisely the interaction of the cultural aspects with the sociopolitical system which creates many of the dilemmas of oppression, racism, etc.

Definition of Cross-Cultural

Counseling/Therapy

Cross-cultural counseling/therapy may be defined as any counseling relationship in which two or more of the participants differ with respect to cultural background, values, and lifestyle. In most cases, the mental health practitioner is generally a member of the majority group and the client is a minority group member or international (a citizen of another country). This definition of cross-cultural counseling also includes situations in which both the counselor/therapist and client are minority individuals, but represent different minority groups (Black-Hispanic, Asian-American—American Indian, Puerto Rican-Black, and so forth). It also includes situations in which the counselor/therapist is a minority person and the client a majority person (Black counselor-white client, Chicano counselor-white client, etc.). Additionally, it may include situations in which the counselor/therapist and client are racially and ethnically similar but may belong to different cultural groups because of other variables such as sex, sexual orientation, socioeconomic factors, religious orientation, and age (white male-white female, Black straight person-Black gay, poor Asian American-wealthy Asian American, etc.) (Atkinson, Morten & D. W. Sue, 1979). In measurement terms, the degree of counselor/therapist-client similarity or dissimilarity in terms of cultural background, values and lifestyles would be the key determinants in discussing cross-cultural counseling/therapy.

The concept of cross-cultural counseling/therapy presented here will no doubt stimulate much debate and discussion. To recognize too many differences might (a) dilute our focus and intent, and/or (b) make all counseling/therapy cross-cultural. However, we recognize that every counseling/therapy interaction is slightly cross-cultural; this recognition may be a source of strength rather than an impediment. What we need to acknowledge is the relative importance and power of each variable in affecting the counseling relationship.

While we do not want to be guilty of focusing upon the negative aspects of a cross-cultural counseling situation, the reality is that in most cases, counseling a person from a culturally different background poses major problems. In a cross-cultural counseling situation, differences between the counselor and client may potentially block, either partially or wholly, a counselor's (a) true understanding of the client's situation, difficulties or strengths; (b) ability to empathize with and understand the world view of the client; and (c) ability to utilize culturally relevant counseling/therapy modes. Cross-cultural counseling problems are most likely to occur when there is a low degree of client-counselor assumed similarity in terms of their respective backgrounds, values and life-styles. Because cross-cultural counseling has been defined in terms of assumed dissimilarity between the counselor and the client, the importance of sociopolitical interpretations of differences must also be an intimate part of the definition. In discussing cross-cultural counseling effectiveness, D. W. Sue (1981) has stated that individuals who share the same world view as their clients are most likely to be helpful. World views are frequently correlated with a person's cultural/racial heritage, ethnic identification and experiences in society. There are many complexities in this statement as many of these variables may conflict with one another. For example, attitudinal/belief similarity tends to facilitate cross-cultural counseling by enhancing counselor credibility and attractiveness. Yet, membership group similarity also tends to facilitate cross-cultural counseling, because it also enhances counselor credibility and attractiveness. Whether membership group similarity is more important than attitudinal similarity in cross-cultural counseling depends on many variables and becomes an empirical question. Cross-Cultural Counseling Competencies.

There is now a growing awareness that the human service professions including counseling and clinical psychology have failed to meet the particular mental health needs of ethnic minorities (Sue, D. W., 1981; Korman, 1973; Dulles Conference, 1978). Most graduate programs give inadequate treatment to mental health issues of ethnic minorities (McFadden & Wilson, 1977). Cultural influences affecting personality formation and the manifestation of behavior disorders are infrequently part of mental health training programs (D. W. Sue, 1981). When minority group experiences are discussed, they are generally seen and analyzed from the "white middle class perspective" (Smith, 1977). As a result, professionals who deal with mental health problems of ethnic minorities lack understanding and knowledge about ethnic values and their consequent interaction with an oppressive society. It is this very issue of cultural encapsulation and its detrimental affects on minorities which have generated training recommendations from the 1973 Vail Conference (Korman, 1973), Austin conference (1975), and the Dulles Conference (1978). All of these conferences noted the serious lack and inadequacy of psychology training programs in dealing with religious, racial, ethnic, sexual and economic groups. Selected recommendations included advocating (a) that professional psychology training programs at all levels provide information on the potential political nature of the practice of psychology, (b) that professionals need to "own" their value positions, (c) that client populations ought to be involved in helping to determine what is "done to them," (d) that education and training programs include not only the content, but also an evaluation of its graduates, and (e) that continuing professional development occur beyond the receipt of any advanced degree.

A recognition of these serious inadequacies and needs in cross-cultural training of mental health professionals have led to the creation of an APA Board of Ethnic Minority Affairs voted upon by APA members in 1980. The new board is charged with formulating policy recommendations and initiating activities related to issues which impinge directly on American Indians/Alaskan Natives, Asians/Pacific Americans, Blacks and Hispanics. The board is expected to focus on three major areas of research, training and service delivery, and to conduct several major activities that include the following: (a) increasing scientific understanding of psychology that pertain to culture and ethnicity; (b) increasing the quality and quantity of educational and training opportunities for ethnic minority persons in psychology; (c) promoting the development of culturally sensitive models for the delivery of psychological services; and (d) serving as a clearing house for the collection and dissemination of information relevant to or pertaining to ethnic minority psychologists and students (True, 1980). There are several other recommendations and charges which deal specifically with organizational factors among the various ethnic groups. However, our focus is primarily concerned with those points outlined above.

One of the most important recommendations and themes arising from the numerous conferences listed above and from the formation of the Board of Ethnic Minority Affairs was the importance of identifying and assessing competencies of psychologists as they relate to the culturally different. The importance of providing educational experiences that generate sensitivity to and the appreciation of the history, current needs, strengths, and resources of minority communities was stressed. Students and faculty members should be helped to understand the development and behavior of the group being studied, thus enabling them to (a) use their knowledge to develop skills in working with minority groups; and (b) develop strategies to modify the effects of political, social and economic forces on minority groups. The curriculum must focus on immediate social needs and problems. It must stimulate an awareness of minority issues caused by economic, social and educational deprivation. The curriculum must also be designed to stimulate this awareness not solely on a cognitive level. It must enable individuals to understand feelings of helplessness and powerlessness, low self-esteem, poor self-concept, and how they contribute to low motivation, frustration, hatred, ambivalence, and apathy. In addition, curriculum should present a balanced positive picture of minority groups. The contributions of various ethnic/ racial minorities, their strengths and assets, the legitimacy of their indigenous help-giving networks, and the advantages of being bicultural need to be recognized. It was felt that the curriculum should contain areas dealing with consciousness raising, knowledge and skills.

Table 1
Characteristics of the Culturally Skilled Counseling Psychologist

Beliefs/Attitudes	1. The culturally skilled counseling psychologist is one who has moved from being culturally unaware to being aware and sensitive to his/her own cultural heritage and to valuing and respecting differences. 2. A culturally skilled counseling psychologist is aware of his/her own values and biases and how they may affect minority clients. 3. A culturally skilled counseling psychologist is one who is comfortable with differences that exist between the counselor and client in terms of race and beliefs. 4. The culturally skilled counseling psychologist is sensitive to circumstances (personal biases, stage of ethnic identity, sociopolitical influences, etc.) which may dictate referral of the minority client to a member of his/her own race/culture.
Knowledges	1. The culturally skilled counseling psychologist will have a good understanding of the sociopolitical system's operation in the United States with respect to its treatment of minorities. 2. The culturally skilled counseling psychologist must possess specific knowledge and information about the particular group he/she is working with. 3. The culturally skilled counseling psychologist must have a clear and explicit knowledge and understanding of the generic characteristics of counseling and therapy. 4. The culturally skilled counseling psychologist is aware of institutional barriers which prevent minorities from using mental health services.
Skills	1. At the skills level, the culturally skilled counseling psychologist must be able to generate a wide variety of verbal and nonverbal responses. 2. The culturally skilled counseling psychologist must be able to send and receive both verbal and nonverbal messages accurately and "appropriately." 3. The culturally skilled counseling psychologist is able to exercise institutional intervention skills on behalf of his/her client when appropriate.

With these issues in mind, the Education and Training Committee of Division 17 feels a strong responsibility to bring to the membership's attention the need for developing minimal cross-cultural counseling competencies to be incorporated into training programs. The following pages contain some general guidelines which we hope will aid in the development of more concrete and sophisticated competencies for working with culturally different clients. In light of our earlier review, it seems imperative that we move quickly to challenge certain assumptions which permeate our training program and to critically evaluate not only the practices of the past, but the present as well. For this reason, we advocate the adoption of the following beliefs/attitudes, knowledges and skills by the Executive Committee and the membership of Division 17. Hopefully, these competencies will be incorporated into graduate schools of counseling psychology as well as other mental health training programs.

Beliefs/Attitudes

1. *The culturally skilled counseling psychologist is one who has moved from being culturally unaware to being aware and sensitive to his/her own cultural heritage and to valuing and respecting differences.* Culturally skilled counselors have moved from ethnocentrism to valuing and respecting differences. Other cultures are seen as equally valuable and legitimate as their own. A culturally unaware counselor is most likely to impose his/her values onto a minority client.

2. *A culturally skilled counseling psychologist is aware of his/her own values and biases and how they may affect minority clients.* They constantly attempt to avoid prejudices, unwarranted labeling and stereotyping. They try not to hold preconceived limitations/notions about their minority clients. As a check upon this process, culturally skilled counseling monitor their functioning via consultation, supervision and continual education.

3. *A culturally skilled counseling psychologist is one who is comfortable with differences that exist between the counselor and client in terms of race and beliefs.* Differences are not seen as being deviant! The culturally skilled counselor does not profess "color blindness" or negate the existence of differences that exist in attitudes/beliefs. The basic concept underlying "color blindness" was the humanity of all people. Regardless of color or other physical differences, each individual is equally human. While its intent was to eliminate bias from counseling, it has served to deny the existence of differences in clients' perceptions of society arising out of membership in different racial groups. The message tends to be "I will like you only if you are the same," instead of "I like you because of and in spite of your differences."

4. *The culturally skilled counseling psychologist is sensitive to circumstances (personal biases, stage of ethnic identity, sociopolitical influences, etc.) which may dictate referral of the minority client to a*

member of his/her own race/culture. A culturally skilled counselor is aware of his/her limitations in cross-cultural counseling and is not threatened by the prospect of referring a client.

Knowledges

1. *The culturally skilled counseling psychologist will have a good understanding of the sociopolitical systems' operation in the United States with respect to its treatment of minorities.* Understanding the impact and operation of oppression (racism, sexism, etc.), the politics of counseling, and the racist concepts that have permeated the mental health/helping professions are important. Especially valuable for the counselor is an understanding of the role cultural racism plays in the development of identity, and world views among minority groups.

2. *The culturally skilled counseling psychologist must possess specific knowledge and information about the particular group he/she is working with.* He/she must be aware of the history, experiences, cultural values and lifestyle of various racial/ethnic groups. The greater the depth of knowledge of a cultural group and the more knowledge he/she has of *many* groups, the more likely the counselor can be an effective helper. Thus, the culturally skilled counselor is one who *continues* to explore and learn about issues related to various minority groups throughout their professional careers.

3. *The culturally skilled counseling psychologist must have a clear and explicit knowledge and understanding of the generic characteristics of counseling and therapy.* These encompass language factors, culture-bound values and class-bound values. The counselor should clearly understand the value assumptions (normality and abnormality) inherent in the major schools of counseling and how they may interact with values of the culturally different. In some cases, the theories or models may limit the potential of persons from different cultures. Likewise, being able to determine those which may have usefulness to culturally different clients is important.

4. *The culturally skilled counseling psychologist is aware of institutional barriers which prevent minorities from using mental health services.* Such factors as the location of a mental health agency, the formality or informality of the decor, the language(s) which are used to advertise their services, the availability of minorities among the different levels, the organizational climate, the hours and days of operation, the offering of the services really needed by the community, etc., are important.

Skills

1. At the skills level, *the culturally skilled counseling psychologist must be able to generate a wide variety of verbal and nonverbal responses.* There is mounting evidence to indicate that minority groups may not only define problems differently from their Anglo counterparts, but

respond differently to counseling/therapy styles (Berman, 1979; Atkinson, Mariyama & Matsui, 1978; D. W. Sue, 1981). Ivey and Authier (1978) state that the wider repertoire of responses the counselor possesses, the better the helper he/she is likely to be. We can no longer rely on a very narrow and limited number of skills in counseling. We need to practice and be comfortable with a multitude of response modalities.

2. *The culturally skilled counseling psychologist must be able to send and receive both verbal and nonverbal messages accurately and "appropriately."* The key words are "send," "receive," "verbal," "nonverbal," "accurately" and "appropriately" are important. These words recognize several things about cross-cultural counseling. First, communication is a two-way process. The culturally skilled counselor must not only be able to communicate (send) his/her thoughts and feelings to the client, but also be able to read (receive) messages from the client. Second, cross-cultural counseling effectiveness may be highly correlated with the counselor's ability to recognize and respond to not only verbal but nonverbal messages. Third, sending and receiving a message accurately means the ability to consider cultural cues operative in the setting. Fourth, accuracy of communication must be tempered by its appropriateness. This is a difficult concept for many to grasp. It deals with communication styles. In many cultures, subtlety and indirectness of communication are highly prized arts. Likewise, directness and confrontation are prized by others.

3. *The culturally skilled counseling psychologist is able to exercise institutional intervention skills on behalf of his/her client when appropriate.* This implies that help-giving may involve out-of-office strategies (outreach, consultant, change agent, ombudsmen roles and facilitator of indigenous support systems) which discard the intrapsychic counseling model and views the problems/barriers as residing outside of the minority client.

A Call for Action

The objectives of the Education and Training Committee of Division 17 have been to provide a rationale for the inclusion of cross-cultural counseling/therapy training in graduate schools of psychology and to briefly outline attitudes/beliefs, knowledges, and skills inherent in such competencies. We have not addressed outselves to the issue of how to implement these recommendations because they have been covered in detail elsewhere (Korman, 1973; McFadden, Quinn & Sweeney, 1978; Blau, 1970; President's Commission on Mental Health, 1978; Dulles Conference 1978; Society for the Psychological Study of Social Issues, 1973; D. W. Sue & S. Sue, 1972). Among the multitudes of suggestions are (a) offering academic and research courses specifically on ethnic/racial minorities,

(b) integrating cross-cultural issues into existing psychology courses, (c) encouraging recruitment and retention of both minority faculty and students, (d) providing practicum and internship experiences in a multi-racial setting, (e) developing resource materials relevant to minority issues, and (f) incorporating such recommendations into current APA and other accreditation criteria. Unfortunately, these strategies and recommendations have made minimal progress partly due to the lack of institutional and professional organizational support beyond the rhetorical level. The Education and Training Committee of Division 17 would like to request that the President in conjunction with the Executive Committee take the following actions:

1. Formal endorsement of the current position paper with respect to the rationale and the delineation of minimal cross-cultural counseling/therapy principles needed outlining the rationale, issues, and need for minimal cross-cultural counseling/therapy competencies.
2. Take whatever steps necessary, to ensure that the current paper receives widespread dissemination among its membership, relevant boards, committees and divisions within APA and in state organizations.
3. Move towards implementing these competencies into current APA accreditation criteria.
4. Establishment of an ongoing process within Division 17 which will continue to develop and define the cross-cultural competencies and issues, and monitor the implementation of these objectives.

Reference Notes

Espin, O. M. Paper on ethno-cultural concerns presented to ACES, May 15, 1979.

McFadden, J., & Wilson, T. Non-white academic training within counselor education, rehabilitation counseling and student personnel programs. Unpublished research, 1977.

Society for the Psychological Study of Social Issues. Document entitled "Graduate programs in psychology, in the sciences, in education, social work, public health, suitable to the needs of minority students," Los Angeles, 1973.

References

Atkinson, D. R., Morten, G., & Sue, D. W. *Counseling American Minorities: A Cross-Cultural Perspective.* Dubuque: Wm. C. Brown Co. Pub., 1979.

Atkinson, D. R., Mariyama, M., & Matsui, S. The effects of counselor race and counseling approach on Asian Americans' perceptions of counselor credibility and utility. *Journal of Counseling Psychology,* 1978, *25,* 76–83.

Baratz, S., & Baratz, J. Early childhood intervention: The social sciences base of institutional racism. *Harvard Educational Review,* 1970, *40,* 29–50.

Berman, J. Counseling skills used by Black and white male and female counselors. *Journal of Counseling Psychology,* 1979, *26,* 81–84.

Billingsley, A. Black families and white social science. *Journal of Social Issues,* 1970, *26,* 127–142.

Blau, T. APA Commission on accelerating Black participation in psychology. *American Psychologist,* 1970, *25,* 1103–1104.

Brislin, R., Lonner, W., & Thorndike, R. *Cross-cultural research methods.* New York: Wiley, 1973.

Bryde, J. F. *Indian students and guidance.* Boston: Houghton-Mifflin Co., 1971.

Carkhuff, R. R., & Pierce, R. Differential effects of therapist race and social class upon patient depth of self-exploration in the initial clinical interview. *Journal of Consulting Psychology,* 1967, *31,* 632–634.

Dorfman, D. D. The Cyril Burt question: New findings. *Science,* 1978, *201,* 1177–1186.

Espin, O. M. Paper on ethno-cultural concerns presented to ACES, May 15, 1979.

Gillie, D. *Phi Delta Kappan,* 1978, *58,* 469.

Hernstein, R. "IQ." *The Atlantic Monthly,* 1971, 43–64.

Ivey, A., & Authier, J. *Microcounseling: Innovations in interviewing training.* Springfield, Illinois: Charles C. Thomas, 1978.

Jensen, A. How much can we boost IQ and school achievement? *Harvard Educational Review,* 1969, *39,* 1–123.

Kamin, L. *The science and politics of I.Q.* Potomac, Md: Eribaum, 1974.

Korman, M. *Levels and patterns of professional training in psychology.* Washington, D.C.: American Psychological Association, 1973.

McFadden, J., Quinn, J. R., & Sweeney, T. J. *Position paper by Commission on Non-white concerns of ACES.* APGA, Washington, D.C.: 1978.

McFadden, J., & Wilson, T. Non-white academic training within counselor education, rehabilitation counseling and student personnel programs. Unpublished research, 1977.

Padilla, A. M., & Ruiz, R. A. *Latino mental health.* Washington, D.C.: DHEW, 1974.

Padilla, E. R. The relationship between psychology and Chicanos: Failures and possibilities. In N. N. Wagner & M. R. Haug (Eds.), *Chicanos: Social and psychological perspectives.* St. Louis, Mo.: Mosby, 1971, pp. 286–294.

Pine, G. J. Counseling minority groups: A review of the literature. *Counseling and Values,* 1972, *17,* 35–44.

President's Commission on Mental Health. Report to the President. Washington, D.C.: U.S. Government Printing Office, 1978.

Ruis, R. A., & Padilla, A. M. Counseling Latinos. *The Personnel and Guidance Journal,* 1977, *55,* 401–408.

Society for the Psychological Study of Social Issues. Document entitled "Graduate programs in psychology, in the sciences, in education, social work, public health, suitable to the needs of minority students." Los Angeles, 1973.

Shockley, W. *Journal of Criminal Law and Criminology,* 1972, *7,* 530–543.

Shuey, A. *The testing of Negro intelligence.* New York: Social Science Press, 1966.

Smith, E. J. Counseling Black individuals: Some stereotypes. *Personnel and Guidance Journal,* 1977, *55,* 390–396.

Smith, E. J. *Counseling the culturally different black youth.* Columbus, Ohio: Charles E. Merrill Book Co., 1973.

Sue, D. W. *Counseling the culturally different: Theory and practice.* New York: John Wiley & Sons, 1981.

Sue, D. W. Asian Americans: Social-psychological forces affecting their life styles. In S. Picou, & R. Campbell (Eds.), *Career behavior of special groups.* Columbus, Ohio: Charles E. Merrill Publishers, 1975.

Sue, D. W., & Sue, D. Barriers to effective cross-cultural counseling. *Journal of Counseling Psychology,* September 1977.

Sue, D. W., & Sue, S. Ethnic minorities: Resistance to being researched. *Professional Psychology,* 1972, *2,* 11–17.

Sue, S. Issues in Asian American psychology curriculum. *Journal of the Asian American Psychological Association,* 1980, *5,* 6–11.

Sue, S., Allen, D., & Conaway, L. The responsiveness and equality of mental health care to Chicanos and Native Americans. *American Journal of Community Psychology,* 1978, *6,* 137–146.

Sue, S., & McKinney, H. Asian Americans in the community mental health care system. *American Journal of Orthopsychiatry,* 1974, *45,* 111–118.

Sue, S., McKinney, H., Allen D., & Hall, J. Delivery of community mental health services to black and white clients. *Journal of Consulting and Clinical Psychology,* 1974, *42,* 794–801.

Sumada, R. J. From ethnocentrism to a multicultural perspective in educational testing. *Journal of Afro-American Issues,* 1975, *3,* 4–18.

Thomas, A., & Sillen, S. *Racism and psychiatry.* New York: Brunner/Mazel, Inc., 1972.

Triandis, H. *The analysis of subjective culture.* New York: Wiley, 1972.

Trimble, J. E. Value differences among American Indians: Concerns for the concerned counselor. In P. Pedersen, W. J. Lonner, & J. G. Draguns (Eds.), *Counseling across cultures.* Honolulu: East West Center Press, 1976.

True, R. H. APA members vote to create Board of Minority Affairs. *Journal of the Asian American Psychological Association,* 1980, *5,* 3–4.

Vontress, C. E. Racial differences: Impediments to rapport. *Journal of Counseling Psychology,* 1971, *18,* 7–13.

Williams, R. L. Black pride, academic relevance and individual achievement. *Counseling Psychologist,* 1970, *2,* 18–22.

Yamamoto, J., James, Q. C., & Palley, N. Cultural problems in psychiatric therapy. *Archives of General Psychiatry,* 1968, *19,* 45–49.

Author Index

Williams, C. T., 133, 135, 155n
Williams, R. L., 15, 31n, 240, 246, 256n, 258, 271n
Wilson, M. E., 164, 166n
Wilson, T., 263, 270n
Wilson, W., 16, 18, 20, 21, 22, 31n, 238, 256n
Wirth, L., 8, 10n
Wolkon, G. H., 187, 203n
Woods, E., 238, 256n
Workneh, F., 109, 119n
Wrenn, C. G., 16, 31n, 143, 147, 153n
Wrenn, R. L., 224, 230n

Yamamoto, J., 14, 31n, 85, 87, 96n, 183, 187, 201, 203n, 221, 230n, 259, 271n
Young, W. M., 129, 131n
Youngman, G., 46, 73

Zangwill, 6
Zimmerman, S., 187, 203n
Zox, M., 14, 28n
Zunin, L., 169, 172n

Subject Index

machismo, 191, 199, 206, 211
Marginal Man, 89, 105
Mason V. Sams, 62
melting pot theory, 6
mestizo, 215–216
minority, 3, 7–8
Minority Group Counseling, 8, 11
Minority Identity Development Model, 35–41
minority typologies, 32–33
model minority, 83, 88
mulato, 216

National Aborigine Conference, 58
National Congress of American Indians,
  58–59
National Indian Youth Council, 58
Negro-to-Black Conversion Experience, 34
Northwest the Survivors of American
  Indians, Inc., 58

ombudsman, 239
oppression, 7
Original Cherokee Community Organization,
  59

Pan American Indians, 58
personalismo, 191, 199, 217
professional adaptation model, 190
pseudoetic approach, 16

race, 3–4
racial types, 4
Rational-Emotive Counseling, 171
reality counseling, 169
representational admission policy, 244
resistance, 22, 26
Resistance and Immersion Stage, 37, 40
respecto, 191, 199, 206, 211

Sansei, 33
second generationitis, 208
Second World, 8
Seymour v. Superintendent, 62
Squire v. Capoeman, 62
stereotypes, 14, 21, 30
stereotyping, 21
super-minority counselor, 24
Synergetic Articulation and Awareness State,
  38

Task Force Report, 55
Theory of Dysgenics, 129
Third World, 8–9
tiers monde, 8
traditional counseling role, 14
transference, 22, 26
Triad Model, 248–249

United States v. Winans, 62

Yellow Peril, 87